BY THE SAME AUTHOR

The Pursuit of Stillwater Trout (1975)

'The most engaging and important book on the subject that has ever been written... So readable and logical, so widely lauded and read that it had a truly profound effect on the sport as a whole.'
– *Fly Fishing and Fly Tying*

'A first-class piece of original thinking. The best book on the subject that I have ever read.' – *Hugh Falkus*

'Completely original... The result of one devoted fly-fisherman's powers of observation ... his understanding and ... his ability to convey it to us without dogma. The value of the book is enhanced by the author's superb writing.' – *Trout and Salmon*

'Without consciously striving to, Brian Clarke has, with a perception remarkably reminiscent of G.E.M. Skues, taken over where that legendary figure left off. With his first book, Brian Clarke has produced an angling classic.' – *Angling Times*

The Trout and the Fly (1980) (with John Goddard)

'A great work... Likely to prove to be the most important contribution to the literature of trout fishing of this century.'
– Richard Walker, *Trout Fisherman*

'Of enormous significance. If you are a fisherman, this book is probably going to change your life... Crisp and witty prose... wonderfully satisfying logic ... extraordinary information on the world that the fish sees... Not only fishermen but anyone with a curiosity about the natural world will be interested in what the authors have discovered.' – *The New York Times*

'Never have I learned as much from reading a book as I learned from this one... A treasure trove of astonishingly new information on the sport.' – *Fly Fisherman*

'An example of the rarest of rarities in angling literature... [It has] shattered dogmas and illuminated many previously puzzling phenomena. The lucid prose at times borders on the poetic.'
– *The Boston Globe*

Trout etcetera (1996) (The author's first collected writings)

'Such authors (Sheringham, Skues, Ransome and Clarke) have the unique gift of providing fresh insights into their subject, acute powers of observation and description and a tolerant and enlightened fishing philosophy. What lifts them above other writers is the quality of their English prose. Anyone who reads Brian Clarke will be aware of this.' – *Flyfishers' Journal*

'A magical collection... evocative ... hilarious ... erudite ... questioning and challenging, but never dogmatic. The author has the enviable ability to paint with words, to conjure up glowing pictures, to capture and recreate moments of drama'.
– *Fly Fishing and Fly Tying*

'Thought-provoking ... penetrating.' – *Stillwater Trout Angler*

'Brian Clarke's voice is an important one in angling. He writes about what he has found to be true, rather than what he thinks ought to be true ... [He has] a rare ability for finding solutions to a particular set of problems by painstaking observation and careful reasoning, then setting them out elegantly and lucidly.' *Waterlog*

'Could be read just for its narrative excitement.' – *Daily Express*

The Stream (1980) (An environmental novel)

'Brian Clarke has unsentimentally delineated the whole, unresolvable dichotomy of human progress versus the natural world. This book strikes a blow for the natural world comparable to Rachel Carson's a generation ago. It is a second *Silent Spring*.'
– Lynne Reid Banks, *critic*

'Devastatingly effective ... ought to be required reading for schoolchildren, government ministers, businessmen, environmentalists and anyone else interested in the environment.'
– *The Times*

'A perfect synergy of knowledge, wisdom, vision and poetry.'
– Guy Morton-Smith, *Director, Environmental Awareness Trust*

'Brilliantly achieves ... a renewal of our perception and experience of nature.' – *The Guardian*

'Magically wrought ... a parable for our times.'– *The Sunday Times*

'An extraordinary book that makes you care ... beautiful and painful as the best books are, yet with not a trace of sentimentality.' – Fay Weldon, *Authors' Club Prize judge*

'The most significant book of its kind I have read since Rachel Carson's *Silent Spring*.' – David Arnold-Forster, *Chief Executive, English Nature*

ON FISHING

BRIAN CLARKE

On Fishing

COLLINS

First published in 2007 by
Collins, an imprint of HarperCollins Publishers
77–85 Fulham Palace Road
London W6 8JB
This paperback edition first published in 2008

www.collins.co.uk

Collins is a registered trademark of HarperCollins Publishers Ltd

Text © Brian Clarke 2007

A catalogue record for this book is available from
the British Library

ISBN-13 978 0 00 728110 7

Designed by Mark Thomson

Publisher - Myles Archibald
Editor - David Price-Goodfellow
Production - Keeley Everitt
Printed and bound in Great Britain by Clays Ltd, St. Ives plc

11 10 09 08
5 4 3 2 1

Mixed Sources
Product group from well-managed
forests and other controlled sources
www.fsc.org Cert no. SW-COC-1806
© 1996 Forest Stewardship Council
FSC

Contents

CONTENTS

Dedication

SOMETIMES, when sitting out there by the river alone, especially at dusk, I begin to fold into myself and my thoughts. Then even thinking fades away. I seem to liquefy, to melt into the physical world shawled about me, to dissolve into the water's curlings and slidings, its soft easings and crinklings, its twiddling little vortices and its washes of light. I go, though not consciously, to some other place.

Later, as if unprompted, the world takes form again, sounds separate and become distinct again and I look at my watch. Ten minutes, 15 minutes, 20 minutes, an hour. I do not know where I have been, but it has been somewhere deep down and I suspect far back, perhaps near that place where everything began.

Wherever that place is, I go there gladly. It is somewhere deep-healing and it makes me whole. It is to that place and space that I dedicate this book: to that place where the physical passes through me like ether – and to fishing, which magics me there.

Acknowledgements

THIS BOOK contains a mixture of new writing and writing of mine that has appeared in various newspapers and magazines in recent years. I am grateful to the following for allowing me to reprint here articles – in many cases significantly amended – that were originally commissioned by them: the Editors of *The Times*, *The Sunday Times*, *Trout and Salmon* magazine, *The Flyfishers' Journal* and *Waterlog*. I am especially grateful to my colleagues at *The Times* who, so long after inviting me to sully their pages, still give me the space to write pieces that have a beginning, a middle and an end.

My particular thanks go to those who have contributed directly to this book. First, of course, they go to my family: to my wife Anne who, with my daughters Vanessa Bennett (and her husband Paul), Lisa Pearce and Jo Hamilton, read the proofs of *On Fishing* as carefully as they read the proofs of my novel *The Stream* – and who continue wonderfully to support me in all that I do; to my dear friends John and Jennifer Payne who also read these proofs as, a lifetime ago, they read the proofs of *The Pursuit of Stillwater Trout* with eagle – and as it happens, legal – eyes; and to my good friend Eric Williams, who likewise endured the proofs and who commented perceptively on the text. I also want to acknowledge the contribution of Myles Archibald, my publisher at HarperCollins, whose idea this book was and who went to such lengths to give me the end result that I wanted.

There are some others I wish to thank. I want to express here my deep gratitude to those whose friendship and whose companionship at the waterside has so enriched my life – in most cases for over 30 years: Timothy Benn, Gary Borger, Fred Buller, Stewart Canham, Ron Clark, John Goddard, Tony Hayter, Peter Lapsley, Nick Lyons and Michael McCarthy, together with Alan and Judi Johnson, Tony and Vicki Barton-Hall, John and the late Rita Jacobs and Barbara and the late John Tomkinson (the affectionately drawn subjects of 'A Fly Fishing Club' in my book *Trout etcetera*); and Sir Peter Cresswell and David Beazley, hitherto unmentioned members of that most civilized of groups The Coarse Tendency, which I am proud to have originated and named.

Lastly, I want to use this opportunity to record my debt to the late Cyril Pybus, English Master at St Mary's Grammar School, Darlington for 38 years until his retirement in 1964. Like many dedicated teachers, I suspect, 'Danny' Pybus can never have anticipated fully the effect on his pupils of quiet encouragement. He greatly encouraged me in my writing – and as a consequence greatly influenced my life. Without him this book, my previous books and anything else that I have published, might never have been written.

Introduction

As I note in the acknowledgements this book contains a mixture of new essays and writing of mine that has appeared in various publications over the years. The new pieces are in the main, the longer pieces. The shorter pieces, though not exclusively, are from *The Times*.

All of the latter, no matter where originally published, have been amended in some way, whether to include points that I did not have the space to include first time around, or to take account of new information, or to accommodate changes in context or circumstance. One or two have been completely reworked.

Because these pieces were individually written for publication at different times, each needed to be self-contained. One consequence is that from time to time information that appears in one article to make it complete appears in another for the same reason. I thought it better to let these very occasional, minor duplications stand than to introduce cross-references which, in my own reading, I tend to find a distraction.

In choosing what to include I have tried to convey something of the diversity of angling, its practices and its refinements; of the absorptions and passions it gives rise to, the places it takes us to, the literature it has stimulated and the threats to it that crowd in all around – many of them, it seems to me, alarmingly unnoticed by the average angler on the bank. Mostly, and perhaps unsurprisingly, the book reflects my own greatest interest – fly fishing for trout – but there are enough other subjects to justify, I think, the generic title my publisher suggested.

The pieces do not appear in any particular sequence: indeed, with minor tweaks I have let them run in a broadly alphabetical order. As I wrote in the introduction to my previous anthology, *Trout etcetera*, I dip into collections like this as though into a bran tub and I am not deceived that my own work will be treated differently by others. However, I began with 'One Long Morning' because I wanted to convey, at the outset, something of what the experience of fishing means to me and does for me. I have ended with 'Angling and the Future' because it self-evidently looks ahead.

I hope that readers will find both essays of interest – and maybe the odd paragraph that comes between them.

Brian Clarke
July, 2007

One Long Morning

THE *appeal of angling is about as easy to define as beauty or truth. We might as well try to weigh what fishing does for us, or measure it with rulers, as reduce it to words – especially for someone who has not fished. To get any sense of it at all, a non-angler would have to be in the one place he cannot possibly get: inside our heads. After all, that is where the real action is.*

* * *

THERE are not many places in Britain where the water is as bright and clean as the day God poured it, but this is one of them.

The road winds down the valley, hemmed in by hedges. Over the hedges, unseen and mostly unknown, the little stream flows scarcely casting-distance away. Looking at it over the old iron gate where I parked the car, I could see how short the fishable length is: maybe 300 yards from the wood just behind me to the place where the sedges grow out so far that they close the water off.

The meadow between the gate and the water is tussocked and flower-strewn, baked by the drought, pitted with the impressions of remembered hooves. Across it, deep within it, the stream hides. It is full of wild trout and it has never been stocked. Never. The great attraction.

Even when I was almost on top of it the water was difficult to see, the only clue it's here at all the line of sedges and rushes, the bright heads of purple loosestrife and the lollipops of reed mace that nod and sway.

The stream's a tiny thing, a rod's length wide here, a rod and a half there and it is extraordinarily deep. At some point, I guess, it must have been dug with a view to draining the land but nature has used the years well. As the reeds and sedges have softened the banks, so starwort and ranunculus have softened the bed. They orchestrate the water and the light.

I'd been told about the depth and the way the rushes and high sedges make bank fishing impossible. It's why, for all the stream's size, I'm waist-deep in chest waders, now.

It's not going to be easy. There's a strong, upstream wind. From down here, deep in the water with my head at meadow height, the sedges and tussocks are rearing high overhead, flailing and thrashing, ready for every back-cast. A procession of ripples is being pushed upstream, as though by an incoming tide. The sky is leaden; the low, grey clouds as long and uniform as plumped feather bolsters, flattening the light. No, it's not going to be easy.

Actually, it's not just the wind and the sedges and the lack of light that are the problem, it's the angle I'm at. This isn't a water for speculative casts. Here, you don't cast until you see a fish, a convention that has a practical edge because by casting blind you'd frighten unseen trout and reduce your already-slender chances still further. But to cast to sighted fish naturally means being able to see them which, if they're not rising, means being able to see into the water.

Which today I cannot do. Not much, anyway. The light and ripples are one thing, the fact that I'm waist-deep is another. This deep in, my eyes are not far above the water and the angle between them and the surface upstream where I need to look, is shallow. It means that, looking more than two or three yards ahead, all I can see is the grey, reflected sky. It's only when I look steeply down, close to my wadered legs, that I can see into the water.

The water is as clear as I'd been told. It's so clear and bright it almost might not be there. It's as clear as melted time.

On the bottom, between the dense growths of the water-plants, channels of flints and chalk gleam up. I can see the roughs and smooths of every stone, every chip and angle. They're so sharp and fine-edged they might have been picked out with scalpels. Caddis cases cover every one. The weed's alive with shrimps, nymphs, the larvae of this and that. This would be a fabulous place in a hatch, but there's little likelihood of one this morning. This morning, it's going to have to be the nymph.

The green canyons between the weed beds and the channels along the bottom will all have fish in them but, because of the angle I'm at, I'll be on top of any trout before I realise it's there. It'll be on the open gravel patches that I'll mostly be concentrating and there aren't many of those. The gravels and chalk reflect the light and any fish on them should be visible from a distance.

I say should be.

I've got company. A water vole sniffle-snuffles towards me on some busy errand, realises that it has got company as well, and dives. A pair of buzzards kee-kees across the narrow strip of sky I can see between the sedges to my left and the sedges to my right. A flock of crows rises like black ashes above one bank and disappears behind the other, leaving its cacophonous caw-cawing behind.

I tuck the little 8ft three-weight under my arm, slide a hand into a pocket and grope and trace among the bottles and spools, seeking the fly-box. I'll start small and change as I need. A size 16 nymph goes onto a 2lbs point.

I put a smear of flotant on the thick end of the leader so that it rides high on the surface, where I can see it. Normally, I'd put a sinking compound onto the leader near the fly as well, to get it off the surface, but the compound is opaque and will make the leader more visible in these conditions, so I'll do without it today. I click the fly onto a rod-ring, loop the leader back around the cage of my reel and tighten up. Ready. The trout have my attention.

Of course, I won't be looking for a trout because I know I won't see one – not an outlined, clearly defined one, anyway. I'll be looking for hints and winks of trout, for linear shades and brushstrokes, for sepia suggestions; for patches of gravel or chalk where, at some point, the stones seem curiously straight-edged. I'll be looking for faint lateral movements, for suggestions of rhythmic pulses that might resolve into a tail. No, I'll not be looking for fish. I'll be looking for water, but in a firmer form.

If finding fish today's going to be one thing, catching them is going to be another. These fish won't only be difficult to see, they'll be hair-triggered, as well. It's not just the clarity of the water and the fact that they are fished for. What's going to make them edgy is that everything else knows they're here and wants them.

This valley's full of otters and herons and cormorants. No-one has a problem with the otters because they're a part of our heritage and here in natural numbers and it's good to have them back after so long. But the herons around here come in vast numbers because of the fish farms on the streams nearby. The cormorants have a roost just a few miles away. The numbers of both birds are unnatural and they take an unnatural toll. A bright thread of tinsel like this, so difficult to see from the road, must glint and beckon from the air.

The fish I'm looking at is up there to the right. It's lying on that patch of gravel at the foot of the little alder, a sepia brush-stroke in front of the stone. It's a half-pounder, maybe a little more. A nice trout.

I can't cast from here. It's not just that the sedges will snatch at my back-cast, it's that any line I throw will fall across that bed of starwort breaking the surface. The line will catch on the weed and the current on the far side will swing the leader around. The leader and the fly. Drag. Fatal, in this place.

That's what I've got to do. I've got to get to the foot of the little alder on my own bank and cast from there. From there, I'll have a diagonal of clear water between myself and the fish. I've got to get up there without disturbing it.

It takes an age. It's not just the weight of weed I've got to push through, or the weight of the water clamped around my legs and middle, it's the need for caution. Every step is so slow and laboured, coiled and taut. Bed my left foot down, take my weight on it, lift my right foot and ease it forward. Push against the weed, push against the water, touch down. Grope and trace over the bottom, reading it like Braille. Find a purchase. Set it down. Take the weight. Now my left foot, ditto.

It's taken five minutes to move five yards, but I'm in position. Me here, the fish there. I'm wound up and locked on, joined to the fish by ancient choreography, by thousands of years, maybe millions.

Crouch lower. Move slowly. Turn my head slowly in case my Polaroids catch the light and semaphore a warning. Keep the rod down. Watch my backcast, watch the flailing sedges, watch the fish, watch everything. The new world fades and the old closes in. The forest and the glade enfold. I am alert for the grunt or the rustle, for the parting of the grasses and the glimpse of fur or hide.

A coot creaks. My eyes are burning through the water, burning into the fish, which still hasn't moved. I drift the rod back, draw the bow tight, take aim along the arrow. I'm at home with this. I've been doing this since I first stood upright. I haven't needed to do it for food for thousands of years but the tug of it, the old compulsion, is still deep inside. Don't tell me this is a game or sport, this is the real thing. I am. The fish is. This is hunting, one on one.

Now! I let go the fly, flick the line into a low, controlled backcast and flick it forward again. It straightens – and the trout does an astonishing thing. It bolts. It bolts, just like that, leaving a little puff of silt drifting down on the current, as if to prove it had been there, once. I'm stunned. How could it? How could it have known? What had I done – or left undone?

I'm also not surprised. This is the way this fishing is. It's the difficulty that's the great attraction. I smile, say 'well done, fish' out loud and without embarrassment and move on.

The morning dissolves. Other patches of gravel, other sepia shades, other sudden boltings and compact dispersals. One fish, pricked and lost. More than two hours gone in a kind of limbo. I've come 250 yards, have maybe 50 more to go before the sedges and the rushes make progress impossible. Now I'm looking at another fish, the one that looks like a tear-drop because I'm right behind it, looking along its fuselage tail-edge on. He's in the gap between the upstream edge of the first weed bed and the tail-end of the one just above. He's a couple of feet down and just three rod-lengths away.

Time for another change. I've been ringing the changes all morning, constantly switching the size and weight of the nymph according to the fish and its depth and the speed of the current. I've been shortening and lengthening the leader according to how exposed I am to the wind and the place in the water where I have to put the fly down and yes, I can see I need another change, now. I take off the size 14 pheasant-tail, rummage through the fly-box and take out a size 12 shrimp, one of those tied with pale green silk, my colour-code for three turns of lead wire under the dressing.

The buzzards are back again. So are the crows. A squadron of swifts is on its way back to Africa. The high grasses thresh and the reed-mace waggles.

Being sheltered here, chest-deep behind this huge bed of star-wort is like standing in an aquarium. The surface is as still as glass and the leader's drooped across it. I can see the surface tension curving in along the nylon, exaggerating its width. It's putting a crack in the mirror. Beneath it, far down in the deep, green cave, first two minnows, then a few, then maybe a dozen come out of the weed-wall on one side and sidle across to the other, right in front of my waders, showing no sense of my presence. It's a God-moment, looking down like this. Such tiny, other-lived lives. They're so separate and contained, close and towered-over, so vulnerable and unaware. So watched. Is something up there, watching me?

No need to cast. I let the shrimp fall into the water, wriggle a couple of yards of line out through the top ring and let the current to my right carry them downstream behind me. Then I bring the rod forward, the leader straightens over the fish – and the wind blasts it to one side.

The trout does nothing. I flick the shrimp again and the same thing happens, but this time the trout turns a fraction towards it before resuming its line. It may have seen the fly, the leader going down, a herringbone of drag, I don't know what. But it certainly saw something. I change pattern, put on a little black-hackled beetle with a little more lead in it. The lead, if I get the cast right and the wind plays the game, will help the leader straighten and give me the entry I want. I pause for a while, waiting for a break between the gusts. My leader puts a crack in the mirror again. Another troupe of minnows. The buzzards and the rooks are back. Again, somewhere, the coot creaks. Creak on, coot.

This time as I cast, I check the line as the leader straightens and the momentum of the weighted nymph loops it suddenly forward and down. The little fly makes a hole in the water and it sinks at once, taking a foot of leader straight down with it. Perfect. A fast sink entry, right for line, right for depth. As the fly's about to pass the fish I move the rod six inches and the nymph rises as though alive and trying to get away.

Again, the inexplicable. The moment I move the nymph the trout hurls itself forward, smacking the fly so hard that the fish comes clean through the surface. I glimpse its head clearly, glimpse its open mouth and its eye, see the leader stab and I tighten. No contact. Nothing at all. How? How? More questions. No more answers than before. Take my weight on my left foot, lift my right, push against the weight of the weed and the water. Move on.

Move on some more. Now I'm 20 yards from the end of the fishable water, the place where it becomes too deep to wade and where the sedges crowd in and make casting impossible. I'm also standing on a hump on the stream bed, which gives me more height and alters the angle of my view. I can see further from here.

Upstream a couple of bushes and a tree are cutting out the surface glare and there, to the right, there's a long patch of open water, really long, the biggest clear area I've seen all morning. It's maybe eight or 10 yards long and a couple wide. A shaft of sunlight, the first of the day, lights it up as if an inspiration.

Half way up, a shadow's sidling sideways over the bottom. That's a fish. So is that sepia brush-stroke to the right of it. Further over still, near the ranunculus, there's a steady throb and pulse. A trout's tail. Three fish together. Riches.

The closest fish is the biggest, maybe a pounder and he's in a crease on the bottom, a fast little run. I'll aim to put the fly two or three yards beyond him and on his line. First, I'll let it sink and trundle loosely back along the bottom. If he ignores that I'll cast again and try inducement.

I snip off the little beetle, knot on a size 12 shrimp tied with orange silk – my colour-code for eight turns of lead under the dressing – look up at the fish, look back at the shrimp and re-read the current. Hmmm. I snip the fly off again, fish a spool of nylon out and add two more feet to the leader. Now it's maybe 11 feet long. Eight or nine have been tricky enough so far, but instinct and experience tell me this is what I need.

Left foot planted and comfortable, right foot likewise. Stay still. Don't take my eyes off the fish. Wait for a pause in the wind. Wait. Wait. The old world creeps up again, the forest's silence enfolds. Any second now. Now! I slow the line as it zips through my left hand and the leader begins to unfurl. The heavy nymph straightens it, dives vertically over and goes in cleanly, right again for line, right again for depth.

The trout scarcely moves. One moment he's riding the water like a slim, tethered kite, the next he's drifting marginally to one side, the next he's back on line. It's a subtle movement, scarcely perceptible, but I'm not fooled. I've seen that a thousand times. I didn't see his mouth open but I know he has it, I know he has to have it and I tighten. The rod goes down, there's a moment's thrashing and splashing then he's charging upstream, doubling back downstream and lodged deep in the weed to my right.

Damn. It all happened in a flash. The only fish of the day and I could lose him in seconds. I wind down, lock tight and the little rod hoops. The weed surges and heaves but he won't come clear.

An old trick. I edge a little nearer, wind in as I go – and then let everything go slack. Sometimes, if you let everything go slack on a weeded fish, it will start to make its own way out. One minute. Two minutes. Three minutes and then, suddenly, from directly behind him, I put maximum pressure on again. The rod jags, jags again, the starwort surges and he's out, weed on the leader, weed over his head and eyes. He stops struggling, drifts towards me on the current, heavy and limp the way an unsighted fish always does. I bend, slip my hand under him and turn him upside down as I lift. Another old trick. He lies perfectly still the moment he's belly-up, again as they so often do. Then I peel away the weed, slip out the barbless hook and look at him.

He's the colour of light honey and pure-white bellied. Red spots and black spots freckle his sides. Each fin is clean-edged and sun-shot and perfect. His pectoral fins are as big as paddles. His tail, for his size, is huge.

What a privilege. Here I am alone in this wild, wonderful place, holding this wonderful wild creature in my hand. I'm conscious I'm maybe the first human to touch him, conscious in that moment that in that touch, I'm taking something from him that can never be replaced.

Time to put him back. I take a last look, lower him upright into the water and little by little loosen my fingers. I watch as his gills slowly open and close, feel the steel start to come back into him and the first, faint shrug. Another shrug or two and I let go completely and he slowly slides away. I watch him going, going, going.

How marvellous. I'm thrilled to have got him in this place, in these conditions, and doubly thrilled to see him go. I feel replete and calm. I've tapped into my roots again, trodden that ancient way again, swum again in those womb-waters dimly remembered.

I bite off the fly, reel the line in and turn to climb out. It's been a long, long morning. Three hours long, 300 yards long, maybe three million years long. Ask me now why I go fishing, ask me now.

Which Fly, When

THE *flies I use now are very different from the flies I used when I first started out. Indeed, they are unrecognisable from those early patterns. There are also far fewer of them.*

I was idly musing on this one day when I realised that my entire fly-fishing career could be plotted through this transition: through my choice of flies as an out-and-out beginner, to those I tied in the middle years, to the sparse collection in which I place all hope, now. Also, I realised, something else could be plotted: not just evolving choices of flies and ways of fishing them, but changes in fishing philosophy and even ultimate goals. Many others will be able to do likewise, for themselves.

In my case, frustration was the catalyst.

* * *

ALTHOUGH I had been an angler since childhood, I did not take up fly fishing until I was in my twenties – and did not take it up seriously until I reached my thirties. As a consequence, I found myself in much the same position as others who discover this wonderful activity at the time of life when they are at their busiest.

Life was so hectic that all time for fly fishing (though, natu-rally, not all time for gardening, washing up, interior decorating, exterior decorating, undertaking minor structural repairs, taking toddlers for walks, helping with the shopping and the school run and earning a living – there seems always time aplenty available for these other delights) had to be squeezed in. Whenever I went fishing, which was infrequently, I found myself beside some huge, intimidating lake, not knowing where to start and relying on shop-bought flies that I knew nothing about.

Naturally, my results reflected this. Most outings ended in disappointment. I would blank, or catch a small one, or miss two offers.

Then, eventually, it dawned. If I wanted better results I could only achieve them on the basis of greater skill, resulting from a better understanding of the business I was about. Only by submitting to that austere, top-hatted and frock-coated taskmaster Effort, I realised, could I hope to capitalise fully on my outings when they came.

And so I decided to stop my mechanistic, chuck-it-out, pull-it-back-and-hope approach. I did not like the drag and dead weight of sinking lines. I did not enjoy stripping lures. I did not know why fancy flies were taken or which to use when, where or how. I did know, though, that to survive a trout had to eat; that it ate flies and bugs; that it could only eat the flies and bugs available to it at a given time of day at a given time of year; and I knew, too, that if I could discover something about these bugs and how they might be imitated, I could improve my chances on the basis of thought and logic rather than on lucky dip and chance. I resolved, from that point on, to concentrate wholly on fishing artificial flies that imitated the real flies that trout regularly consume.

And so, as I recounted fully in *The Pursuit of Stillwater Trout*, I began to autopsy my own fish and to seek out the results of autopsies conducted by others. Then I constructed a small aquarium and stocked it with the kinds of insects I was finding inside fish: that is, with the kinds of insects that I knew for sure, trout ate.

It was as though the road to Damascus had become floodlit. Now I could see close-up not only what important nymphs and bugs looked like but how they moved, lived and hatched. I saw how pathetic as imitations the shop-bought articles were and what sensible representations would need to look like. I saw, as well, how those representations needed be moved on the end of my line: it was, of course, in the way the naturals themselves moved in my aquarium. In other words I began, for the first time, to understand what imitation and presentation were really about. I saw them not as some horns-locked, competing alternatives as much writing of the time seemed to suggest, but as necessary co-conspirators in the deception process.

Before long I was creating my own stillwater patterns and was moving them in the way I had watched the naturals move – sometimes exaggerating this movement to attract attention to the fly or to prompt a predatory reflex from any following fish. My results improved and my confidence improved. The more confident I became, the more fish I caught. In that first year on stillwaters – the only kind of fishing available to me – my catch rate went up 600 per cent.

Then fate stepped in. My work moved out of London and took me to Hampshire. Rivers as well as lakes – many of them glass-clear – became accessible for the first time.

New circumstances, new opportunities. I was able to get close to trout and to study them in their natural habitat. I watched how they responded to natural insects in and on the currents and began to imitate these river insects as I had imitated the bugs of stillwater. I watched how fish responded to the artificial flies cast by my friends and I amended my tactics and presentation in light of what I saw. I continued an interest in feeding behaviour and rise-forms because of the clues I realised they could reveal about the insects being taken. Over time, I took thousands of photographs and studied each one to see what it revealed. Gradually, almost unrecognised, a new factor was creeping into my fishing: it was the fascination of study and experiment in its own right.

It was around this time that John Goddard and I began to fish together and before long we decided to collaborate on a book. We decided from the outset to study not only the fish's behaviour, but the underwater world in which the fish lived.

We constructed large tanks with specially angled sides so that, crouched down beneath them, we could see the world as perceived by the trout: more particularly the fly, the angler and his equipment as perceived by the trout. We set cameras in waterproof housings onto the river bed.

We photographed flies from every angle, from both above water and below. We even, on a few memorable occasions, photographed flies' feet from under water, at night. (Yes, really. We were trying to understand how trout could go on rising unerringly to flies floating on the surface at night when we, peering down at the surface in the dark, could see no flies at all. Obviously, the fish could see something – but how and what it was we did not know).

With this work, for each of us, the search had moved from dressings that might catch trout or dressings that looked broadly like certain species of fly. Now, the goal had become the creation of dressings – and especially dry fly dressings – that would give a fish everything that we believed it might look for or expect to see. Dry fly dressings, we had realised from the outset, posed a special challenge: because they sit on the water's surface (i.e. in air) and are seen by the fish from below (i.e. through water), any view of them must be distorted by refraction.

Refraction influences the trout's view of the world in several ways. One of the things it does is to make it impossible for any trout below the surface to look up and see the world outside the water as clearly as we can see the world below water, when looking down at it from the bank. For reasons too complex to go into here, refraction turns most of the underside of the surface into a mirror that reflects the river or lake bed – or the water's gloomy depths. So in most places the ceiling of the trout's world is green or brown or sombrely dark. The exception, again for complex reasons, is a circle of daylight above the fish's head that acts as a kind of port-hole. The trout can see out into the world above water, but only through this porthole – and everything it does see is distorted. The common term for the mirrored area is, unsurprisingly, 'the mirror' and the round porthole through which the trout can see above water is 'the window'. (All of these extraordinary effects, and some of those that follow, are clearly shown in photographs in *The Trout and the Fly*, the book we eventually published).

John and I were keen to take account of these effects in our fly designs. In particular, we wanted to provide the trout with two visual features which are present in any fly sitting on the surface when it is viewed from below. The first was a tiny prickle of light spots that the feet of a fly transmit through the darkness of the mirror where they touch it. The second was wings that would appear to become separated from the body (rather in the manner of a flame from a gas jet) when the fly drifted from the mirror into the window.

One result of this work was a fly that was aerodynamically designed to land upside down, with the hook point uppermost, when cast. We did not set out to design a fly that landed upside down. Our aim was to design a fly that gave out the signals described above, to a trout looking up at the surface for approaching food: light dimples on the surface and wings that would flare over the edge of the window.

However, as we worked on such a fly, it became clear that the only way we could achieve our goal was by turning the fly upside-down. We were almost surprised – though more sensible men would not have been – when our end-product looked quite like a real fly, even to us.

John and I both knew, of course, that such refinements were not necessary for 99 per cent of the trout we tackled. Indeed, I believe that any effort to turn the hook upside down as an objective in its own right is wasted, offering aesthetic appeal but no observable, practical advantage. However, our upside-down (USD) patterns did bring about the downfall of some of those tantalising, pernickety, wary fish in the 1 per cent category – and that had been our aim.

This whole period was fascinating for us both. We had rummaged through the technicalities of fly design and presentation to an extent which, it is probably fair to say, few others had done. We had photographed much of what we had seen; we had documented it meticulously and we had put our work, through the resulting book, on record.

The period also marked a particular stage in my evolution as an angler: my absorption with the most difficult fish. Soon after the book was completed – and perhaps even as a reaction to such a long period of locked-away, esoteric study – my interest began to turn in the opposite direction. I began to look for simplicity.

The flies I have carried in the years since have become fewer and fewer and ever-more simple. They reflect my belief that appearance (i.e.pattern) in a dry fly is vastly less important than most writers would have us believe – and that the only really important requirement of a dry fly is that it be of correct size. Colour comes a distant second. I fish these few flies in the knowledge that most feeding trout are catchable if they do not know they are being fished for and are presented with flies that look as though they might be food, in a natural and unalarming way, when and where the trout expects to see them.

And so, these days, I do not drive to the waterside towing a trailer burdened with copies of every fly and bug known since Genesis, in triplicate. I do not carry representations of *Centroptilum pennulatum*. Nor of *Heptagenia lateralis*. Nor of *Rhithrogena haarupi*. *Ecdyonurus torrentis* is not in my box. *Hydropsyche pellucidula* has slung his hook. *Leptophlebia vespertina* might be in Argentina.

If anyone looks in my box these days – even fly box was an over-statement for years because I actually used those little plastic tubs that rolls of 35mm film come in – they will find only two kinds of general-purpose dry flies: little brown jobs and little black jobs. All the brown patterns are identical to one another and all the black patterns are identical to one another: it is only the hook sizes that differ.

The little black flies have a black seal's fur body with a short black hackle at the head. Nothing more. I carry these in sizes 14, 16 and 18. I use the largest size when hawthorn flies are about, the middle size to suggest black gnats and the 18s to suggest smuts.

The other flies are all sedge-style dressings. They have a seal's fur body, the overall hue of which is a warm olive-brown (I do not agonise over the shade of olive brown: each mixture varies and I do not find it matters a jot). The wings are fibres taken from a brown saddle hackle, tied horizontally along the back and clipped off square just beyond the hook bend. A short, brown hackle wound just behind the eye completes the job.

I do not carry a dun pattern at all for the smaller upwinged flies, because I know I do not need to. I know that virtually every surface-feeding trout that is eating small duns will accept the sedge pattern – and the sedge pattern has marginally more bulk (which makes it easier to see), floats longer (all those tiny bubbles trapped in all that seal's fur) and will last for several fish because it is more robust than a dun.

The only other brown fly I carry is a spinner pattern in sizes 14 and 16 and again, all are identical. They have the same olive-brown seal's fur body, a few brown hackle fibres for the tail and a strip of very thin plastic tied in the middle, just behind the hook eye, to suggest the spread wings of the egg-laying or dead natural. There is no hackle. If the wings are nicked at the base with scissors, on the rear edge, close to the body, they will not take on a propeller shape and cause the leader to kink. They will also collapse as though hinged when a trout sips the fly in.

Beyond these, the only dry flies I carry are for use on special occasions: mayflies for when the mayflies are up, daddy-long-legs for when the naturals are on the water. And that's it.

My nymph box is similarly sparse because, again, just a

handful of patterns meets most of my needs.

To cover any deep-lying fish or to explore a likely lie on a rain-fed river, the fly I most commonly use is an artificial shrimp. I tie these shrimps mostly on size 12s, with a few size 10s. I tie them with different amounts of lead wire under the dressing and distinguish one from another by tying each weight with its own colour of tying silk: in other words, I colour-code them. Unweighted, these dressings are deadly for fish on the fin, high in the water. Weighted, they are also useful for fishing deep down from reservoir banks – and as stalking flies on clear stillwaters.

The shrimp usually has the same seal's fur mix for the body as my dry flies. I rib the fur with gold wire and tie a thin, clear strip of plastic along the top of the body to suggest the natural shrimp's shell-like back. Other nymphs I use for general river fishing are size 16 and 18 midge pupa-style dressings, which have a tiny tungsten bead behind the eye. These little flies, attached to ultra-fine leaders, can be very effective when used against difficult fish – and when fishing for coarse fish, which I do quite often. If I need to get down fast in deep, heavy water, a hare's ear with a large tungsten bead head, often fished on the end of a long leader, does the job.

For fishing on lakes I am never without a range of midge pupa dressings in sizes 16 to eight, variously weighted. I also have a couple of long-hackled spider patterns which can be fished slowly while still suggesting life on a large scale; a damsel nymph; an absolutely deadly, weighted mayfly nymph that I tie with a marabou tail, dyed ivory; and a short, highly mobile black leech dressing that I will try if all else fails.

Add to these flies a few others accumulated over the years – those that have been given, bought or removed from overhanging branches – and you have my entire collection. Honest.

The pleasure I now take in simplicity does not mean that I need not have gone through all those earlier stages. Rather, it is something that I have arrived at, having been through all else. The early frustration, the resolve to learn more, the experiments with tanks and underwater cameras and, yes, those photographs of flies' feet from underwater at night and the rest have been, for me, essential. They have provided me with hours of fascination and have given me insights that I would not otherwise have achieved. They have, above all, taught me something about trout and have given me, as a consequence, a degree of confidence when I tie on one fly in preference to another and fish it this way instead of that.

But now I am content to follow a sublimely simpler path, dipping in and out of intensity as I please. Sometimes I do get locked-on and involved, but mostly I sit and watch, soak up the wonders of nature and all her works, talk with my friends and relax.

At the end of *A River Never Sleeps*, Roderick Haig-Brown wrote that 'perhaps fishing is, for me, only an excuse to be near rivers.' Like many others, I suspect, I know exactly what he means. The only difference between us is that I wouldn't go that far. Not quite that far.

Just yet.

A Second-hand Book

I ONCE met a man who told me he collected fishing books. He had 35,000, he said. Later – and maybe not surprisingly – I learned that he was well-known in collecting circles and that his library was one of the most valuable in the world. He had agents and scouts everywhere looking for rare volumes to buy. He kept some in his house in Washington, DC, but most of them were in vaults in a bank.

Most of us are not like that and could not afford to be like that. Lots of us have a few titles, many of us have dozens, some have hundreds. But we do not collect on an industrial scale. We find our books ourselves, one by one. We find them in jumble sales and charity stores and little local auctions. We find them in tucked-away corners of second-hand book shops and we are tickled pink if we find something exceptional.

That, anyway, is how it is for me. I found an exceptional book, once.

* * *

NO SPORT has a finer literature than angling and no sport's great works are more avidly sought.

The market in second-hand and antiquarian angling books is immense and world-wide. Some dealers handle little or nothing else, their catalogues offering hundreds of titles and thousands of volumes. There are periodic auctions in London, New York, Paris and elsewhere. Prices regularly reach four figures, sometimes five depending, naturally, on an individual book's significance, rarity and condition.

In a small way, I dabble myself. I am not on the London–New York–Paris circuit. Like lots of others, I am at the 'tenner, go-on-then, twenty' end of the market. My haunts are second-hand book shops, ideally tucked away and dimly lit: the kinds of places where time stops and all sound fades; cocooned places where the world resolves to spines and titles, dates and editions; to the whisper of turned pages and the occasional creak from a bare floorboard in the room overhead.

Everyone in such shops is hunting a bargain as he or she defines it, the angling collector's equivalent of landing a whopper. I have landed one or two – only one or two – myself. One of them was a seemingly ordinary reprint of Sir Edward Grey's classic *Fly-Fishing*. It is set to stand as prominently on my shelves as books of far greater historical importance and value.

Viscount Grey of Fallodon was Foreign Secretary from 1905 to 1916 and the man who, shortly before the First World War, famously saw the lights going out across Europe. Grey published his sensitive insight to his fishing life, times and philosophies in 1899 and it has been much sought-after ever since. A nice first edition of *Fly-Fishing* would, at turn-of-millennium prices, have fetched £200-plus. The 1928 reprint I have just acquired cost less than a tenth of that.

It seemed, as I reached it down from its tucked-away niche in the tucked-away little shop, just the kind of thing that would make a present for a friend. Then I noticed that it had a couple of dents on the cover and, on ends of the pages when the book was closed, a couple of faint red stains where water, presumably at some time splashed onto the cover, had run.

I was on the point of rejecting it when the edge of something inside the back cover caught my eye. It was a cracked, yellow-and brown cutting from the Liverpool *Daily Post* dated Tuesday, August 29, 1933. The headline read 'Sinking Yacht Rescue' and then 'Liverpool Men's Thrilling Escape'.

Beside the cutting there was an inscription, written in hand-writing that was scarcely bigger than the print used in the book itself. I started to decipher it but my eye was drawn relentlessly back to the cutting and I began to read.

It told how Mr A. McKie Reid, clearly a prominent Liverpool medical man, had set off on a sailing holiday with his friend Mr Leo Gradwell, a barrister. They had left Mostyn, in Wales, on the hired ketch *Lalage*, with two professional deckhands aboard. The plan was to sail up the west coast to Scotland but, in high winds and heavy seas in Caernarvon Bay, they found themselves in trouble. They used the engine for a time, then it broke down. Eventually finding themselves being driven towards the Skerries and with the seas running higher and higher, they made out to open water to run before the wind.

McKie Reid told the *Daily Post* how, as darkness fell, the boat began to take in water and they had to bail continuously. Finally, after what must have been a terrifying night, a trawler was sighted. Someone on the *Lalage* managed to flash a lamp briefly and the vessel – itself far off its own intended course – turned towards them.

Once alongside one another, the two boats rearing and plunging on the waves, McKie Reid made what he called 'the biggest jump of my life. The two deckhands jumped next and Mr

Gradwell made fast a towing line before he jumped. By this time the vessels had drifted apart and he nearly fell between them. About an hour after the trawler had taken the yacht in tow, it foundered. But for the trawler's arrival, we should have been lost.'

Dramatic stuff, all right – but why was the cutting here, in this fishing book? I flicked to the front and looked again at the name and address I had noticed written inside it: 'A. McKie Reid, 86 Rodney Street, Liverpool.' I turned back to the inscription alongside the cutting. Deciphered, it read: 'This book was with me on the *Lalage*. I threw it inside a rucksack, on board the trawler, before the boats were near enough for me to jump.' And then the initials 'A. McKie R.'

What I was holding in that shop – and what will now stay in my own collection instead of being passed on to someone else – was a book of little cash value yet one containing a text that generations of anglers have prized; a volume clearly so loved by its fly-fishing owner that in that dire, life-and-death situation, he took the time to grab it and hurl it to safety before jumping himself, even as the boat beneath his feet was making ready to go down.

I closed the book, went to the counter and handed over the £15 that was being asked for it. It was a bargain to me, if not to anyone else: this collector's whopper literally in the bag. I'd have been happy to pay twice the price for a book with that kind of history – and for the tell-tale water stains, extra.

A Shattered Dream

THE *affection that many of us hold for our rods can border on the irrational. There is something about a rod that, once owned, can make it highly personal whether mass-produced or not. I don't mean carbon fibre rods, marvellously functional though they are. I mean cane rods. Once cut and tapered, glued and varnished, cane comes to life again in the hand. Or, at least, we fancy it does. We fancy we can feel the throb and pulse of it clean through the corks.*

With carbon fibre, all this wonderful subjectivity is lost. Carbon fibre performs better. It can be manufactured to produce any action required of it. We can abuse it constantly without impairing its performance. Carbon fibre has replaced cane for very good reasons. But still it is synthetic stuff, inert and characterless. It cannot tap into the emotions the way split cane used to do.

To lose a cherished split cane rod – worse still, to break one – can be a shattering experience in every sense. I know it only too well.

* * *

I HAVE many fishing rods, but I have only ever loved three. All were made of cane. One is a Wallis Wizard, the brilliant whole-cane butt, split cane middle-and-top design by F.W.K. Wallis, the legendary Avon barbel specialist. I bought it as a lad by doing a newspaper round. I have it still. It is still in good heart and, more to the point, still in its original number of pieces.

The second rod is a Fario Club, one of the great creations of

Charles Ritz, the famous hotelier who, in fly-fishing circles, is infinitely more famous as a designer of trout rods. I bought this 8ft 5in piece of honey-coloured delight with the first royalty cheque from my first book, half a lifetime ago.

I did most of my dry fly and nymph fishing with the Fario Club for ten years after that. Eventually, I broke its back – literally – when trying to keep low on a treeless bank while casting to a fish in distant mid-river. Down on one knee, while concentrating hard on the fish and reaching for distance, the line fell too low on the back cast, snagged a meadow buttercup – and did not come forward.

The third rod, a 6ft 9in AFTM-4 brook rod built by Constable, was as light and delicate as a fairy's wand and it cast spells as well as lines. It was as crisp and precise as a rapier – and as deadly. My wife gave it to me on one of my Big Zero birthdays, and I was thrilled to have it.

Cliff Constable was one of the finest builders of split cane this country has produced and his staggered-ferrule brook rod was his finest achievement. I asked my friend Stewart Canham, master fly-tyer and furnisher of cane rods so exquisite that they would not have looked out of place in a Bond Street window, to finish the cane for me.

Now Stewart is an extraordinary man, a big, multi-talented man with hands the size of bin lids. For all that he has an exquisite delicacy of touch and specialises in creating delicate things. One of his one-time interests, for example, was icing cakes and he iced the wedding cake he made for one of my daughters. It was so wonderfully done, so decorated about with sprays of flowers he had made from icing that guests were peering at them this way and that, wondering if they were real. His fly-tying was, a doctor friend of mine said, more delicate than brain surgery. At one time, interested in butterflies, he bred them by the hundred and produced cases of them so delicately spread and pinned that they could have been exhibits in the Natural History Museum. Everything that Stewart Canham decides to do, he does to perfection.

When it came to my rod, he never produced a more personalised thing. All the usual restrained touches were there, from the subtlety of the matt varnish instead of gloss to the near-transparent whippings, tipped with black. But it was the rest, the attention to so much tiny detail, that made the rod truly unique.

When he delivered it, I found that Stewart had got Constable to autograph the cane. A tiny ephermerid nymph, beautifully drawn in Indian ink, was crawling up the butt amid the details of rod length and line weight and the like. The 20-inch stopper that extended the butt section to the length of the top section for carrying purposes was wound about with ivy, drawn in Indian ink, in-filled with white. And so on and so on. He had produced less a rod, more an artwork and it carried a freight of sentiment for me.

Mayfly time in Dorset. A friend invited me down. It was a lovely day, warm and sunny but with – note it – a downstream breeze. The hawthorn blossom was out. The ranunculus was in flower. Swifts curved and sculpted the air. From time to time, wagtails wagged and kingfishers skimmed. In a sidestream, we saw a fish lying awkwardly just downstream of a tree. Mike suggested I give it a go. I slipped under a barbed wire fence and slid into the deep water.

It took several minutes to get into position and feel comfortable. All the time, the fish went on rising and moving steadily upstream towards the tree, narrowing the angle where my fly would have to go. To have any chance, the leader would have to overshoot the fish and be squeezed into the space between the water and the branches. It would take a driven cast, all wrist, to create the tight loop I was going to need. And I would have to take care with the back-cast to avoid the alder that grew over the water behind me. I studied the situation and looked back at my friend. 'Thanks a lot, Mike,' I remember saying.

It must have been on the fourth or fifth attempt that the breeze suddenly strengthened. In mid false-cast I took account of it. I tightened the loop still more. I applied yet more wrist. I let the final back cast straighten and then drove it forward.

It did not come. There was an odd sensation, impossible to describe, but something, somehow, somewhere seemed to grate. In the concentration of the moment, I assumed that I had snagged the alder. I have snagged trees a thousand times. Foolishly, I did not bother to turn. I flicked the rod again, expecting either the fly to come free or the branch to give and cushion the movement. I have done that and seen that a thousand times, too.

Nothing. No give. Absolutely no give, but again a grating feeling and this time a sound. I turned and instinctively looked for my line and fly. The line was well clear of the alder and to the right. The fly was on the barbed wire fence that I had forgotten about. My eyes followed the line back from the fence to my rod. I saw the oddity of an angle in the silken curve, two rings back from the tip. I saw the cane splintered and light shining through the long, loved fibres.

For a long time, I could not take it in. I suppose the realisation of what I was seeing, the pain of it, was somehow dulled, the way that the shock of an injury sometimes can be. Then, all the things I had loved about the rod – its exquisite beauty, the occasion it commemorated, the scores of magical moments I had experienced with it – rushed through my mind in a torrent.

Mike said it was two minutes before I spoke. I simply stood there uncomprehending, staring at one of the three or four possessions I treasured most in the world, now utterly ruined. I know we all have such moments, but that gives no comfort. It was – it still is – terrible.

Wildlife, the Media and Us

As sports go, angling is well-provided with media. Coarse, trout and sea anglers all have several magazines apiece and fishing as a whole has long supported two weekly newspapers. Together, they help us to keep abreast of developments in and around the waterside and to stay on top of new tackle and techniques. By and large, they serve us well.

But not always. Every now and then an editor has a rush of blood to the head. Then, it is as though he loses all sense of proportion. It is as though he sees angling and our small world as the whole world – or else he consciously disregards the wider world completely. Neither is a great idea, but for the most part this matters little. In the main, no-one in the wider world cares much about what anglers think and say – and why should they?

When angling editors go overboard about something which the public holds dear, though, everything changes. Then, real problems can arise – some of them profoundly damaging.

* * *

Pretty well every issue of every publication in Britain is bought by news agencies as a matter of course, angling publications not excluded. Journalists – mostly freelance journalists who live by the column-inches they can generate and the air time they can clock up – read them in the hope of picking up a snippet here, a story there. Insofar as angling is concerned, they know that the

British public is besotted with the furred, the feathered and the cuddly and if some angling editor's rush of blood appears to put him at odds with this, then the telephones ring, news editors get busy and a view that was originally aimed at an angling audience alone hits several million breakfast tables overnight.

This is why, whatever concerns might exist in angling's media about creatures other than fish – and concerns do arise from time to time – a cautious and measured response is wisest. The temptation to rant to readers for the sake of short-term impact, needs to be tempered with a realisation that outside eyes will be watching and that long-term damage might ensue.

We have seen it over the years with swans and otters– and with cormorants in particular. All three, at one level or another, can have an impact on our sport but the article that begins with pointing this out, that moves on to an indignant 'something should be done about it' (always, note, by someone else) and that then demands that populations of whatever it is be controlled, is destined to become 'Anglers demand cull of swans/otters/cormorants/babies/old people/the halt and the lame', or whatever.

It is then that the perceived, short-term editorial satisfactions of 'making a stand on behalf of our readers' as fishing editors love to put it, can lead to huge and lasting damage outside angling. Then it is not swans/otters/cormorants or whatever that is most likely to end up in the dock, but angling itself.

Because of one particular incident I want to focus on cormorants, but there are a couple of points on swans and otters to be made, first.

Swans (dealt with at more length elsewhere) can create two problems when, as sometimes happens, they descend in their scores and their hundreds on a short length of water. The first is that they can make fishing, even the simple act of casting, physically impossible. The second is that they can so denude the water of the plants on which they feed that they devastate the cover and bug life on which fish depend.

Given the right of swans to exist, their grace and beauty, the affection in which the public holds them and the power of the Royal Society for the Protection of Birds, any approach to problem flocks has to be measured and thought out. It may well be possible to get the public to recognise the birds' impact on fish and fisheries, but that progress will only come through education and negotiation and it will take many years to achieve.

The same principle applies to otters, which have made a dramatic recovery after numbers collapsed in the second half of the 20th century. This recovery has been stimulated by the release into the wild of artificially reared cubs over a period of years. Through natural breeding and because there is so much virgin territory to be reoccupied, numbers have gone up significantly.

Otters eat fish, but they also have huge territories and so the impact on a given section of a river is likely to be small. It is a different story on lakes, especially if an otter occupies a holt near a commercial stillwater fishery stocked with carp and rears her cubs there. Then, significant numbers of carp – some of them costing thousands of pounds apiece – may be taken, the quality of fishing is likely to decline and the owner's livelihood may well be threatened. The answer is not for anglers and editors to demand impotently that 'something be done' (as some have) but for us all to recognise that the otter, like the swan, is an iconic species much loved by the public and that, if push ever came to shove, the public would unhesitatingly back otters against smelly old fish and those who support them.

The only sensible course of action for anyone concerned for fish and fishing is to accept that the otter is here to stay – I, for one, am delighted about it – and for fishery owners to take whatever steps they can to protect their waters. If fencing and the like cannot be afforded and no public funds are forthcoming to help build them, then the loss of fish will need to be offset through the prices charged: and if the market will not stand that, then the fishery, like any other enterprise caught by changing market conditions, is likely to close. We may think that brutal but the public is likely to see it as simply a fact of life. The only safe and effective solutions to concerns about swans, otters or any other form of wildlife are ones that public opinion will support.

Enter cormorants. If anglers want to see the potential for damage that can be caused by editors getting it wrong, let them consider the impact, many years ago, of a rant against cormorants in a national angling newspaper.

In 1996 a campaign against cormorants was launched by the publication concerned. The report, over several pages, set out the damage that cormorants can do to fisheries, was headlined in huge type on the front page 'These birds must be killed' and was accompanied by a picture of a man crouching down with a shotgun at the ready.

The story implied that anglers were shooting cormorants on a large scale and that large numbers more needed to be shot; that organised bands of militants were roaming the countryside blasting at every black bird in sight and that many of their fellows condoned it. The whole episode was a text-book example of how not to handle an emotive issue and, not surprisingly, a national out-cry resulted. Many of our fellow-conservationists rightly deplored it. Politicians of varying hues leapt on the bandwagon. Animal rights extremists whipped up the horses. The entire sport, along with its furious and hapless spokesmen, was put on the back foot.

Then the inevitable happened. The media spotlight fell onto something else and the row calmed down. But it left dreadful damage behind. Those images and headlines and that whipped-up outcry had gone deep into the public psyche. In the minds of many, the image of angling as a harmless and rather dotty pursuit had been tarnished. We are continuing to live with the conse-quences. In a climate in which, increasingly, all creatures are seen as fellow passengers on planet earth, angling – given the demise of foxhunting – is now in the sights.

It was all so short-sighted and unnecessary. The issue is not that cormorants do great damage – there is no doubt that, locally, they do – but how best the problem might be tackled. If we are to make real progress on this, as on other sensitive issues, rants must be avoided and loudly condemned when they occur. We need to deal with the world as it exists and not as we would like it to be. We need to deal with facts. Here, in relation to cormorants, are a few.

First, there is no doubt that cormorant numbers are rising rapidly. By the year 2000 it was estimated that there were up to half a million birds in Europe, of which around 15,000 nested in Britain, many of them inland. This indigenous population was even then being steadily supplemented by an influx of birds from the mainland. These incomers boosted the number of birds over-wintering here to around 25,000. Around 10,000 of these birds wintered inland and it was recognised that even birds living on the coasts will fly many miles inland to find food. Cormorant numbers have gone on rising ever since. There are single colonies of many hundred of birds close to some of our biggest lakes.

A range of factors is likely to be involved in this population growth. The first is that the free control of cormorants was banned under the Wildlife and Countryside Act of 1981, a piece of UK legislation giving effect to the European Union's Birds Directive. Other factors include the fishing-out by commercial boats of inshore waters where cormorants would normally hunt; the creation of more and more self-stocking reservoirs and lakes as a result of gravel extraction and the like; a growth in the numbers of waters artificially stocked with trout both for food and for sport; a growth in the numbers of heavily stocked commercial coarse fisheries and a reduction in poisons like DDT in the food chain which, in the past, have kept cormorant numbers down.

What has it all meant for anglers? It has given us two problems. The first is the sheer tonnage of fish that cormorants eat. The second is the vast number of fish that the birds injure and kill but do not eat.

At the most conservative estimate (conservative estimates are best because exaggeration simply undermines our case) the average cormorant eats 1lb of fish a day, which means that in a year six birds will eat one ton, 600 birds will eat 100 tons, 6,000 birds will eat 1,000 tons. While grossing up figures gives staggering totals, the net impact of this predation is not easy to calculate, not least because no-one knows what freshwater fish populations are, overall. What we can assume, however, is that the birds will get their food from the easiest places (most likely small, heavily stocked waters of the kind anglers have created); and what we know is that the damage comes in the particular, not the general – that is, that the damage done to individual fisheries, whatever is happening to fisheries at large, can be dire.

But that is only part of it. While natural mortalities in fish stocks, spawning failures, predation by other creatures and the like all have to go into the negative mix, so do all those fish not eaten but fatally injured by cormorants. When hunting, cormorants often behave like pack animals or sharks: they seem to go into a feeding frenzy. Then, anglers' concerns become even more clear. Cormorants have large, sharp, hooked bills and will chase most fish that swim, other than the very largest. The injuries they inflict are quite unmistakable – lines across the sides of a fish showing where the bill has taken hold and one or more short, deep slashes, usually in the belly, where the bill hook has gone in. Fish injured in this way but not eaten, are likely to die quickly from their injuries or to die later from disease.

I can speak of it all personally. For some seasons, many of the fish I have been catching from my local river have shown signs of cormorant damage. I have caught many trout weighing around 3lbs that have had cormorant wounds across their flanks, indicating that they had been attacked by birds even though the birds could not cope with their size. One of the biggest grayling I have ever caught – it came from a stream so small and overgrown I cannot imagine how a cormorant got into it – weighed 2lbs 13oz and had cormorant marks across its sides. On another river I found a 6lbs salmon kelt dying in the margins, with cormorant slashes deep in its gut. A fish farmer I know was able to walk right up to one bird because it had so gorged on small trout that it could not take off.

Many a regular angler has similar stories to tell. There is no doubt that cormorants are not just one more big bird. In large numbers they are an obvious menace to waters within flying distance, whatever statistical evidence might currently be lacking.

Politics, however, is the art of the possible. If the birds cannot be fully controlled – and under both British and European law they cannot – then anglers and those who represent them must make the best use of circumstances as they stand. This is what angling's representative bodies have been doing, with some limited success. Thanks to their efforts, where significant damage to a fishery can be proven, a licence to shoot a small number of birds as a means of scaring away others (albeit only to make them fly to someone else's water nearby) can now be obtained.

To gain further concessions will take a steady accumulation of credible case histories, wider research (when did researchers ever recommend less?), bridge-building with other conservation groups, reasoned explanation of our concerns to them, to the public and to the politicians who hold the levers of power and, not least, education of the angling community itself.

An important part of this effort must be to win public recognition of the fact that our environment needs to be seen in the round. Specifically, we need acknowledgement of two points. The first is that, of necessity, we have created on our island a landscape that is wholly artificial – and hence everything within it needs to be managed to maintain balances that, for better or worse, we have long since upset in our search for food, shelter and diversion. The second is conscious acknowledgment that, although they may not be as cuddly or as photogenic as their furred and feathered friends, fish are a part in our wildlife heritage and have a place in that wider equation, too.

In the meantime, any relief from cormorants that can be achieved – tweaks to legislation here, alleviations there – are likely to fall short of what anglers would like to see. High bird numbers, and the problems that come with them, are here for years to come.

They will be around longer – and maybe longer than angling itself – if the hotheads have their way.

All You Need to Know

I READ *somewhere that more books have been written about angling than about any other subject except mathematics. I have no idea who made the calculation, but it was probably a mathematician – and not a very good one, at that.*

Even so, there are many thousands of angling books in print and they have come in all guises: factual books, fishing guides and diaries, reminiscences, anthologies like this. A few, among the very best, break new ground – not an easy thing to do in this ancient sport. Others, also among the best, have a literary quality that makes them timeless. Lots, alas, add only to the word mountain.

* * *

I WAS fishing with one of my closest friends, a man who, because of his many excellent books and articles, has become a household name in the fly-fishing world. We fell to talking about the tide of angling literature – the hundreds of books, the thousands – that has been published since Dame Juliana Berners gave us the first work on angling in English, in 1496.

My friend and I were as one. We agreed that while there had been works of technical brilliance over the years, and many sublimely written texts, vast numbers of books had contributed nothing, at great length. 'In fact', I said, 'it would be interesting to go the other way, as an exercise – to see how much information you could squeeze into the fewest possible words.' A light bulb pinged in my head. 'Actually, the really essential things about angling can be very simply stated. I think I'll write a new book, myself. It will be called *All you Really Need to Know about Fly-fishing*. It will be about seven pages long.'

My friend's stride faltered and his jaw dropped. 'Blimey', he said, somehow conveying that his entire past life – all those books, all those articles – was passing before his eyes, 'you can't do that, you'll put me out of business.'

It was a joke, of course, but for all that, the essentials of fly fishing would consume very few trees. I once tried to squeeze quite a few of them into a reply to the youngest reader of *The Times* to have written to me up to that point. Peter was 13. He enjoyed coarse fishing but, on a holiday in Wales, had seen someone catch a grayling on a dry fly and had been fascinated. His father had suggested he write to me. What exactly was dry fly fishing and how could he get started?

Here, more or less, is what I told him.

Dry fly fishing is a way of catching fish – mostly trout or grayling, but plenty of other species as well – on imitations of the kinds of natural flies they are accustomed to taking from the surface.

To do it, I told Peter, he would be best off with a fly-rod about 9ft long, rated what is called AFTM-6. He would need an AFTM-6, double-tapered, floating flyline to use with it and a reel to put the line on. This outfit would do the job he wanted and be versatile enough for lots of other fishing as well. He should persuade his father to buy him a couple of lessons with a professional fly-casting instructor. The instructor would teach him how to cast correctly and practice would take care of distance and accuracy. He would also be shown how to do fiddly things like joining a nylon 'leader' to the line and a fly to the leader. He would be using only one fly at a time and it would be treated to float. At the water, the aim would be to get that fly to the surface in front of a targeted, rising fish, in a natural and unalarming way.

When Peter approached a river, I said, it should be in the knowledge that a fish is a wild and wary thing, easily 'put down'. What is more, he should know that in a river fish have to face the flow and so, when they are hungry, they look upstream for the flies and bugs the current brings downstream towards them.

What did all of this mean? It meant that he should avoid alerting the fish to his presence either by the way he dressed or the way he moved and that the best approach to a fish looking upstream was from downstream – from its blind side.

On the flies to be cast, I explained that most of the natural flies fish eat are not much more than a centimetre long and that if Peter wanted to maximise his chances, his artificial flies should be tiny as well. This question of size, I wrote, was the single most important factor where artificial flies were concerned. The only other important factor was colour and because most natural flies are drab as well as small, his flies needed to be drab also: browns and blacks would cover most situations.

With all of these matters taken care of, the need was to ensure that the cast fly floated towards the fish as daintily and unhindered as the naturals all around it. That meant avoiding drag. Drag is what Peter would often see, after casting out: the current would push on the line and leader floating on the water and would create a downstream curve in them. Sooner or later and sometimes instantly, this push on the line and leader would pull on the fly and cause it to skate across the surface in an unnatural way. Minute amounts of such drag, quite invisible from the banks, could be enough to kill all chances.

Drag can best be avoided, I wrote, by having the minimum amount of line lying on the surface in the first place and by careful choice of the position from which the cast is made. Most often, the best place will be from just behind the fish and a little to one side of it; but often, paradoxically, it will be from directly opposite the quarry, as well.

When he had got everything right and his fish had tilted up, opened its mouth and taken his fly, I told Peter he should give it a moment to close its mouth and tilt down again before lifting – not yanking – the rod end upwards and setting the hook. A few words about landing the fish, fishing barbless, the value of joining a local club and – well, all right, then, recommendations for a couple of books, my own astonishingly among them – rounded the letter off.

I knew that success would not take long if Peter followed these simple suggestions – and so it proved. I also know that in my letter I have the makings of Chapter 1 – All you Really Need to Know About Dry Fly Fishing in that seven-page book I had talked about. Chapter 2 – All You Really Need to Know About Wet Fly and Nymph Fishing – surely cannot be far behind.

Naturally, I told my famous writer-friend. He was gratifyingly appalled.

Arthur Ransome

IT MUST *be fascinating to have someone we thought we knew well, cast in a new light by a sudden turn of events. The mere possibility that long-held assumptions could be wrong would have us sitting bolt upright and curious.*

Even news about someone remote can, we all know, have this effect: for example, when damaging allegations surface about a national figure. The charges do not have to be based on fact to set the weevils at work – all they need to do is to appear. Ideally, for the media, they should surface about a revered figure who is long since dead and so cannot lodge a defence. Tarnished Idol Syndrome always makes news.

*   *   *

IT'S NOT EVERY day that I get to think kindly about Lenin or Trotsky or even, come to think of it, about certain personages in MI5 and MI6. I mean it wouldn't be, would it? We angling correspondents have plenty to do without getting mixed up in politics and revolutions and counter-intelligence, thank you very much.

Still, credit where credit is due. Had it not been for the foregoing folk, Arthur Ransome would not have been making the news the way he has in recent years, at first identified and then exonerated as a possible Bolshevik spy – and then I would have had no peg on which to hang my own information about him.

Of course, it had long been known that the famous foreign

correspondent and children's author got close to the revolutionary leaders while reporting from Russia around 1917. And we can assume that he got a lot closer still to Trotsky's secretary, Evgenia Shelepina, because he had an affair with her before the two eventually married.

Yet the fact that Ransome might, just might, have been a spy or a double agent was not aired until some of his private papers came to light in 2002. In 2005, the National Archive released MI5 files relating to the time Ransome was a journalist in Russia, between 1913 and 1925 – and raised similar questions.

The MI5 files made it clear that Ransome had been watched by the security services because they feared he had become a propagandist for the Bolsheviks while working in Petrograd, then the Russian capital. One informant claimed that Ransome was expected to move into the Kremlin to live. Another report said that Ransome had been considered such a potential risk to British interests that a top-secret paper on him was circulated to the 'King and the War Cabinet'.

As late as 1927, by which time he was back in England and domestically ensconced, a 'confidential source' was reporting that 'Arthur Ransome is a traitor, married to a Bolshevik woman, he is an undoubted Communist and in the pay of the Russian Secret Service'.

While all of this was being filed away by MI5, other material was giving rise in the agency to the contrary view: that Ransome was not only not a traitor but actually a spy for MI6, working against the new Russian leadership. (How, it must have seemed as reasonable to ask then as now, could MI5 not have known for certain, one way or the other? What does it tell us of communication between the two in those tumultuous times?).

Whatever the truth, such exotic possibilities in Ransome's background will have surprised many a reader of *Swallows and Amazons*. More prosaically, perhaps, some others may be surprised to learn of Ransome's background as an angler. Ransome was not only a passionate angler but wrote extensively about his sport. He became one of the finest angling correspondents to write for a national newspaper in the 20th century.

Though many aspects of Ransome's life have been extensively chronicled, Ransome's work as an angling correspondent has been as submerged from view of late as split-shot beneath a float.

Fishing and fishermen stimulated some of Ransome's best writing and led to one of the best collections of essays in a sporting literature that goes back to 1496. It led to a second collection of angling pieces and to a fine exploration of Ransome as both writer and angler by Jeremy Swift – *Arthur Ransome on Fishing* – published in 1994.

Ransome was born in Leeds in 1884, the son of an angling professor of history who was himself the son of an angling father. Early family holidays were spent near Coniston, in the Lake District, walking, boating and learning to fish – experiences that were later to be deeply mined for his children's books and which, between his travels, constantly drew him back.

A somewhat chequered education that took in an unhappy spell at Rugby, eventually led to a place at Yorkshire College – later Leeds University – where Ransome surprisingly began to read science before dropping out. He headed for the bright lights of Chelsea, having determined to become a writer and threw himself into it with huge energy. By the time he had reached his mid-20s he had a string of books behind him – including a critical study of Edgar Allan Poe – and had married for the first time.

This marriage, to Ivy Walker, of Bournemouth, was a disaster and Ransome was soon looking for an escape. From 1913 on, Ransome spent much of his time in Russia, writing the kinds of insider reports for the *Daily News* and the *Observer* that caused the security services to take an interest, dallying with Evgenia – and fishing wherever and whenever he could. He returned to England with Evgenia in 1925 and settled in the Lake District. The same year he began an angling column for the then *Manchester Guardian*.

Between August that year and September 1929, Ransome produced 150 pieces, most of them as polished as gemstones. He wrote on people and places, tackle and trout, wet flies and the weather. He wrote on 'Bulls and Kindred Phenomena', on 'Talking to the Fish', on 'Failing to Catch Tench' and on scores of other subjects besides. He wrote about them all with knowledge and insight and warmth and wry humour. He crafted every piece in a style that engaged the non-angling reader as well as the smitten.

Fifty of the best pieces, plus a translation of angling passages from Sergei Aksakov, the great chronicler of Russian life, appeared in *Rod and Line* (1929) – a book which Sir Michael Hordern, another keen angler, brought memorably to life for television.

The opening sentence of the first piece in *Rod and Line*, is a corker: 'The pleasures of fishing are chiefly to be found in rivers, lakes and tackle shops and, of the three, the last are least affected by the weather.'

Among several later penetrating essays is one on the theme that angling is 'a frank resumption of Palaeolithic life without the spur of Palaeolithic hunger'. In that piece, as often elsewhere,

Ransome goes to the heart of it: 'Escaping to the Stone Age by the morning train from Manchester, the fisherman engages in an activity that allows him to shed the centuries as a dog shakes off water and to recapture not his own youth merely, but the youth of the world'.

Ransome's second collection, which included the scripts of some of his radio broadcasts, was published as *Mainly About Fishing* (1959). A portrait of Ransome tying one of the flies shown on the cover of this book, his favourite Elver Fly, still hangs in his old club, the Garrick, in London.

Ransome finally gave up his angling column when he decided that the pressure of producing it weekly was beginning to take the edge off his own fishing. He gave his editor three months' notice of his intention to quit in March, 1929. By May he was well into *Swallows and Amazons*.

Ransome fished – and on and off wrote about fishing – late into a life that was increasingly plagued by ill-health. He caught his last fish, a salmon, in 1960. By 1963 he was confined to a wheel-chair. He died in 1967, aged 83. Among the papers he left were parts of a new novel. It had, like so much else in this public man's private world, an underlying angling theme.

Coarse Fish on the Move

OFFICIALLY it is the salmon and the sea trout that are the 'migratory fish' – the fish that begin their lives in rivers and that go to sea before coming back, in turn, to spawn. The rest – eels excepted – are the 'non-migratory' species: the stay-at-homes and the moochers-about; the sidlers from this side of the river to that; the fish that limit their forays to a trip to the shallows downstream from time to time, or just occasionally to the deeps around the bend.

That, anyway, is the official view and, as it happens, the view of many anglers. The reality, though, is more complex – and surprising.

* * *

BIOLOGISTS have known for years that coarse fish, for all their stick-around reputations, are given to travelling astonishing distances – often at astonishing speeds. It is just that somehow the results of their researches rarely reach the riverbank and even long-established facts will come as news to most on it.

Like, for example, the fact that barbel can range tens of kilometres upstream and downstream in a single season. Like, for example, the fact that bream can leave their daytime swim at dusk, roam several kilometres during the night – and be back where they started off by next morning, leaving the local anglers no wiser.

Research into behaviour like this is highlighted from time to time at fisheries management conferences and when biologists get together, but not on many other occasions. In fact, an Aquatic Animal Research Group at Durham University has been studying fish movements for years. Scientists there have tagged and tracked barbel, chub, dace, bream, roach and a range of other species on the Nidd, the Ouse and the Derwent in Yorkshire, and on other rivers and lakes further south.

Much of this work has been undertaken in an attempt to understand the effects on river life of man-made interventions – from the building of weirs and fish passes to flood prevention works and significant water abstraction. It is the insights into fish behaviour coming out of it all that will fascinate anglers most.

Barbel have been tagged and tracked five and even ten kilometres upstream and down again in a single season, with individual fish undertaking round-trips of 60 kilometres to find suitable spawning gravels. Chub heading upstream for places to spawn have been found to make repeated attempts to use fish passes built for sea trout and salmon – one memorable fish on the Derwent entering a pass seven times in seven nights before finally giving up.

A study of bream on the River Trent revealed that individual shoals covered beats of up to six kilometres long in the course of a season. Within a shoal, different fish would behave differently as dusk approached. Some would leave the 'home' reach occupied during the day and move several hundred metres upstream and down in the course of a night. Others would range three and even four kilometres afield and still be back before morning. The extent to which a given reach meets the needs of the fish in it is likely to dictate when, how far and how often fish will travel.

Studies have thrown up other fascinating insights – like the disadvantage of being released into the wild after being bred in captivity. Stocked coarse fish, it seems, can travel at the wrong times. Whereas native fish lie doggo while the sun is up and travel under the cover of darkness, farm-bred fish will shift location in broad daylight.

'Presumably there is an advantage in native fish moving at night – they may be less susceptible then to predation by birds, pike and otters', one of the study team has suggested. 'The movements of reared fish – if they're looking for food – may reflect the times of day when they've been fed in captivity and that could prove a disadvantage.'

It is not only the extent to which fish move and when that is surprising, but also the speeds at which they move. Twelve-hour round-trips of six and eight kilometres by bream are startling enough, but the speeds of other fish – and especially the speeds of small fish relative to the speeds of large – can leave the portly bream standing.

Whereas a metre-long adult salmon can swim at better than two metres a second for hours and days on end – a formidable feat of strength and endurance – tracking has shown that salmon smolts a sixth of that length can sustain close on half a metre a second without difficulty. River lampreys have been recorded travelling 10 kilometres a night upstream, against a steady current – a distance and speed many would find surprising in a fully grown sea-trout.

What does it all amount to for the angler on the bank? In the case of swimming speeds, probably not much, other than to cause him or her to marvel yet again at the wonders of nature. In the case of in-river migration, it will be to cause anglers to see coarse fish in a new way – and to encourage them to be more adventurous in their choices of swim as daylight fades and each season progresses.

Fish movements also throw two of angling's most commonly heard statements into a new light. The fact that a fishless day for one angler is followed by a night of frenzied action for another in the same place might not be simply because 'fish come on at night' – a well-known saw – but because a hitherto fishless swim has had travelling fish come into it.

And the heartfelt 'there are no bloody fish in this bloody swim' might sometimes not only be an excuse of a kind but that rarest commodity in angling – the truth.

Buying Tackle

I AGONISED over my first fly-rod. I was a wholly self-taught fisherman and, when I became interested in the sport, I had no-one to guide me. So, like count-less others, I went to a tackle shop to seek advice. This was not a local tackle shop, because I did not have one. This was a big, posh tackle shop in a big city.

The staff saw me coming. I ended up paying far more than I should have for a big-name rod that in the event, was an indifferent performer. It is a trap that newcomers especially can fall into. Every beginner would benefit from independent advice on what rod, reel and line to buy. Here is some.

* * *

A FEW years ago I went to buy a new fly-rod. I did not need a new rod – I have accumulated more rods than you could shake a wad-ing stick at – but I had convinced myself I needed one. All anglers, I know, will have sympathy with this sensation. Perceived Tackle Deficit Disorder (PTDD) is a kind of medical condition and tackle shops are the places where it is treated.

I went to a well-known store and told the dealer what I wanted – a fast-actioned, 9ft five-weight. He listened sympathetically and made soothing noises. Then he turned to a glass case behind him, opened it with a key and lifted out a 9ft wand. Naturally, this was not any old fast-actioned, 9ft five-weight, he explained. This was the Dollar-Sign Flabbergast fast-actioned, 9ft five-weight. It looked fabulous. It was made of deep-green carbon fibre and was wonderfully varnished. It had lots of gilt lettering on the butt and the kind of maker's name that evokes candles and incense.

The Dollar-sign Flabbergast – the dealer turned and angled it so that it flashed in the light – was made of the latest High-Modulus, High-Five Technology. It provided faster back-loading of the thingy than any rod before it. In tests, five spindles of torque had been achieved. This rod was practically guaranteed to improve my casting distance by 50 per cent and my Accuracy Quotient Factor (AQF) by very nearly the same.

How much did it cost and where could I try it, I asked? Naturally, the dealer inferred, a rod like the Dollar-Sign Flabbergast did not come cheap but I was clearly a man who not only appreciated the best but would positively demand it.

Yes, but the price? The figure he mentioned sounded like the distance to Mars. Outside, the rod cast like a piece of wet string. *Caveat emptor* can be as good advice in the fishing business as it is in the motor trade – especially at the start of a new season. Then, spring is in the air, cuckoos are on the wing and the air is filled with the song of tackle-dealers pushing wheelbarrows to their banks.

When choosing tackle it is essential to keep function in mind, above all. The principal job of rods, reels, lines and the rest are to help an angler put his fly where he wants it and to handle effectively any fish hooked as a result. Many an angler buys tackle for other reasons – for example, assumed status – but among the sensible the ability to do the job required, comes first. The truth is that many a lowly priced outfit will do that as well as some top-priced kit, though the actual rods may appear much the same.

A fly fisherman on small streams will want a rod in the 7ft to

8ft range, carrying maybe a 4-weight line. An angler tackling larger rivers and many stillwaters will want something between 8ft and 9ft 6ins, carrying 5-weight to 7-weight lines. For some lake fishing and angling for sea trout, rods of up to 10ft or a little more carrying lines up to 8-weight or so, will be useful.

Large numbers of rods for all these purposes are priced at astronomical levels while entire and wholly serviceable outfits – rods, reels, lines, leaders and flies together – can be bought for a third of their price. The two rods I use for virtually all my own stream and lake fishing cost £120 apiece in 1990 – a fraction of top prices, even then – yet they have had the users of rods costing four times as much gasp at the silken ease with which each puts out a line. My favourite loch-style rod cost me £25 second-hand and its original owner £70 new. When, in the mid-1990s I wanted a salmon 15-footer, I sought advice from a hugely experienced, money-no-object salmon angler. What did he recommend out of all the rods available, most of which he had tried? Why, the same rod he used himself – a product costing less than half many on the market. That is the rod I bought – second-hand, again – and it performs like a dream.

The reality is that few rods and anglers are born for one another. Often enough we buy a rod that feels good in the hand and that gives the impression of being up to the job we want doing. If, having bought it, the rod shows a less-than-fatal quirk we often fish on and find we adjust to it. More often than not, the rod we fish with ends up becoming the rod we know and learn to love. When the time comes for a change, use of the old rod will likely have made the next new rod feel strange – and we repeat the cycle.

It is much the same with fly reels. Plenty of fly reels now cost hundreds of pounds. I have never spent more than £50 on a fly reel and the two of that price I do own both incorporate superb disc drags. Some of my expert friends are wedded to reels that cost between £20 and £40 apiece. The reel I use on my 7ft 3-weight cost £14 in 2003 and does everything I ask of it, which is not much.

On the high-priced reel options, this or that gizmo justifies a little extra cost and hype delivers the rest. Statements like 'the days are long gone when a reel was regarded largely as a place to store line' are now heard repeatedly – and are wrong. The prime function of a reel will always be to store and, of course, dispense and recover line. The essential qualities – lightness, reliability and an exposed rim – cost very little in themselves.

In truth, the rod has not yet been priced that will turn an indifferent caster into a good caster and no rod-reel-line outfit has been assembled that will make up for a lack of fishing skills. Unless the angler behind the rod knows the value of a cautious approach to the water, can read the currents when he gets there, knows where a fish is likely to lie and can present the right fly in such a way that it comes to his quarry's attention naturally, every penny spent on gear will be money down the drain.

This is not to say that much expensive tackle is not superb or that good tackle will not give a good fisherman an edge: simply that expensive tackle will not necessarily be good tackle and that quite superb gear can be had at a very modest price. Telling the difference in the shop or from the products in the catalogue is, of course, the problem.

For the angler who can be persuaded that he needs the most expensive in anything and can afford it – or who just wants the top names regardless – the issue is neither here nor there. For many more – and especially gullible newcomers confronted by honey-tongued salesmen – the issue is often central.

My advice to anyone inexperienced who wants new gear is to seek independent, experienced advice if he or she can and to spend any money saved on instruction.

Dry Fly, Wet Fly, Nymph

FISHERY managers love rules. On some trout waters, the list is as long as your rod. There are rules about fly sizes, net and mesh sizes, the distance one angler must stay from another on the bank, the distance boat anglers must stay from the shore. There are size limits and bag limits, guidance on how fish should be returned and when not to return them; directions on when fishing may start and must stop and all else.

One of the most common rules, applied almost exclusively on rivers, is whether a water is dry-fly only or whether nymphs may be used. Naturally, this invites definitions of what exactly an artificial nymph is and what exactly constitutes a dry fly.

Quite rightly, everyone has a view.

* * *

MY OLD English master might well have shed a tear. Cyril Pybus was not only one of the great influences on my life but the man who named two kinds of question, frequently raised in his classes, after me.

One was the 'Clarke's Worrif', as in – when he was putting forward some proposition or other – 'Sir, worrif this or worrif that?' He would sometimes use the other to cut short a classmate, as in 'Bloggs, this is beginning to sound suspiciously like a Clarke's Worrabout'.

Both questions were hijacked on a fly-fishing web site I once dipped into. Someone foolishly asked 'how many angels can dance on the head of a pin?' Or, in angling-speak, they asked 'exactly how do you define a dry fly?' The hair-splitters and devil's advocates, the leg-pullers and the ayatollahs were out in force. The Worrifers and Worrabouters had their hands up in a flash.

Frederic Halford is to blame. Up to the late 19th century, the flies anglers used on rivers were motley collections of feathers that were mostly cast out across the current in the hope that a fish would make a grab as they swung around, below the surface.

Then, in the 1880s, Halford and his pal George Selwyn Marryat embarked on an intense study of the kinds of winged flies most often taken by trout. Two books resulted. The first, *Floating Flies and How to Dress Them* (1886), described how these winged, natural flies could be imitated more precisely on hooks. The second, *Dry Fly Fishing in Theory and Practice* (1889) described how these imitations could best be fished to individual trout that the angler could see.

The advantages of Halford's new 'dry fly' strategy over the old, random, underwater 'wet' approach, caused a sensation. Halford found himself at the head of a 'dry fly cult' – a position he reinforced by eventually declaring that dry fly fishing was not only more effective than wet fly fishing, but more sporting. Before long, extensive reaches of rivers became restricted to 'dry fly only'.

Then G.E.M. Skues bobbed up. Whereas Halford and Marryat had studied the adult, winged flies at the surface, Skues studied the underwater nymphs that the adults had hatched from – and developed wonderful imitations of several species. Like Halford, Skues cast his flies only to fish he could see and he, too, attracted a large following. The Halfordians were unmoved. They classed Skues' underwater nymphs with the old-style wet flies, declared they were just as 'unsporting' – and banned them from their waters. Battle was joined between the two camps and raged for decades.

The cordite still hangs on the air. Even today, some fisheries restrict angling to the dry fly in the belief it is more sporting. Hence the short fuses on the web-site when someone asked what is and is not a 'dry fly' – a question complicated, of late, by the arrival of new flies designed for fishing not on the surface film or under it but actually in it, part in and part out of the water. Could emergers be fished on dry fly-only waters, as well?

Internet hackles were up in a flash. We had this response, that response, the other response, some of them extraordinarily acrid. They went on and on. The high point for me came when someone decided he could cut through it all. When is a dry fly a dry fly? No problem. You dropped your fly into a glass of water. If 50 percent of it floated above the surface, then it was dry and okay to use on dry fly-only streams. If not, it should be kept for wet-fly waters.

Cyril Pybus would have groaned. He'd have seen it coming a mile off. Worrif, someone said, a fly is 50.1 per cent above the surface in the tumbler test and 49.9 per cent below – or, if it comes to that, vice-versa. Where did these flies stand – or in the latter case, sink? Worrabout eddies and flows, another wanted to know. There were none of these in a glass but they were all over the place on rivers and these could influence the way a fly appeared. Exactly, said someone else – and worrif the glass itself influenced the thickness of the surface tension, and made it different from the surface tension in open water? That could affect a fly, too. And, and, and.

The debate went on for pages and pages, but I eventually fell asleep at my terminal. Many of the contributions – they ran well into three figures – were inordinately long and split every previously splat hair, several times over. Thousands of visitor-hits had been recorded, leaving many readers – no doubt like me – variously fascinated, appalled and amused.

My own view? In my experience, the best fisheries are those that have no rules at all and where the rods can be left to fish as much in the interests of the river and other members, as in their own results on the day. These waters tend, however, to be in the hands of small syndicates whose members are carefully selected and who get to know one another well.

Most other waters do have rules. It is clear that an owner or fishery manager can make any rules he chooses and that if an angler doesn't like them, he can go elsewhere. There are excellent reasons on some rivers – reasons not connected with prejudice but with conservation – for limiting techniques and catches and the pressures on the water. Restricting fishing to dry fly-only is one of them, but there are others. Finally, where a rule like dry-fly only does exist, it is incumbent on the fishery to make any special refinements crystal clear.

Speaking personally, I carry no tumblers of water and no measuring devices. Where an unelaborated dry fly rule exists, anything I can see on the surface is a dry fly and anything I can't is a wet. That's it.

And as to angels on a pin head, who said they can dance, anyway? I mean, sir – worrif they've all got two left feet?

Fun in the Grass

FISH will, on their day, take pretty well anything. There is scarcely a comestible you can think of that has not, at some time or another, caught them. Undeniably, though, some baits are more consistently successful than others and we all have our favourites.

Many of the best baits can be bought from tackle shops and lots of others come free from the wide outdoors. Acquiring the former is straightforward. Getting our hands on the latter can lead to excitements and delights, not all of them obvious or expected. I once risked the censors to write about them – and in a family newspaper, at that.

   *   *   *

ONE of angling's weeklies marked the opening of a new coarse season on rivers with a supplement devoted to the 'Top 50 Baits'.

The supplement was structured rather in the manner of the dance-of-seven-veils. The revelations came little by little. They were made from the outside in. It was only at the very end that the Top Two – the tit-bits, so to speak – were revealed. Before them came as extraordinary a smorgasbord of fishy temptations as can have been served up in one place at one time.

Squid was Bait No 50. Marshmallows, the 'Floating Kings of Confectionery' as the weekly described them, came in at 49, elder-berries at 46, beef steak and mince at 45. Potatoes came to the boil at 35, artificial spinners and spoons wobbled into view at 34 and cheese got a sniff in at 19. As might be expected whole fish, fillets of fish, bits of fish littered the list of delights for the carnivores and plenty of cereals, fruits and cooked pulses were there for the veggies.

When the last veils were whipped aside, we found ourselves ogling The Big Two. Top Bait No 1 was maggots, Top Bait No 2 was bread. It was the lack of detail on Top Bait No 3 that was surprising. Top Bait No 3 was that anaconda of the lawn and vegetable patch, the lobworm. What was missing was an appreciation of the sporting opportunities the lobworm offers in its own wriggly right. It is an omission I want to make good, now.

Only a masochist digs for worms. Every angler knows that lobworms aplenty will be found lying right out in the open, on top of the lawn at night. All that is required to catch them is a torch, a tin, the stalking skills of a Kalahari bushman and the fastest forefinger and thumb in the west.

I don't know why lobworms come up at night, but I can guess. Some say it's because they are attracted by the cool night air. Others say they want to drink the dew from the grass. More likely, I suspect, is the prospect of getting up to what nature expects all of us to get up to on the grass under the cover of darkness at some time or other – only faster and more cheaply.

When it comes to courtship, remember, lobworms have little use for chat. When pursuing their wriggly ends, they have no need to splash out on drinks and dinner, quite possibly wasted. There are no clothes to be fumbled off. All they have to do is lie out there in the buff, waiting for a touch from another pointy nose and they're away. So lobworms are on the top because they're on the pull.

Which appears to leave them vulnerable. To the uninitiated, it looks the simplest thing in the world to bend down and pick them up. But the lobworm has lots of tiny little hooks in the sides of its tail and while its body is in the open, it usually leaves its tail in its tunnel. The challenge is to spot the worm, grab it and whip it into the can before it can set the hooks into the earth and pull itself down to safety – which it can do at reflex-defying speed. Obviously, easier said than done.

Also, because lobworms are light-sensitive, the torch beam cannot be shone directly onto one for more than a moment or it will be gone. One solution is to point the beam into the grass and to look for your quarry in the periphery of the light it throws. The other is to soften the beam's glare.

A friend told me about his preferred way of doing the latter, long ago. He recommended – you can see why no-one digs for lobworms any more – covering the torch end with several layers cut from a woman's silk or sheer nylon stocking, ideally still warm ('they're more stretchy, then') and taken from the thigh end, which for some reason was 'better'. Tights, I remember him saying fervently, 'just aren't the same'.

There is no doubt that the thicker, thigh end of a sheer nylon stocking doubled and redoubled over the end of a torch, diffuses the beam nicely. The problem is that the time taken to negotiate one from the wearer's legs can sometimes leave little time for fishing itself. Which, my friend said, was okay by him.

But let us say that these preliminary challenges have been risen to. Let us say you have your stocking-tops, that your worm has been sighted, that it does not bolt and that you have managed, with a lightning stab down of forefinger and thumb, to grab it. Now what?

Usually, not much. The worm will have its hooks firmly set into the sides of its tunnel. You will be pulling with the aim of extracting it. But you cannot pull too hard in case the worm snaps – and you want the whole worm. So you find yourself in a protracted battle of finely judged strength and wills.

What is required is a steady pull that does not slacken for an instant. If the pull does slacken, the worm will sense weakness and take heart. If the pull can be sustained, the worm will over time begin to give up hope and little by little its grip will ease. Eventually, if you judge things aright, the lobworm will release its grip all of a sudden and the prize will be yours.

So yes, though the Top 50 Baits supplement did not mention it, there is more challenge in getting your hands on a lobworm than in acquiring the 49 other baits put together. It can take ages. That is the down-side. The upside is that in getting the requisite gear together – the stocking-tops especially – you can end up with more than one kind of result. Which, as my old friend would say, has always been okay by me.

Arthur Oglesby

ANYONE who reads the angling press regularly sees the same writers featured, time after time. If they go on long enough and have enough to say, such writers can acquire a kind of fame – though it is fame only within the closed world of fishing. Then, sooner or later, they disappear: either they lose interest, or they are displaced by younger, fresher writers or else, naturally, the man with the scythe intervenes. And that is that.

Every now and then, though, a fishing writer reaches a wider audience and is remembered by the national press when he dies. Arthur Oglesby was one of them. Oglesby was not a mover of mountains in angling, like a Falkus or a Walker, but he was a skilled writer and teacher who featured in the game fishing magazines for over three decades. He also lived in an exotic way. Oglesby had Brylcreemed good looks, money and social connections. Together with his fishing and writing skills, they took him to places, and into company, of which most anglers could only read. And he caught fish. Boy, did he catch fish. It was because of all this that I obituarised him in The Times.

* * *

WHEN Arthur Oglesby died on December 2, 2000 – the same day as his long-time friend Jack Hemingway (son of Ernest) – British angling lost a legendary salmon fisher: a man who repaid the privilege of a private income and the ability to fish pretty well when and where he pleased, by passing his encyclopaedic knowledge on to thousands of others through four decades of teaching and writing.

Oglesby was able to enjoy the cream of Atlantic salmon fishing on the international circuit in the days before disease, loss of habitat and pollution took its toll of this heroic fish, reducing it in many places to the point of extinction. He amassed a tally – it was over 2,000 fish in Britain alone – sufficient to take an ordinary mortal's breath clean away. He counted among his friends many glittering names inside and outside the sport.

Indeed, Oglesby had been due to fish with Hemingway in Alaska earlier that year, but looming heart surgery prevented him from going. Then Hemingway himself underwent heart surgery and it was complications following their operations that claimed both men's lives.

Arthur Victor Oglesby was born into comfortable family circumstances in December, 1923 and lived the early part of his life in York, close to the family business of Harvey Scruton Ltd., a firm of manufacturing chemists. He started to train as an industrial chemist immediately on leaving school, enlisted with the Black Watch at the age of 18, led his men into battle in the D-Day landings as a young officer – and was wounded in both chest and leg.

Oglesby left the Army as a captain and went into the family firm, which had been built on a widely known product of the time, Nurse Harvey's Gripe Water, the first gripe water to come onto the market. In 1955 his father came into the younger Oglesby's office – and collapsed and died in his arms. Arthur was catapulted into the managing director's chair, struggled to overcome the burden of heavy death duties – and built the business up. By the mid-1960s he was able to hand over the reins to his brother

David so that he could do what he had always wanted to do: devote his life to angling. Soon after he moved to Harrogate, where he settled.

Oglesby had been a passionate angler since childhood. In the 1950s he took to fishing the Yorkshire Esk, in those days an excellent salmon and sea trout river – and it was there that he met the man who was to prove, he was later to write, the greatest single influence on his fishing life: Eric Horsfall Turner.

Horsfall Turner, then Town Clerk of Scarborough, made an international name for himself in the late 1940s and early 1950s as captor of a string of giant blue-fin tunny – fish weighing 500lbs and 600lbs apiece – that put in a brief appearance along the north-east coast: but he was also a brilliant salmon angler, knew everyone in the business – and introduced Oglesby around.

In 1957 Oglesby went to Scotland with Horsfall Turner and there found himself introduced to Captain Tommy Edwards. Edwards was, by common consent, the finest fly-casting instructor of his day and had a fishing school on the Spey. Oglesby went back several years to act as Edwards' unpaid assistant – and took over the fishing school himself on Edwards' death in 1968. In 1969 he helped to found the Association of Professional Game Angling Instructors, the body that put until-then unregulated game fishing tuition onto a formal footing. He went on to run fishing courses personally until close to his death, teaching over 3,000 students on the Spey alone. Over the same time he regularly led paying clients on fishing expeditions to Russia, Alaska and Iceland.

By the time he started teaching, Oglesby had already made a name for himself through journalism. He first began to write for angling publications, then additionally for *The Field* and *Shooting Times* – at one time producing so much copy that he had to adopt a *nom de plume* to spread his name more thinly. He became European Editor of the American *Field and Stream*. He edited the *Angler's Annual* for three years. He taught himself to fly and regularly presented field events for Yorkshire Television, from time to time adding glamour for participants and audiences alike by flying in and out on his own aircraft.

Like many successful anglers in their later years, Oglesby found that he needed to fish less and less, but he did not become the outstanding performer he was without being fish-hungry at the outset. This fish hunger – and resulting success – bred some jealousy and led others to spread rumours of how his captures might actually be achieved. In Oglesby's case it led to some wonderful stories. A family favourite is of the time he arrived at the Yorkshire Esk for a day in the middle of what was proving, for him, a terrific season. Another angler, who did not recognise him, was on the bank when he arrived and saw that he was about to head upstream. 'I wouldn't go up there', the other angler called, inferring by his tone the possibility of nets and maybe a little dynamiting, 'I hear that bugger Oglesby's up there'. A pause. 'Oh, good', Oglesby replied – 'I think I'll go and join him.'

It was in 1966 that Oglesby's international career took off. Again, through Horsfall Turner, he met Odd Haraldsen, a Norwegian who had a prime beat of the Vosso, at that time the finest big-salmon river in the world and one on which spring fish averaged 28lbs apiece. Oglesby and Haraldsen hit it off and Oglesby came home with an invitation to return every year 'until you catch a 50-pounder'.

He did not quite make the 50lbs but over the years pictures of Oglesby and his amazing Vosso captures became part of the page furniture of the angling and sometimes of the national press. At the time of his death, among the stag heads and books and other mementoes of a 60-year sporting life that looked down from the walls of his study were four salmon. They weighed 45lbs, 46lbs, 46lbs and 49lbs-plus. The biggest fish was caught on June 17, 1973. The three others were, remarkably, all caught on June 18 of their respective years. In 1981 Oglesby caught a bag of four Vosso fish that weighed 151lbs – an incredible total and one which now seems unlikely to be beaten anywhere.

Oglesby's fame and wherewithal took him to many exotic places – and as a result he made many famous friends. Hemingway was one. Another was Charles Ritz, the Parisian hotelier and a man who, in private life, was a brilliant designer of fly rods. He fished with the Americans Joe Brooks, Lee and Joan Wulff and Al McClane. In Britain he knew and fished with pretty well every famous angler who wafted a salmon rod, most important among them being Hugh Falkus, with whom he made a number of films. It is a point of interest that it was Oglesby who first taught Falkus to Spey-cast – a fact that Falkus did not publicise widely.

Arthur Oglesby wrote several books, among them *Salmon* (1971), *Fly fishing for Salmon and Sea Trout* (1986) and an autobiography, *Reeling In* (1988). But it will be for his extraordinary captures – and the whirl and the world he lived in – that he will be remembered by most.

The Weakest Link

FOR most of us, the challenge of the fish alone is enough. Just getting a fish onto the line and then onto the bank takes all the knowledge and wristy skills we can muster. It also takes the tackle to do the job, properly maintained. There is nothing worse than losing a fish through carelessness or through tackle that, in one way or another, has been allowed to deteriorate. Everything is hostage to the weakest link.

* * *

A FORLORN friend, relatively new to angling but mad keen, told me how, on one of the first casts of his first outing of the new trout season, he had hooked a substantial fish that came unstuck in seconds. When he wound in, the leader had broken a little above what had been a well-tied knot.

This sad little everyday tale, garnished by the fact that – naturally – not another fish was touched all day, will strike a chord in us all. Every new season brings its crop of challenges. Mostly they are concerned with the intransigence of fishes. For the newcomer or the inexperienced, they can concern tackle as well.

The breaking leader problem is typical. Quite often, when a leader breaks under the circumstances described, the problem is not that the nylon chosen was too fine – though, of course, it can be – or that the breaking strain marked on the spool overstated the breaking strain of the line wound onto it. It is that, in the months since last used – or in the time on display in the tackle shop – the nylon has steadily weakened.

The problem is light. I am not sure what the process is, but the ability of light, and especially sunlight, to weaken spooled nylon is well-established. A few days' use at the water is one thing; continuous exposure for weeks and months on end is another. The answer is to store leader material in the dark. I keep my spools stacked one on top of another in a long, old sock.

The sock lives in my fishing bag. At the start of each season, every spool in the sock is tested and any suspect nylon is discarded. Then, the spools I will need on my next outing are transferred from the sock in my fishing bag to the pockets of my fishing jacket. If the same spools are needed for the following outing, they stay there. If others are required, the appropriate switches are made. At the end of the season, all spools are socked up and rebagged. It is a simple, if somewhat inelegant ploy that ensures no spool is left open to the light and every spool is available when and where needed. The nods and nudges in the car park, when a loosely jointed leg is noticed hanging out of the boot, add to the ploy's attractions.

Flylines can present problems, too.

A line that has had some use and that is then left wound on a reel through a close season, tends to acquire 'memory': that is, when it is taken out and used again, it does not cast silkily and lie flat on the water. Instead, it casts like wire and spirals across the surface like a loosely wound spring. This is especially true of the inner coils, which have been wound in the smallest, tightest turns around the reel spindle.

The problem this time is not light but lubrication. Modern lines are coated in plastics to which a form of lubricant – a plasticiser – has been added. The job of the plasticiser is to keep the line supple. In preventing the line from becoming stiff the plasticiser assists casting and reduces the risk of cracking. But over time – and especially, it seems, if stored in high temperatures – plasticiser leaches out.

One way of alleviating the effects of stiffness in a line is to stretch it. The permanent answer is periodically to replace the plasticiser that has been lost.

Replasticising agents are available from any good shop that deals in fly-fishing equipment. The line is laid out straight or coiled in wide, loose loops and the plasticiser is smeared along its whole length. After five or six hours the line will have absorbed as much as it needs and the surplus can be wiped off. That is it. The line is ready for use. The effect of this simple operation is magical: it not only abolishes memory and transforms the line's casting ability but lengthens line life. I treat my lines once a season and they behave perfectly for anything up to five or six.

There is another little wrinkle about lines and leaders. At the waterside they have to be threaded through the rod-rings. Ninety-nine anglers in 100 take the fine tip of the leader and poke that through successive rings, drawing the much-heavier flyline behind it. On most days that works perfectly well. But every angler experiences the other days: those days when, in the eagerness to get started or some moment of distraction, the leader-end is accidentally dropped. Then, pulled by the weight of the flyline behind it, the whole ensemble rattles back down through the rings into the grass – and the process has to be started again.

A far better method – and one that does not demand the eyesight of a hawk before fine nylon can be guided through tiny rings – is to thread the flyline up the rings and not the leader.

How? The leader, plus a few feet of flyline, are pulled straight off the reel. The end of the flyline is doubled back on itself to form a tight loop and the loop is passed through the rings, in the process pulling more line and leader behind it. Held between forefinger and thumb, the loop can be closed tightly enough to pass through even the tiniest rings on the top-piece.

Done this way, getting a line up a rod is not only far easier for those with less than nimble fingers and good eyesight, it overcomes the falling line problem as well. If the line is inadvertently released, the held loop springs open and jams in the last rod ring to have been threaded. In other words, line and leader are held where they are so that threading can be continued as before.

With the line on the rod and a reliable leader on the end of it, all is ready. Only the challenge of the fish remains: that, and finding a strong, sharp hook.

Always and Never

IT HAS been said many times that the two least appropriate words in angling are 'always' and 'never'. We can say that this or that usually happens or almost always happens – even that we have never known it not happen – but the moment we become dogmatic and absolute, the exception will pop up to prove us wrong.

Likewise with 'never'. Fishing is so wide and deep a sport, conditions and circumstances so infinitely variable, fish so varied and unpredictable that, sooner or later, the highly unlikely, even the seemingly impossible, will occur. You can bet on it.

A well-known angling writer and professional biologist, a man whose work I know and admire, wrote in an angling journal that 'grayling always lie on the bottom. Always! There is no reliable scientific observation published of a grayling resting, like a trout "on the fin", just below the surface.'

* * *

ON THE afternoon of September 16, 1983, I was walking upriver looking for trout when, on a bend I know well, over seven feet or so of water, I saw a big fish on the fin, inches under the surface. I naturally assumed it was a trout – this was a big trout lie – but before I could cast to it the fish saw me, turned and rushed downstream. From high on the bank on that sunlit day, I had a perfect view of it. I saw every detail of the fish as it passed. It was a huge grayling.

The incident was so remarkable and the grayling so big that, for future reference, I marked precisely the position the fish had been, by drawing mental lines across it from features on my own bank to features on the bank opposite. Then I went downstream, waded across the river and came up the other side to find a position I could cast from, while keeping well below the skyline.

A week later, on the afternoon of September 23, I returned to the bend in the hope of finding the fish there again, high in the water, because I knew I would not be able to see it if it were deep. This time, though, I crept unseen up the opposite bank and went straight to the casting position I had marked. I could see nothing of the fish from that place and so cast a small shrimp 'blind' a yard or two upstream of the fish's previous lie. I got it at once. The shrimp could not have sunk six inches before the fish took, indicating that again it had been just under the surface. It weighed 2lbs 14oz and remained my biggest grayling for the next 20 years.

In July, 1987, I was on a camping and fishing trip in the Swedish Arctic with a group of Swedish friends. On a river one evening – there was, of course, still plenty of light in those parts at night – we found a great raft of fish lying just under the surface, again over deep water. The fish were smutting, tilting up to sip down flies with the regularity of metronomes, again just like trout. We could see that they were grayling. We got only one – a monster, 3lbs 4oz – before the wind got up and the fish went down.

One evening in July, 1989, immense numbers of fish were lying just under the surface on a Hampshire carrier. Although it was evening I could, with the light behind me, see them clearly.

They were almost all grayling – again, all smutting, simply tilting up, taking a fly, realigning themselves horizontally and then taking again. I caught several. They were grayling in the water and grayling on the bank.

I have seen similar behaviour several times since: two or three times below a particular hatch pool on a river in Dorset where, over very deep water, the fish will range about on the fin, only two or three feet below the surface. I have even taken a photograph of a grayling on the fin, again just below the surface over deep water, in the back-eddy downstream of a hatch-pool on a river in Berkshire.

The writer of the article on grayling also mentioned barbel. I have not seen it myself but I know a wholly reliable barbel fisher, another professional biologist, who has watched these archetypal bottom-hugging fish feeding from the surface when it has been worth their while. Faced with a continuous stream of floating bread, he tells me, some fish will rise right to the top to take it. They deal with the underslung mouth problem by rolling at the last moment, so that the mouth is uppermost.

Even more improbably – I have written about it elsewhere in this book – I have watched video footage taken by a keeper on the Test, showing a group of eels lying just under the surface like trout, wholly preoccupied with a heavy fall of mayfly spinners. That, it seems to me, is the *coup de grace* in this debate.

The explanation? I am personally convinced that all fish are opportunistic feeders and that when everything comes together to make 'abnormal' behaviour more productive and energy-saving than 'normal', they will adopt it. Not always or frequently, but when it pays dividends. Dense hatches of smuts, which might not always repay repeated journeys from bottom to top and back again for each single fly, would clearly be a starting point for such a combination of events. On the other hand the 2lbs 14oz fish, like the fish I photographed in the eddy, was not smutting: it was simply near the surface, over deep water, on the lookout for food exactly like a trout.

Perhaps part of the problem for anglers may be that grayling are so obviously bottom-dwellers, and the received wisdom has so long been that grayling never lie on the fin, that in the main we never expect anything else and so do not look for it. And if we are moved to look for it, either circumstances might not be right to induce grayling to lie high in the water or visibility might be such that, if they are high, the fish cannot be seen.

Either way, in angling, the lesson is the same: 'always' and 'never' should be given a wide berth.

Barbless Hooks

WHEN, in the late 1970s, John Goddard and I were working on our book The Trout and the Fly, we conducted all manner of experiments. One was to test the efficiency of barbed hooks versus barbless: did we lose more fish with the latter than the former, we wanted to know.

It was the welfare of the fish we had in mind. Though the barbed hooks we used for our flies were tiny – sizes 12 to 18, mainly – they nevertheless, like all barbed hooks, had to be wriggled and teased out. Fish often had to be lifted from the water during the process and the possibility of stress on the trout was further increased.

If we could use barbless hooks without greatly impacting our results, most fish could be set free without being touched. Once beaten they could be brought to the bankside or the wadered leg and the hook could be slipped out with the merest twist of the fingers. The fish would benefit and so, through the sheer convenience of it, would we.

Appropriate barbless hooks were not available so we started removing existing barbs, ourselves. We hooked fish, then gave them every opportunity to escape. We let the line go slack when the fish was in open water, we let it go slack as usual when they jumped, we allowed them to get into weed beds. It made little or no difference to the numbers of fish we banked. We were happy and the fish were happier. We both wrote about it extensively. But for some, old habits die hard.

* * *

A TRAWL of tackle shops has confirmed yet again what a hide-bound, tradition-driven and often unthinking animal the average angler is. It was almost impossible to find a suitable hook for fly-tying that had no barb. The reason so few shops stock barbless hooks is because so few anglers demand them. And it makes no sense.

It is now decades since I last fished with a fly tied on a barbed hook. Indeed, even when coarse fishing, I almost always fish barbless because the advantages are so obvious and significant.

A barb on a hook serves only two purposes. The first, in coarse fishing, is that it helps to keep a bait on board. The second, in any fishing, is that it gives some anglers peace of mind. The idea that a bait is less likely to have wriggled or fallen off the hook is, of course, comforting to a coarse or sea angler – though the notion is irrelevant to a fly fisherman, who is not using bait. The thought that a hook with a barb on should in theory not be able to come out, can comfort some in the middle of a fight.

It is worth setting against these ideas, some facts. Chief among them – as anyone who habitually fishes barbless knows – is that no more fish are lost from barbless hooks than from barbed. Many will say that fewer fish come adrift.

Anyone in doubt should consider what happens – and can test the principles involved with a short length of line, a hook and a piece of wood into which the hook point has been clicked.

A fish rises to a fly or takes a bait and the angler responds by striking. In an instant the line tightens, exerts its pull on the hook eye and the hook point begins to go home. Alas, it does not always arrive. A barb sticking out from a hook just behind the point creates a wider part of the wire that slows penetration. Sometimes it stops penetration completely and the hook gains the merest purchase.

All sorts of things can then ensue. One is that the fish, held only by the tip of the hook point, comes off instantly – it has 'been pricked'. Another common occurrence – especially for dry fly anglers, who need to use fine-wire hooks in the interests of lightness – is that as the point slows penetration and the pull of the line on the eye increases, leverage causes the hook bend to open, again enabling the fish to slip free.

There is a third possibility. A barb is not added to a hook, but is cut into it and the spot at which the cut is made naturally represents a weak-point. Too often the result – especially with cheap, fine-wire hooks – is that the great leverage exerted on the point by the pull on the hook's eye, causes the point to snap clean off. Another lost fish.

With a barbless hook, none of this happens. Without a barb, a hook has no weak point and no wider point to slow penetration. If a barbless hook gains a purchase, the odds are that it will go home, first time.

Once home, it is much less likely to come out than might be imagined. Any angler playing a fish needs to keep a tight line to stay in control – which helps to keep the hook in place. But even if the line is allowed to fall slack it is extremely unusual for a hook to come free. The mere action of a fish swimming means that it tows the line, which exerts enough drag on the hook to keep it secure. In a river, even if a fish stops swimming and the line is allowed to fall slack, the hook stays in place. The reason is that in a river the fish is obliged to face upstream, into the current and the current carries the line downstream behind the fish – again exerting drag on the hook.

There is another, overriding consideration why I not only always fish barbless with a fly but almost always fish barbless when using bait. It is because even the tiniest barb can make a hook difficult to remove and the fish often has to be taken from the water to get the hook out. Any time a fish spends out of the water adds stress for it and, in inexpert hands, there is an added risk in the process of the fish being damaged.

In contrast, a fish taken on a barbless hook can be set free with ease, the hook simply sliding out. Indeed, there is rarely a need for a fish taken on a barbless hook to leave the water at all – a reason why, when trout fishing on most rivers, I not only do not use barbed hooks but do not carry a landing net, either.

It is in spite of all of this that anglers keep on demanding hooks with barbs and why the trade, not unnaturally, keeps on supplying them to the exclusion of pretty well all else.

There are fixes: a barb on a hook can be pressed flat in the vice before fly-tying begins or – caught at the waterside with a shop-bought article – the barb can be pressed down with a pair of small, flat-nosed pliers, a tool that has many other uses besides.

Both actions are the work of a moment, but still that weak spot remains and the odd point snaps off. If only more anglers would recognise the benefits of barbless hooks and would ask for them, the problem – and not the fish – would go away.

Bernard Venables

ASK A NON-ANGLER to name the best-selling angling book of all time and the most likely answer will be Izaak Walton's The Compleat Angler. Ask a fisherman – one over 40, anyway – and the one-word response will be 'Crabtree'.

It is hard to find a middle-aged angler who does not have Bernard Venables' marvellous book. In the 20 years to 1970 Mr Crabtree Goes Fishing was almost a compulsory buy. My own copy – yellowing, frayed and dated 'Christmas, 1952' in a childish hand – is beside me as I write.

No-one knows how many copies Izaak Walton's pastoral hymn has sold, though in the 350 years since it appeared it has run to more than 400 editions, printed in dozens of languages. Anglers know that Venables' paperback story of father showing son how to fish through the angling year – largely through wonderfully executed, cartoon-style strips with informative bubbles – sold hugely. Few know what the true figure was. All knew its impact on them. Its importance, the way it enthralled two generations of young angling minds, was so great that, in later life, Venables became positively revered, the first Izaak Walton since Izaak Walton.

I got to know Bernard quite well. I first met him in the early 1990s when I interviewed him for one of my columns for The Times. Subsequently we found ourselves, quite independently, guests at a fishing dinner in Wales and we jiggled the place-names about so that we could sit together and talk. The next meeting was at a small lunch party, held in a mutual friend's home, to mark Bernard's 90th birthday. I met him several times more before he died on

April 21, 2001 – and subsequently was invited by Eileen, his wife, to speak at the memorial gathering held to celebrate his life. It was one of the greatest gatherings of anglers – eminent anglers – that can have ever been brought together in one place. I did not write about that, but I did write about his extraordinary burial.

* * *

ON MAY DAY, under a cherry tree just breaking into blossom and not a fly-cast from one of the rivers he lived much of his life for, the most-widely known and best-loved angler since Izaak Walton, was laid to rest.

Bernard Venables, creator of Mr Crabtree and author of the extraordinary Mr Crabtree Goes Fishing, a work that sold over two million copies and that lit the torch in two generations of young angling minds, was not a religious man and there was not a trace of formal religion in the two events of the day.

The first was a simple, private gathering of family and friends – if it had been public, there would have been thousands there – in a village hall deep in Hampshire. Friends recalled their memories of the man they knew and one read a marvellously crafted, humorous piece that Venables wrote in 1953 about the dangers of leaving groundbait in the vicinity of horses. Later there was the simple interment ceremony conducted on the side of the sloping downland hill in the wind and the rain.

For all that there was no religion in the day, it was a spiritual occasion. Venables had lived his 94-plus years in tune with nature, close to the earth, marvelling at its wonders, secure in his mortality. When he died on April 21, after a mercifully short illness, he was ready and content.

Venables was devoid of pretension. He genuinely wanted to be buried in a cardboard box – he saw his own return to the earth as the landing of just another dust-speck on the turning wheel of time and felt that to use anything else would be pointless. But it was not to be. When he was lowered into the pure, white chalk it was in a more startlingly appropriate way: in a wicker basket made to take his own tiny frame, as light and natural a coffin as one of Old Izaak's creels.

At the precise moment of his burial the heavens opened and a wind-driven rain riveted down. Someone said 'typical fishing weather' and we smiled and nodded before drifting away. A few held back. Someone dropped an old cork float onto Bernard's creel. Someone else dropped down an artificial mayfly. Yet a third old friend dropped down another artificial fly and a fourth a small slip of wood which, he later said, had long-ago been harvested from the garden of Izaak Walton's Staffordshire cottage.

A couple of minutes later a blackbird, gripping its swaying cherry branch tightly, burst into full-throated song. It was as if the clouds had parted and the sun had come out.

It is impossible to overstate the impact that Bernard Venables had on angling – and on young minds especially – with Mr Crabtree Goes Fishing. Crabtree was not Venables' first book or his only book – Venables wrote a shelf-full of books, including one on tanks, one on a journey down the Zambesi and one about the open-boat whalers of the Azores. But Crabtree was his masterpiece.

Crabtree the angler hatched from a highly popular strip cartoon that Venables drew for the Daily Mirror in the years immediately after the war. In 1949 the Mirror decided the strips should be turned into a book. Venables pulled several of the strips together, added some new bits, a few watercolours and some linking text. The resulting marriage – of images so vibrantly crafted to words marvellously honed – proved a soft-backed, 96-page publishing wonder. All it seemed to do was follow a father and son fishing through the year – for pike in winter, for trout in spring, for bream, tench and carp in summer, for perch, roach and rudd in autumn. But it sold in its hundreds, its thousands, its millions, earning its author not an extra penny in the process because the *Mirror* took the view that he was an employee when he did the work and so all rights were the paper's own.

There is no doubt that, in his later years, Venables came to view *Crabtree* with ambivalence. In a real sense he lived his later life struggling to get out of *Crabtree*'s shadow but whatever he did, the shadow lengthened and followed. Venables had much to feel frustrated about: not least the fact that his high artistic talents – 'I live and breath for my art', he once told me, 'I am hell-driven by it' – did not receive the recognition that was their due. Venables was a painter of a high order in oils and watercolours, a wonderful carver of wood and sculptor of stone. His work was hung several times in the Royal Academy's summer exhibition. His cottage near Salisbury was crammed with the artillery of these inner conflicts: paintings, busts, easels, paints, brushes and inks jostled for space with rods, reels, bags, boxes, books and wellies.

The overriding question Venables leaves behind is as much – he would not like this – about *Crabtree* as it is about himself. Why did that tiny book with its both timeless and dated, working-class yet oddly classless team of father and son fishing and talking, become the publishing wonder that it was?

Acumen on the part of the Mirror Group obviously played its part. The timing was perfect. After the war, in drab days, long before television or videos or computers, most people were thrown back on their own resources for diversion and the reach and promotional clout of the paper made sure that anyone who might remotely be interested in the book, saw it. Venables' great skill with brush and pen also played a key role.

But there has to be more, something that accounts for the book's success with, above all, young boys.

A key feature, I believe, is that for the first time Venables took young minds which to that point had been physically marooned on the bank, down into the water and into the world of their quarry. He showed Crabtree and Peter at one end of the rod, fishing to the barrier of the reflecting surface. He showed the fish at the other end reacting to what the pair did and did not do. So Venables, for the first time, completed the circle: he made fishing come alive in the reader's own mind, in the process giving each action at one end of the rod a visible consequence at the other. Naturally, also, his fish were great fish – and we knew that if we did what Crabtree and Peter did, whoppers would end up in our nets, too.

Moreover, because Venables was a romantic as well as an artist, he did not destroy the wonder when he communicated the clinical: because everything was shown through the prism of his own mind, the awe and mystery – the very things that attract boys to water and fish in the first place – came through as well. So in reading Crabtree, everything was gained and nothing at all was lost.

Venables did it all so personally. He did it in language that any one of us could understand. He did it for each one of us individually, by the million upon the million, lighting our lights and altering lives in the process.

When Bernard Venables went back to his beloved nature, he went replete with affection and filled with awe to the end. He went with his creel and he took *Crabtree* with him, as if to fish on in that deep, wide pool.

The Power of the Close-up

I HAVE always been fascinated by slow-motion, by that frame-by-frame view of things which, occasionally, can give a sense of pulling alongside some parallel universe and being given a glimpse inside. Slow-motion can enable eyes and brains accustomed to one reality to become aware of another: sometimes to see that what appears to happen is not what actually happens, at all.

Likewise I am fascinated by the close-up, especially the close-up of small, living things and isolated events. In its proximity and involvement, a close-up can act as metaphor, which is to say that in showing us the particular, it can illuminate the general. Take water and water life, for example.

* * *

SOME time in the mid-1980s, around the time that global warming was first being mooted, I was walking the banks of the river Kennet in Berkshire. A slight movement in a bay cut off from the main river, caught my eye.

Looking close I saw a pike and a trout, as much predator and prey as lion and lamb, lying side by side together in water that scarcely covered them. They were ignoring one another completely, bent only on survival. Only the occasional sudden clutching of a gill, as one of them tried to extract what oxygen the warm water carried, gave them away.

In the early 1990s I was walking up a small stream in Yorkshire.

Again the river had shrunken into its bones and the blazing sun had warmed it. This time, though, fertilisers sprayed onto the great prairies all about had obviously leached into the water. The result was a massive growth of blanket weed, that matted-hair algae which, increasingly, is choking waters of all kinds in summer. The river was full of the stuff. Even as I watched, a small section at my feet, for reasons best known to itself, rolled right over. It left a tiny water snail high and dry, its small flat foot sucking wetly at the air.

I am not Francis of Assisi. Mostly when I walk in the countryside it is to absorb and be absorbed; to watch, look, listen and move on. Yet for a few minutes in the case of the fish and moments in the case of the snail, I became intimately involved with those creatures' lives. I picked up the pike and the trout in turn, carried each to the main river and held it into the flow until it was strong enough to shrug my holding hands aside. I turned the snail the right way up and put it back into the water, deep down.

The power of small incidents like these, seen in close-up, is that they bring great and complex issues vividly to life. They make the ungraspable, comprehensible and real.

Talk to me about the environment debate in general, tell me about a five-degree Centigrade rise in global temperatures over the next 100 years, about the melting of the ice-caps, the uncountable tonnages of unpronounceable chemicals being tipped onto the land, the hundreds of thousands of new houses that need to be supplied with water in the dry south-east and I understand the implication but miss the actuality. It is a bit like discussing lottery odds or the distances between stars.

But show me two fish cut off from an abstracted river, a small snail set to dry out atop a chemical soup and I can see it all clearly. I can see it when a report on crashing salmon numbers tells me that ever-more spawning gravels are being choked with silt. I can see it when a river keeper tells me he has seen fields crusted with dead mayflies frozen in the open, because the hedgerows that once sheltered them at night have been grubbed out to achieve economies of scale.

I can see our meddling in a different way when a pal rings me to say that a mink that someone must have recently set free, has stood hissing and spitting at him over the body of a moorhen with its throat ripped out.

So it isn't just the cuddly and the pretty wildlife that is under pressure – the otters and the red squirrels, the skylarks and the Adonis blues, though you could be forgiven for believing it: all wildlife is under pressure. Somewhere, out of sight and mind, some part of our natural heritage is being edged back, compromised or destroyed, every day for every upward tweak in national housing requirement, every increase in farmland productivity, every new bypass and motorway. There is Messianic interest at the bunny end of the spectrum, but it tapers off sharply. By and large interest and knowledge stop dead at the water's surface. If you are a fish, forget it.

The major conservation groups, for all their excellent work, can be depressingly narrow in outlook. I am an active member of several. As I mention elsewhere, the only times I have heard aquatic life discussed at any of the countless local Wildlife Trust meetings I have attended has been when I have raised it myself. When I was invited to speak at a large, public meeting of the Campaign for the Protection of Rural England, the CPRE had posters and displays about the threatened landscape aplenty, dotted about the hall. There was not a mention anywhere on them, of water. My subject was rivers.

The general lack of interest in water and the life it supports is naturally reflected in Government policy and funding. Grants to the Environment Agency (EA), the body that looks after 40,000 kilometres of river and tens of thousands of hectares of lake in England and Wales, are being cut relentlessly.

While the EA is making efforts to cut abstraction – though not enough because it lacks the cash – some rivers flowing now are almost entirely man-made and others are held together by the equivalent of sticking plaster and string.

As climate change begins to grip and rainfall distribution alters, river banks are being narrowed to maintain water velocity, water levels are being maintained by supplies sucked up through boreholes and some streams are having their beds artificially lined to prevent loss through seepage. When, in the late 1990s, the river Darent, in Kent, infamously dried up overnight it was no act of God: it was because someone had accidentally turned off the power that drove the pumps that lifted water from deep underground and channelled it into what otherwise would have been a dry river bed.

There are no easy solutions to the pressures on water and the life in it and around it, but there are three certainties.

The first is that, if we hope to pass on as much of our heritage as our grandchildren have a right to expect, we cannot go on as we are.

The second is that we will continue to demand individual homes, private transport, inexpensive food and more and more power-consuming gizmos. We will go on doing it because we are not on the outside of everything and looking in, but in the living business ourselves and want the best of it. We will do it because we are human and can do it. Naturally, there will be no ill-intent.

The third certainty is that if we do not alter focus and learn to value our rivers and lakes more – the amount of water in them, the state of the water in them, how we conserve it and use it and treat it – the same price as now will continue to be exacted. It will be paid by pike and trout, water snail and salmon, water vole and water caterpillar, mayfly and damsel-fly, crayfish and heron, kingfisher and dabchick and all else besides.

Our grandchildren will see the results of it all in slow-motion and in close-up – and will rightly condemn our inaction.

Best Day, Worst Day

I WAS once asked by an editor to write about my best day and my worst day. He gave me no guidance beyond that and so, given that there are about as many ways of defining 'best' and 'worst' as there are of losing fish, I defined the first as the day that produced my most memorable catch and the second as the one delivering my most crushing loss.

Also, in the absence of guidance, I decided that neither day need have anything to do with fly fishing (though this was a fly-fishing magazine) and so neither did. Likewise, neither had to have anything to do with the sizes of the fish involved or their numbers but – surprise, surprise – both do.

I described the crushing loss first, so that I could end on a high.

*   *   *

IT WAS A baking summer's day on the River Tees at Croft, downstream from Darlington and I was about 12 at the time (12 turned out to be a significant age for me and Croft a significant place – see 'The Otter', elsewhere in these pages). I was spinning for chub, trout, anything that would latch on; prospecting with the little quill minnow in the weak-tea, north-country water; dropping it into likely spots on the layered rock slabs that covered the bottom.

I was using the little Japanese split-cane spinning rod that I had bought by doing a paper round – a rod, as it happens, that I still possess, along with others funded from the same source.

I had covered, I suppose, maybe 300 yards of water upstream from the old bridge and was opposite the place where the little Skerne flowed in when I made maybe the 80th, the 100th cast of that afternoon. I gave the rod a wristy flick, the line whirred and arced and the lightly weighted lure on the end went in, sank a bit – and stuck fast.

Oh, no! The second or third time, already. I pulled tentatively this way and that, as concerned for the rod as the line. Nothing. I moved upstream a little and hauled and downstream a little and hauled. Still nothing. Eventually I pointed the rod at the water and began to back off, pulling for a break. Light winked. Water crinkled. The line played a highly strung, oriental tune.

Something shifted. Then it shifted some more. I kept the pressure on and whatever it was kept on giving. I stared into the water, expecting to see a branch slowly lifting – but no angular arm broke the surface, no silt drifted downstream.

It took an age, but shadows coalesced and lines took form. What was this? What was it? Was it a branch? An old, laden sack? A body? It was like lifting the unspoken from my own imagination. And then, little by little a monstrous pike, a gigantic thing, the first pike I had ever seen, much less hooked and still the biggest pike I have ever had on my line, broke the surface. It came up as though a dead thing, unmoving – first its skull and then its back. I saw water peeling from it like ancient time.

Disappointment gave way to excitement gave way to awe, tinged with dread. I had read about pike. They were fierce, everyone knew that. They had millions of teeth that all curved inwards. They lived on other fish and birds and small dogs, anything. One had drowned a drinking horse by hanging onto its nose, I'd read that, as well. When you landed them, their eyes followed you about the bank, even when they were dead. How was I going to land this fish? How was I going to cope with it? My biggest fish up to then had been a 2lbs chub.

I would like to say that the fight was savage, but it wasn't really a fight at all. Actually, the pike hardly seemed to realise anything was amiss. It simply turned it head towards the far bank, swam idly to the mouth of the Skerne and then swam back. Then it did the same again. Then it did it again. On the seventh excursion of that pike's afternoon the little reel jammed, the rod was dragged down to a shallow curve and the line snapped. Just like that. There was no sudden crack, no sound like a pistol shot: the line just broke with a sickening, low-key switch.

It was a terrible moment then and it is still terrible. I can see myself standing there now, short-trousered, black-wellied, motionless and numb, held in a kind of emotional death. I can see myself looking down at the reel, studying it this way and that, then looking out at where the pike had been, then looking back at the reel, uncomprehending. Unbelieving. I can see myself reeling slowly in and trudging leadenly out.

How big was the fish? It weighed twenty-one and a quarter pounds exactly. How do I know? Because it was caught and landed by someone else soon after – a fish so big that it was reported in The Northern Despatch, picture and all. You can't get much bigger than that.

Such heartache.

My most memorable day came a few years later.

By now I was 18 or 19, a reporter for The Northern Echo and The Darlington and Stockton Times, covering a fair chunk of North

Yorkshire from the lino-floored, single-bare-bulb-lit office above Smurthwaites' Garage, in Northallerton. The River Swale was 20 minutes away by bike. Sometimes, on a summer evening, I would go there after work to waltz a float down its runs.

One evening, after batting out deathless prose for my breathless readers, I headed for the river near Ainderby Steeple, parked the bike by the bridge and headed upstream.

After a while I came to a broad shallow that gathered into a racing tail at a bend. The tail had cut into the high bank on the outside of the bend and dug a deep channel beneath it. Under that high, sheltered bank for 30 or 40 yards, the river ran narrow and deep and fast. The slower thread just this side of the fast water, screamed fish.

This time I was using my paper-round Wallis Wizard and a centrepin, the same centrepin that I use for my coarse fishing, even now. I trickled a steady stream of maggots into the head of the run as I tackled up, got into the water at a point where I could control the float absolutely and dropped in. Ten yards downstream, it stabbed away: a dace. Second trot, ditto. Third, likewise. Fourth and fifth casts, a chub. Sixth and seventh casts, a trout apiece. And so it went all evening long, as the martins wheeled and the high clouds reddened and the world all about stayed on hold. There was, in those caught-breath moments only rod and line, water and float, tugs and runs. Flashes and splashes. Pulsing cane.

I cannot remember how many fish I caught or how much they weighed, only that they showed no relent. It was common, then, to use a keep-net. That was the only time in my life that I have emptied a net and half-filled it again.

More was to follow. At last light I headed upstream through

the shallows, to make my way home. Half way up I saw a likely run in maybe 18 inches of water. On the 'just one more absolutely last cast' principle I paused and flicked the float into it. I let it run a while, checked it a moment – and saw it slide away. I found myself attached to what felt like a motorbike, a fish of immense speed and power. Eventually it came to the net: an all-muscle barbel of about 4lbs. I flicked the float out again and again it slid away: another barbel, about ditto. The same again and again, maybe half a dozen times.

When, in the darkness, I finally stepped from the water and headed for the bridge it was in the knowledge that I had taken by far my biggest catch to date. It had been the kind of catch I read about every week in *Angling Times*, the kind of catch that Mr Crabtree and Peter would have made. To this day it remains the biggest bag of coarse fish I have taken.

Since then I have fished all over the world, in freshwater and in the oceans. I have caught everything from minnows to marlin, blennies to bonefish, salmon to shark. There have been vastly bigger fish and vastly greater overall weights. But none of them have been as memorable as that catch and that loss. The fact that they came so early, were so out of proportion to all my experience at that time, is the most likely reason for their unfading power.

And unfading both still are. I think about them quite often. Here I am, a lifetime later, writing about them now and not for the first time. There was no rummaging for examples when I was asked to write this piece because I could have written about nothing else. It had to be about those two incidents. That pike. All those fish off the Swale. Astonishing, a lifetime on. Astonishing, isn't it?

Big Noreen

THERE was a time when we could get away from it all. At home we simply had to close the door and turn off the telephone. In the country, there were no telephones anyway. Then the mobile arrived and everything changed. First, employers demanded that we should always be in reach. Then our friends wanted us on tap and we wanted them on tap. Now, our mobiles go everywhere with us and there is no escape, even at the waterside. Equipment suppliers, though, are trying to make the intrusions more acceptable. Some are trying to make them more acceptable to anglers in particular. One of them is using ring-tones as a tool.

* * *

AN enterprising company has come up with a new set of ring tones for anglers' mobile phones – the recorded clicks and whirrs of classic reels, as the line is ripped from them by imagined monsters.

All the reels used were made by Hardy of Alnwick who, for the better part of a century, had the reputation of making the finest in the world. Hardy made lots of reels and each had its own triumphal note when a fish took line, so there are plenty of distinctive tones to choose from. They include the sound of the Zane Grey big game reel – 'the best big-game reel ever made', the blurb says. We can have *The Field* salmon reel, a reverential recording of the 1895 model named after that well-known sporting journal. We can have the monstrous, nine-inch Fortuna, a reel made for tuna anglers: the Fortuna for tuna, so to speak.

In the interests of my readers, I have tested a few. All the ring-tones I tried were fine in their way. Indeed, there was only one reel which, to this untrained ear, jarred or maybe night-jarred: an old Hardy Perfect that, on the basis of the frenetic, fits-and-starts recording I heard calls to mind an elderly South American bird approaching what it hopes will be orgasm.

Now, not even my best friends will accuse me of being a busi-nessman. I would not normally recognise a business opportunity were it to roll itself into a tight ball, pitch from a high roof and hit me on the head, drawing blood. But in the matter of ring-tones for anglers I am on home ground.

While the reel-sounds idea has a certain novelty, it does seem limited. A reel is a reel is a reel, as it were. There are lots of other sounds that, if supplied as ring tones, could not only lend variety but grab any angler's attention – which, after all, is what they are there for. Such sounds could be of pretty much anything associ-ated with fishing, but the most vivid and effective will recall impressionable youth. Experiences and impressions in youth can, under certain conditions, go right in. Some, if sufficiently high-wired when first encountered, never leave us.

A ring-tone that would electrify me, for example, would be the sound of a dangerously close and irate north-country farmer shouting 'Oi, you – gerroff that bloody tractor'. Purists might complain that this is merely a traditional 'countryside call' and not really a fishing sound, but it is the kind of thing millions of young anglers out for the day, will have heard. Certainly, it will forever be associated with fishing in my mind, as I first heard it when Tony Richardson and I, then about 12 or 13, somehow found ourselves trying to start some rusted, oil-dripping monster we saw in a field while fishing on the Tees, near Croft.

Were I able to download it now, a sudden 'Oi, you – gerroff that bloody tractor' would be capable of getting my attention any-where. It would seize my brain on the underground in rush-hour. It would take determination to ignore it in even the tensest business meeting.

Another ring-tone to grab attention would be a sharp, parrot-like 'Where's-yer-permit? Where's-yer-permit?' Millions of young anglers will have heard this cry, too. I often heard it on the posh Darlington Anglers' Club water at Blackwell, usually after David Buckle and I had inadvertently walked past three No Fishing signs and wriggled under a taut, barbed wire fence without noticing.

Another thought. Surely, if carefully chosen, some tones associated with fishing could be used not as alarms of various kinds, but as the bringers to weary anglers of deep, happy sleep. They could open up an entire new market segment. The recorded slow arch and collapse of waves on a coral island while bonefishing would be one example. The sound of some burbling brook, per-haps casting the listener back to some childhood, gudgeon-strewn, high-summer idyll would be another. Had one been made, a recording of a later idyll when Big Noreen from No. 12 asked if she could come fishing with me to a particularly well-treed and out-of-the-way stretch of water, would have this old heart a-flutter. Recordings of such moments could create a customized market and a diligent company could soon have thousands of them out there: we all have our Big Noreens from No. 12.

As to pricing, I see that the reel-tones currently on offer are billed at £3 to £5 apiece. The inclusion of other angling sounds would not only introduce more variety but the possibility of a more diversified – and more lucrative – pricing structure. Individual recordings could, if sufficiently appealing and vivid, be broken down and sold in, say, two-second segments to different kinds of customer.

Take, for example, the news that Mr Votesnatcher, an unpopular politician, had fallen in from a high bank while trying to land a chub. So many of us would rejoice at the news that, were his fall to be captured on tape and sold, even snippets from it used as ring-tones could fetch hefty prices.

A segment that captured the moment Mr X realized his fall was unstoppable – a strangulated 'Uh-uh-uh!' for example – could be offered at £3 a time at the low end of the market. The same followed by 'Aaaargh!' might fetch £5 in the middle market. The full tape – 'Uh!' followed by 'Aaargh!' followed by 'Kersploosh' – could go well at a tenner. Thousands with this on their phones would ring themselves up, just to hear it.

Other angling sounds used as ring-tones could be fitted into this basic structure. Except, of course, for those of Big Noreen at No 12 – of all our Big Noreens at No. 12. These would be in a price bracket all of their own. Any company that could take me back to those heady afternoons – and stay this side of the law in the process – could ask what it liked as far as I'm concerned and I'd still have to have its products. I imagine we'd all feel the same. If it were up to me, I would sell recordings like that split-second by split-second and start high. I mean, the sound of the zips alone could be premium-rated.

Brain-boxes on Fins?

IT IS A wonder we anglers catch anything at all. Scarcely a month passes without some scientist or other telling us how brainy and resourceful and sensitive fish are. Listen to some of them and gudgeon are practically human. Soon carp will be declared cleverer than the angler who pursues them.

When that time comes, non-anglers will say they suspected it all along. Our friends will smile sadly and tap the sides of their heads. But we know the truth and we have always known it – and in one piece I blurted it out.

* * *

I ONCE saw a cartoon that showed an angler looking at a trout that was looking back at him. Bubbles showed what each was thinking. The bubble over the man said 'A Trout'. The bubble over the fish contained a mass of chemical and mathematical formulae that analysed the man down to his last trace element.

What the cartoonist was saying, of course, was that the fish is much cleverer than the man trying to catch it. Now, it seems, scientists are bobbing up every other day to claim the same. One group said that fish had individual personalities and that some species were more brave and clever than others. Another group suggested that fish lived in social groups and knew how to get on with their neighbours. 'Fish Machiavellis swim rings around anglers', one headline on that research said.

That story – a silly season story, naturally – suggested that fish were brain-boxes on fins. Scientists had found that the likes of gudgeon and bleak pursued social strategies of manipulation, punishment and reconciliation that would have had The Prince himself taking notes. Fish could recognise their chums in shoals, had been found using tools only a little this side of laptops and were dab hands at backgammon and pastry-making. Something like that.

What angler wouldn't like to think so? I mean, the more intelligent we believe fish to be, the more kudos there is in catching one.

But it's not true. No matter what scientists say – and what have Bunsen burners and pipettes ever had to do with trying to fool a trout? – fish are just what anglers have always known them to be, but have never admitted: mere gloopers and idlers and moochers-about; suckers in every sense.

That is why, for millennia, anglers have been handicapping themselves to make fish harder to catch. Want a trout? Chuck in a worm or a spam sandwich on a hook. Want to make it interesting and give the fish a chance? Use an artificial fly.

Anglers, we know, have been imitating natural flies with slips of feather and fancy silks – instead of using the real thing – since Claudius Aelianus was a lad. It is almost 2000 years since, in *De Animalium Natura*, he described how the Macedonians caught 'fishes of a speckled hue' with red wool on hooks.

The first book on angling in the English language, published in 1496, went further. The *Treatyse of Fysshynge wyth an Angle* – attributed, as we likewise know, to Dame Juliana Berners, alleged Abbess of Sopwell Priory, in Hertfordshire – carried instructions for tying 12 different kinds of imitation fly. As it happens The Dame also gave 'twelue manere of ympedimentes whyche cause a man to take noo fysshe'. The wrong tackle, bad weather and scaring the fish were all in there, but of the fish's intelligence and cunning, not a mention. And an abbess, with her contacts, should know.

Since the *Treatyse*, angling literature has been in full spate and every kind of big name has swept into view, among them – fishy researchers humbly note – some major scientists. Sir Robert Boyle of Boyle's Law and Sir Humphrey Davy of the miner's lamp, both wrote at length about their sport. So, among the writers, did Charles Kingsley of *The Water Babies*. Ditto, among the politicos, Lord Grey of Fallodon, the sometime Foreign Secretary who saw the lights going out across Europe. Arthur Ransome was Angling Correspondent of the *Manchester Guardian* in the 1920s. Ted Hughes, the sometime Poet Laureate, wrote extensively, in poetry and prose, about his love of rivers and his passion for angling. Andrew Motion, Hughes' successor as Poet Laureate, did something of the same. The list goes on and on – with not a fishy contribution to anything other than a dinner plate being mentioned by any of them.

Izaak Walton in *The Compleat Angler* (1653) came nearest to hinting at intelligence or sensitivity – really, just wariness – when he declared the chub to be 'the fearfullest of fishes'. And if the researchers can take some comfort from that, they're welcome.

Boyle was brutal. Boyle not only did not rate any fish intelligent, he rubbished the lot. In *Occasional Reflections Upon Several Subjects* (1665) – a work so stupefyingly dull and wordy that it could have provided the raw material for his work on the expansion of gases – Boyle wrote a 'Discourse Upon Fishing with a Counterfeit Fly'. What word did he choose to sum fish up? 'Silly', that's what: fish were just 'silly', he concluded. Apparently, not a thought in their heads.

Sir Humphrey Davy seemed to conclude little more. For all his studies, Davy failed to point to a single advance in either the arts or the sciences, made by a fish. In fact, in his book *Salmonia* (1828), he not only failed to contradict Boyle but inferred that Lord Nelson, another keen angler, would have agreed with Boyle's view. Indeed, the admiral must have found fish dismissively easy to catch because, Davy says, Nelson at one point taught himself to fish with one arm behind him.

Several years behind him, as it happens.

Which just leaves the moderns and the practical men. Not one of them goes along with the brainy-fish view. In fact, about the only thing modern anglers do agree on is that the carp, a fish with a brain the size of a pea, is the most intelligent freshwater fish or, at least, the hardest one to catch. Which, in the context of things, is not saying much.

So no, fish are not intelligent, no matter what any scientist writes. In fact, far from 'swimming rings around anglers' as that headline said, fish might be described as perfectly unintelligent from an angling point of view. Once tactics like fly fishing are in place to limit their capture, they go on rising in a way that keeps us all wanting to go back for more.

I ask you, how stupid can you get?

Frank Sawyer and Oliver Kite

ANGLING is perceived by many as a kind of sleepy backwater, a place to which, all passions spent, men and a few women repair to idle their time away.

And so it is. But, of course, that is not all that it is. Angling is no different from any other activity that attracts people in large numbers. It appeals to all kinds, for all reasons. For every idler there is an enthusiast, for every dabbler there is an expert, for every passion-spent soul there is a man on fire.

Mostly, we all rub along quite well together, but there are exceptions. When two strong-minded and contrasting individuals find themselves in close proximity – either physically or through their writings, for example – then sparks can fly. Likewise, when two clear and radically different philosophies emerge at the same time and each is advocated with Messianic zeal by its followers, tempers can flair and resentments, smoulder.

The small, inward-looking world of the south-country chalk streams has seen more than its share of such situations – and of resulting feuds. One, between the Halford and Skues, dry-fly-purist versus nymph schools, came in the early years of the 20th century and has been extensively chronicled. Another came towards the century's end and is less well known. Like the first, the second was kept running long after the principal parties were dead.

* * *

I HAVE, no doubt like plenty of others, heard many an impassioned exchange between the followers of Frank Sawyer and

Oliver Kite, two of the best-known fly-fishing writers to emerge in modern times. Always the questions at issue are the same: to what extent, if at all, did Kite over-exploit Sawyer's work and, if he did, was it this that caused the estrangement between these once-close friends?

In the great scheme of things these questions are, of course, side-issues, though that does not make them go away. More interesting by far are the unadorned stories of the two as individuals and the coincidences which marked their lives.

On any historical perspective, Sawyer was by far the more important of the two – a shy, close-counselled man, formally little-educated: a local country river keeper who became world famous and the sought-after fishing companion of the rich and the titled.

Kite was an extrovert, as brilliant a communicator as Sawyer was awkward; an army major turned television personality confident enough to say he could catch fish blindfold – and then to invite the cameras to watch him do it for an audience of millions, not once but several times.

Both men were befriended by Charles Ritz, the Parisian hotelier and rod designer. Both, for all their different backgrounds, found themselves whisked away from time to time from the same tiny street in the same tiny Wiltshire village, to be Ritz's guests in the hotel he owned in the Place Vendôme.

Sawyer was born in Bulford, on the banks of the River Avon in Wiltshire, in 1907. He came to know the river intimately and, in 1928, was appointed keeper on the stretch run by the Officers' Fishing Association, a body formed to cater for the fly-fishing enthusiasts in the large military population on Salisbury Plain.

Sawyer was a born naturalist and made an intense, lonely

study of the fish and insects of the river. In the process, he made himself so knowledgeable an entomologist that he could confound the experts of the Natural History Museum in London – and eventually several of his insect specimens were given a home in the permanent collection there.

Encouraged by distinguished anglers who had contacts in the media, Sawyer – who by this time had moved to Netheravon – began to write articles for country magazines. Over time, his painstaking work attracted admirers and followers. Then he produced two books. The first was about the Avon and the life in and around it. The second, published in 1958, was an angling book, Nymphs and the Trout. It moved chalk-stream fly fishing on from the close-imitation, scarcely sinking style of artificial nymph pioneered by Skues, to fast-sinking nymphs of radical design – an original contribution that brought him lasting fame.

Sawyer's approach, the 'Netheravon style', involved the use of nymphs that emphasised profile and weight: minimalist affairs typified by his now world-famous Pheasant Tail Nymph, that were tied with copper wire. These sleek, life-sized creations were designed for casting to sighted, deep-lying, individual fish. Once at or below the depth of the fish in the water, they were animated with a lift of the rod-top, an action that caused the nymph to rise and accelerate past the quarry as if escaping. It was a movement that prompted a feeding reflex from the fish reminiscent of the behaviour of Pavlov's dogs. These 'induced takes' were indicated by the reaction of the fish in the water or by movements of the leader as it floated on the surface. Sawyer's nymphs, and his way of fishing them, were deadly.

In 1955 the Monmouthshire-born Kite was, after service with

the army overseas, posted to Bulford, Sawyer's birthplace. In 1956 he joined the Officers' Fishing Association, where Sawyer was now head keeper. In 1958 he likewise moved to Netheravon. The house he chose was directly across the street from Sawyer's own.

The two men got to know one another well. With Sawyer's help, Kite became a dazzling Netheravon-style performer in his own right and – he was already a superb, all-round naturalist – a fine entomologist. Kite moved ahead under his own steam. He continued to study fish and insects – and to experiment with his own angling. In 1963 he published a book of his own, *Nymph Fishing in Practice*.

By this time Kite, too, was making a career in the media. He went on to write scores of articles and contributed to several books. Above all he made a big name for himself in regional television, making a total of 230 television programmes, including 115 editions of his own nature programme, the hugely popular 'Kite's Country'. Many of these involved fishing. He likewise went on to attract international attention – and a postbag that could run to several hundred letters a week.

At the height of it all – on June 15, 1968, after many years of heart problems – Kite collapsed and died on a riverbank. He was just 47. Two thousand admirers packed Netheravon church and its grounds for his memorial service.

Two years after Kite's death, Sawyer produced a much-expanded second edition of *Nymphs and the Trout*. His own media career went on to embrace many magazine articles, a dozen television programmes and over 50 radio broadcasts. On April 14, 1980, Sawyer collapsed and died – also on the river bank.

And the estrangement, that now well-established shift from

warmth to chill? It occurred around the time Kite published *Nymph Fishing in Practice* – a book which, for all its own not-inconsiderable insights, was based in fundamentals on Sawyer's original work. In due course, Kite's programmes were to make him vastly better known to the general public and they often showed him fishing 'Netheravon-style'. They helped to generate an income which was reflected in his lifestyle, every nuance of which – a gleaming white Jaguar not excluded – must have been visible from across the street.

Humans being human, it is not difficult to see that Sawyer might have felt to some extent exploited. After all, to him it might have seemed that his former pupil was effectively peddling his master's wares. Given the hot-house proximity of the two men, their radically different personalities and Kite's natural showmanship, who is to know what resentments might have welled in the quiet keeper's breast?

On the other hand, Kite was a brilliant and creative man in his own right and there may well have come a time when he was stimulating Sawyer's work just as Sawyer stimulated his. What is more, of course, who is to deny Kite the right to exploit his own gifts to the full provided credit was given where credit was due which, to a significant degree, it was?

It is this outcome of the relationship that causes sides to be taken and passions to flare, even now. It is the stuff of fiction that two such remarkable men – as remarkable in their differences as in their achievements – should have found their lives and interests so tightly bound together, in such a tiny, out-of-the-way place. In a very real sense, there can have been no escape for either of them. Perhaps the outcome we now see, was inevitable.

The Man Who Dressed as a Tree

ANGLERS *are no different from anyone else. We have the same kinds of hopes and ambitions, fears and concerns, strengths and weaknesses. We walk the same, talk the same, do the same, dress the same. All right, then, we don't dress the same. Not always. Not all of us.*

* * *

IT IS COMMON knowledge that readers seeking a dodgy thrill – not just angling readers but readers without the remotest interest in the fishy arts – have, over the years, been turning to my *Times* column in droves. Word has got around that, once in a while, I am prepared to slip into tabloid mode: to reveal some of the tip-offs that come my way about angling's allegedly squeaky-clean past.

I have a simple formula for deciding whether or not to run such a piece. It is – would *The News of the World* like to publish it first? I am quite sure that in the current case, it would. And so to the facts: Thomas Birch FRS (1705–1766), biographer, historian, editor and, if we are to believe it, respectable married man – the same Thomas Birch who published the vast *A General Dictionary, Historical and Critical* (1734–1741), the same Thomas Birch who wrote up the lives of Sir Isaac Newton, Sir Robert Boyle and many other worthies – liked to dress up as a tree.

I am indebted for this arboreal tit-bit to Mr Eric Williams, of

Esher, in Surrey. Mr Williams is one of a band of readers who has written to me regularly about this, that and just occasionally the other. Mr Williams says he picked up his information from the *Oxford Book of Literary Anecdotes* (OBLA), a claim I was at first naturally reluctant to check in case it turned out to be false and the facts got in the way of a story. But it proved to be true.

The OBLA says:

'Dr Birch was very fond of angling and devoted much time to that amusement. In order to deceive the fish he had a dress constructed which, when he put it on, made him appear like an old tree. His arms, he conceived, would appear like branches and the line like a long spray. In this sylvan attire he would take root by the side of a favourite stream and imagined that his motions might seem to the fish to be the effects of wind. He pursued this amusement for some years in the habit till he was ridiculed out of it by friends.'

Now we all have our little foibles. I always wear subdued clothing when fishing and have often been looked at askance for the way I bob and weave my way to the waterside, taking advantage of every scrap of cover on my approach to a fish close in. I once got myself into terrible trouble when, crawling on my hands and knees to get at a chub under a willow, I became enmeshed in a young couple lying in its shade. My friends and I routinely sneak up behind cows on the bank-side in the hope of casting unseen to our quarry. Anglers do these kinds of things every day. We know full well that once alerted to our presence, any decent fish will be sent bow-waving towards the antipodes, towing all hope in its wake.

But dress up as a tree? Even in the knowledge that fish like chub will come close to trees so that they can gloop down the bugs that are forever falling from them? Hmmm.

Though the questions pop and fizz like fireworks, the OBLA answers not a one. We are not told whether the doctor preferred to dress as a willow or an alder or for that matter, a birch. To what extent did he adapt to the seasons, maybe thrilling to the prospect of autumn's slow revelations and then to the nakedness of winter? We are left to guess at the indignities visited upon him by dogs.

And how did it all begin?

Was it, for example, a rush of blood, some 'moment of madness' that caused Dr Birch suddenly to branch out – or was he long in the grip of some secret and unhealthy compulsion? Did he first start off in childhood, perhaps dressing up as a shrub when his parents were out? Did he then find himself drawn further along that slippery slope until suddenly there he was, out on the riverbank, brazenly in leaf and not caring who saw?

And what of his catches? Did he fool more fish when he was in disguise than when he was not? If not, why did he persist for years with it in the face of ridicule from his friends? If yes, why did his friends not dress likewise so that, instead of suggesting just one chub-attracting tree they could have clustered together and formed an entire thicket? Again, the OBLA is silent.

If there is much we cannot know, there are some things we can deduce. One of them is that Dr Birch will not have been alone. If one man in such circles felt compelled to dress as a tree, we can be sure there will have been others. Who were they? Did they ever meet? Was there a secret society of cross-tree dressers? What actually goes on in the Woodlands Trust and would *The News of the World* take an interest?

Come to that, what else might not be hidden in angling's literary past? How did Frederic Halford become so absorbed with flies – and were they always his own? Who were Charles Kingsley's 'Water Babies' and were there any three-in-a-beat romps? How did Herman Melville come by his Moby Dick (mercifully, even then, a treatable condition)?

Mr Williams, of Esher and his team are investigating every one and it is not only anglers who will be shocked by his findings. So keep buying – and keep watching this space. All will soon be revealed in a hot new series.

Next time around: Izaak Walton – the truth about the man and his 'incompleat' tackle.

You can read about it all first, right here.

A Definition of the Impossible

THINK. *Think of the most extraordinary thing you can imagine happening in an angling context. Do not think of pigs flying overhead. Do not think of marlin running a small mountain stream. Do not imagine that, after heavy rain, a trout comes out of your tap with a fly in its mouth. Think seriously about something involving real fish in real rivers, that could just about define the impossible.*

To my mind, the following comes pretty close. It does not report an earth-shattering event and, in the great scheme of things, the incident it puts on record is not terribly important. But this angler found it astonishing, nevertheless.

* * *

EVEN after a lifetime of fishing over much of the globe, I had seen nothing more extraordinary.

The fly hatch had been building for days and the spinners were laying, en masse. Close into the bank, over deep slack water, the spent flies were packed closely together. Suddenly, a shadow long enough to set any angler's heart pounding, materialised from the ranunculus and began to lift. The shadow resolved and took shape as it neared the surface. I could see the whole length of the fish as clear as day: the fin on its back, the sharp bright eyes, the mouth, the miles and miles of flank. A head lifted to the surface and sucked a fly down.

Even though it was the kind of rise any trout would make, it was an astonishing thing to see. The fish lifted and took another fly and then lifted and took a third. Small rings ebbed out.

From beneath the first fish a second then appeared, just as dark, just as long. Soon a third joined them. One of the three spent some time feeding just under the surface, rather than from it: I could see its jaws gleaming white from time to time, presumably because, as trout often do, this fish was taking nymphs or else the bodies of dead flies that were drifting, submerged. It was all just as Guy Robinson had said, a few days before, when he told me of the video he had taken.

The Test, in Hampshire, is a remarkable river, all right. The most famous trout stream in the world flows for 11 miles through the estate where Guy is the head keeper, and then heads on to Southampton. Extraordinary events must occur between its banks, every day. And yet still Guy's warning had not prepared me sufficiently well for what I was about to see. Indeed, what angler could be adequately prepared for the sight of three large eels videoed at the surface, sipping down a hatch of mayflies as steadily and deliberately as well-bred trout?

Eels, as we all know, live on the river and lake bed: they are the insinuators around rocks and the sliders under logs, the threaders-through of weedbeds and of the gaps between stones. They are the definitive bottom feeders. For anyone hoping to catch an eel, a bait fished midwater would guarantee a blank day because the fish would simply ignore it. Yet here these eels were, not in midwater but right at the top, feeding for all they were worth.

Guy had taken the sequence at the height of the mayfly hatch a season or two before. He had come upon the eels by chance and had videoed them because he knew how rare their behaviour was. The clip he took is probably unique and a copy of it deserves a place in some natural history archive.

Of course, anyone who spends a lot of time by the water – and few spend as much time beside it as a river keeper – sees some curious sights. But eels feeding on surface fly? It is as near as we could get to a definition of the impossible.

Why did it happen? It is anyone's guess. All creatures in the wild are opportunists, of course. Few will turn down a sudden glut of food if it appears – and it is easy to think this is what happened that day.

The mayfly is big as aquatic flies go and the stretch of the Test in question gets a wonderful hatch. The flies can come off so densely that they almost cloud the air. When the stored-up hatches of females return to the water to lay, their bodies can carpet the surface. Here and there, currents funnel wide swathes of river into tight, thin lines, concentrating any food they carry. Mayfly bodies in such places can become so dense that they form a near-slurry. It was in this kind of place that the eels were rising and so, perhaps, like all of nature's opportunists, they were simply taking advantage of a conveyor belt of food.

It is easy to think so. It is tempting to think so. But given that an eel feeding at the surface is a bizarre eccentricity in any circumstance, why three eels and not one? And why all in one place instead of spread along the banks? And if it was an understandable response to plenitude, why just three eels and not 3,000? After all, the Test is famed for its eels. On the estate in question, so many eels run the river that they are fished for, commercially.

I have no answers. What I do know is that it really did happen and that Guy Robinson has taken a video to prove it. Nature surprises. Nature surprises at every turn. How fascinating it can be.

The Beatrix Potter Syndrome

NOT MANY Government reviews cause a stir among anglers. Mostly, reviews and commissions are the equivalent of the politician's three-card trick, a means of buying time until (now you see it, now you don't) some contentious issue has lost its steam, or circumstances have changed or someone else is in office to carry the can.

One such review, though – a study of the state of Britain's salmon and freshwater fisheries at the millennium – came up with a great and troubling truth. The distinguished group which produced it wrote that after taking evidence from hundreds of organisations and individuals, 'it became apparent to us that fish are often regarded as the poor relations in conservation terms when compared to other animals and birds, particularly where conflicts between species arise.... Fish are an integral part of the aquatic eco-system and share equal importance with other organisms, including birds and animals; this needs to be recognised more widely'.

It is a statement that defines the most fundamental of all angling's problems, which is that aquatic life just does not count in the wider equation. Because it does not count, it gets little protection – and because it has had little protection, it has been reduced to the state we have seen it in for so long.

However, we need more than a statement of the problem. What we need is a solution – in the first instance, a route to a solution. That lies in understanding how such a problem can have come to exist in the first place.

At least some of the origins lie, I believe, in what might be called the Beatrix Potter Syndrome.

FOR MOST of the last 100 years, when writing about wild creatures, authors of fiction have been turning animals and birds into furred and feathered little people with human senses and sensibilities. Birds, rabbits, cats, dogs, moles, voles – you name it – have all been given the power of speech. They have been shown thinking and planning, being happy and sad. Often enough they stand up and walk about on hind legs – those that have hind legs – once they have got their braces hitched to their trousers, their dresses buttoned up and their bonnets in place.

The ploy is a powerful literary device. It has been the means that writers have used to get their readers to identify with their subjects. Every writer understands that if a reader is to become involved in the fate of anything, he or she has to become emotionally involved with it. And for that to happen, the reader has to be able to relate to it in terms which he or she can understand: which is to say, largely in human terms.

We have, all of us, been encouraged at some point to see animals and birds in this way. Beatrix Potter, Rudyard Kipling and Walt Disney were among those who started it. Others have followed. Squirrel Nutkin, the Jungle Books, Tom and Jerry, the rabbits of Watership Down, the moles of Duncton Wood, the bankside pals of Wind in the Willows are deep in our psyches. George Orwell, in Animal Farm, turned domesticated creatures into human beings to get a strong message across to adults.

'Factual' television documentaries often do the same. Television, as an entertainment medium, overly concentrates on creatures that have either photogenic looks or endearing behaviour – or both. Some scripts are saccharine-coated. Some others follow a pre-determined storyline to which a creature's filmed, natural behaviour is force-fitted. In the process, thought-out motivations and reactions are often attributed to wild creatures behaving in wholly instinctive and unreflective ways.

In other words, not only fictional creatures but real birds and animals are presented as if they are a bit like us. And naturally, being a bit like us, they matter.

Aquatic life is different. It is not furry and feathered, cuddly and friendly. Some of it is 'ugly'. Much of it in a real way – it comes from another element, from unbreathable water – is positively alien. Creatures like this are manifestly not like us. They are difficult to study because of where and how they live. So we study them less. The less we study them, the less we see of them and know about them. The less we see of them, the further they are from our minds. The less we know about them, the less important they are to us. And the less important they are to us, the less we are interested in their fates.

I was a founder-member of the Wild Trout Trust and, at the time of writing, I am its President. I am a member of the Royal Society for the Protection of Birds. I am active in and on behalf of the Wildlife Trusts. I have done my bit for the Council for the Protection of Rural England. I am interested in all of these organisations and most of their aims – even if I do not agree with all that they do. But it is a one-way street.

It is a constant source of frustration how so many members of these groups are single-issue naturalists; why so few of them give a moment's thought to fish or aquatic life. For every three hours I have heard discussions of skylarks and water voles, otters and marsh orchids, I have heard a second's-worth of discussion – usually stimulated by myself – about the plight of the salmon and the eel; about the way abstraction is sucking rivers dry; about the hormone-mimicking chemicals that are feminising male fish; about the feeding and breeding pressures on fish and insects alike as water and habitat qualities decline.

Members of the fisheries review group found the same lack of interest among the biologists and environmentalists they consulted: 'We were surprised at how little evidence we received on fish conservation and the conservation of the freshwater environment from environmental non-Governmental organisations... despite the fact that we invited a number of such organisations to submit evidence. We concluded that, as with the statutory nature conservation bodies, these organisations do not attach high priority to fish and their environment.'

In other words – who should be surprised at it? – the Beatrix Potter Syndrome is at work not only on the folk we rub shoulders with in our local conservation groups but at the policy-influencing, decision-making levels of Government. At Parliamentary timetabling and law-drafting levels. At Treasury funding levels. At the levels at which political advantage is weighed and votes are counted.

It is in large part the Beatrix Potter Syndrome that has placed so much publicly funded research alongside emotion on one side of the scales, anglers and a few others on the other side – and that has resulted in the skewed environmental priorities we have had so long.

Until such perceptions can be changed, real progress on protecting rivers and lakes and the fascinating but unfamiliar life in them, will be limited. And the right of aquatic life to its equal place in public concern is unlikely to be realised.

So what can be done?

People care about what they know about and become involved with. If we are to make progress in protecting aquatic life, it seems to me, we have to engage the public's imagination: those of us who care already have to get as many others as possible to become interested in aquatic life – not exclusively nor to the detriment of anything else, but in the round, along with everything else.

I made my own attempt at this with my novel, *The Stream*. This is not a book about fishing or even a book written with fishing in mind. It is an entirely fictional work, written with the whole of the natural world in mind.

My purpose in writing it was to show what happens at the point of impact when the interests of human beings collide with the needs of other creatures – a conflict which only ever has one outcome. Specifically *The Stream* shows the price paid by real animals and birds, fish and insects, for every greenfield site that is developed, every motorway that is built, every abstraction licence that is approved, every pollution incident that occurs.

From an angler's point of view there is, of course, a danger in any attempt to focus greater public attention on aquatic life along with other life. It is that in the process, greater attention might well be focused on fishing which, of course, exploits aquatic life.

There are three good reasons for doing it. The first is that, with the abolition of fox-hunting, angling is going to get greater public focus in any event, not all of it helpful – so we had better get used to the idea and plan for its challenges. The second, as the review group recognised, is that we cannot have our cake and eat it: that there is a greater danger to aquatic life – and hence ultimately to fishing – if we fail to attract attention to our concerns and things continue to slide.

Thirdly, most of us would agree that fish are more important than fishing: that the right of our grandchildren to inherit as complete an environment as we ourselves did is every bit as important – many would say far more important – than our own natural wish to pursue a sport that we love.

If we denied the first two, we would be burying our heads in the sand. If we could not agree on the last, all we said would be hollow. And then we would get what we would rightly deserve – which would be no public hearing at all.

Fishing at Night

SOME *anglers love to fish at night. Sea trout enthusiasts do it all the time. So do carp anglers. At night, they say, their fish come out to play and that is when their best bags come.*

We are not all like that. Many of us, when the sun goes down and the moon comes up, are happy to reel in and go home. If we are near home. When we are abroad, things can be different – as different, sometimes, as night and day.

*   *   *

I HAVE not often fished the whole night through but I have, countless times, stayed late at the water, quietly sitting, long after the last cast has been wound back on the reel.

To be absorbed by the dusk – to sit listening to the soft, liquid easings and crinklings all around me, to hear the trout planting kisses on the warm night air, to see the barn owl float and hawk, the bat flicker and falter, the solemn procession of swans moving upstream in the gloaming – is like pillow-talk with nature. A sense of completeness often enfolds me. Ancient truths seem to make themselves known.

Of course, not every night is the same and not every place is the same. I am not always the same, either.

Fishing through the pitch dark of a moonless night alone, is not unalloyed fun. Then, the huddling caveman stirs. I hear every snapping twig, every settling stone, every hair-raising shuffle and call. My imagination makes monsters and furnace-eyed things, mostly creeping up from behind.

I have never forgotten the night I camped by the Arkle Beck in Swaledale with my school pal, Dave; hearing his voice drain away on the other side of the fire, turning to follow his palsied gaze, watching the grey shade in the trees slowly materialise through the mist, hearing the low sudden moan, feeling the hair stand on my neck and prickle on my arms; watching as the lone white bullock – what on earth was it doing there? – took form.

Night fishing does not have to mean fishing in the dark. In the Arctic at night in summer, it means fishing beneath the circling sun.

The biggest grayling I ever saw came from Sweden. It weighed 3lbs 4oz and was caught in broad daylight at the dead of night from a river deep in the Arctic Circle. Lars-Äke caught it on a tiny dry fly cast to a group of fish sipping in spinners from a deep, wide pool.

We guessed instinctively, of course, that the fish were trout: they had to be, hadn't they, lying like that, so close to the surface, rising with continual, punctilious sips? The thought of grayling did not enter our minds. Grayling, as every fishing book has ever said, lie on the bottom. If they want a surface fly they dash up to get it, then return to the depths again.

But as we proved – and as Lars-Äke magnificently proved – they were almost all grayling and, what is more, grayling behaving in a way that grayling elsewhere sometimes do, especially when night gives them a cloak of confidence and there are lots of flies about.

I have caught fish other than grayling in the dead of a sunlit night, memorably salmon in Russia. I caught them after a long, white-knuckle ride in a helicopter that was so crowded with passengers and piled-high luggage that the door to the flight deck had to be left open to make use of the extra space.

I shared the navigator's seat, back-to-back with an unsmiling Russian for whom the novelty of such conditions had long worn off. He perched on the front of his seat scowling across his charts and the endless tundra ahead. I looked back down the fuselage at two rows of grim faces, never quite coming to terms with the fact that one of the windows really had been opened at 150 knots at 1,000 feet because the stench of fuel in the cabin would otherwise have choked us.

One of the best sea trout I ever took was taken at night. Well, at sunset. The Times, God bless it, had ordered me to South America. 'Go to Patagonia and fish the Andean foothills', I was sternly instructed. 'Then carry on to Tierra del Fuego and try to get some of the big sea trout there. Come back. Write about it.' I shrugged. I knew not to argue. You have to take the smooth with the smooth in the writing trade.

The river in the Andes was a dream of a stream. It was, like most of Argentina's waters, clear, fast, unsullied and mostly unfished. It was full of wild brown and rainbow trout. It wound through a baking desert where, on the day we took the temperature, it was 105 Fahrenheit by the water.

The river in that stifling, rock-strewn oven, was chalkstream cool: the water was snow-melt draining the high peaks. The fish grew to immense size, their staple diet a small crab-like creature called the pancora. The pancora was the starter and main course on that river. The sedges were dessert.

One memorable evening there, fishing in the long-shadowed dusk beneath a snow-capped volcano as high and conical as Mount Fuji itself, Jorge and I took half a dozen fish apiece, to 3lbs apiece, in not much more than 30 minutes – all on the drifted or skated dry fly.

The sea trout of the Rio Grande river, in Tierra del Fuego, were something else again.

The Rio Grande runs like a crack across the coccyx of South America's spine. Undulating, honey-coloured plains lie all around. The wind howls from Cape Horn like banshees run amok. No trees can stand upright to grow. Muskrat scramble along the river's margins. Llama-like guanacos stand edgily and stare. Condors slide and circle far overhead. All around, heavy fish forge and roll.

They are impossibly big, impossibly broad and deep. Anyone capable of standing up in the wind and slicing a weight-forward line through it can, in the right place, catch them.

By my last evening I had taken my share, but no more. It was close to midnight. I was on a long pool, wading chest-deep. The sun was bleeding over the horizon. I had worked my way down the pool, shuffling and groping, tracing the bottom with my feet, enjoying the novelty of casting in a near-calm, when suddenly the line stopped, tightened – and the sea trout jumped.

It might have been on film played back in slow motion. The fish hauled itself from the water, climbed up the air. It went higher and higher – shoulder height, head height and on into the night sky so that I, chest-deep, was actually below it. Then it arched clean over the set sun and the smouldering light. Pieces of water, wobbling globules of water, drops and spots of water streamed, turned into rubies, fell into the cavernous foaming its re-entry made.

A long, hard fight, a reaching net, a click of the torch and light on the scales. Thirteen and a half pounds exactly. I took his picture, slipped him back and bit off the fly though there was a good hour to go. How could I possibly follow that? How could anyone ask more? I left it there, ended a memorable trip on that memorably high note.

No, I have not often fished through the night but I have often fished into it, just as I have often sat quietly and become absorbed. The half-light has given some of my finest fishing. Its ancient truths mostly dissolve with the dawn.

Flies, Hooks and Leaders

THE relationship between the size of a fly and the best leader to fish it on often seems little understood. Simply expressed, it is that a tiny fly cannot convincingly be fished on a heavy leader and that a large fly – especially a large fly on a large hook – cannot effectively be presented on a fine leader. The two need to be complementary.

Precisely why and how they should be matched becomes apparent when big flies like the mayfly are on the water. Then, too often, excitement pushes common sense aside. Though the fish are surging and splashing all about, disappointingly few are risen and too many risen fish are lost.

A little thought can fix both problems.

* * *

IT IS NOT for nothing that the brief hatch of the mayfly is called Duffers' Fortnight. Trout become so preoccupied with huge, beautiful Ephemera danica and its cousins that they seem to lose all discrimination and fear. Even the rawest tyro launching the crudest pattern at the water will take the occasional fish and, sometimes, a bagful. For all that, disappointment often attends the annual appearance of this exotic insect and it is sharpened because expectations are so high.

The problems that many anglers have when fishing the mayfly arise for just two reasons. The first is a simple failure of technique, which is easily put right; the second is largely a failure of observation.

The failure of technique centres on the leader. Most beginners and a large number of old hands fish imitations of the huge mayfly from the same leaders that they would use to fish small flies. In other words they tie flies dressed on hooks as big as size 8 to leaders of 2lbs and 3lbs breaking strain.

Three problems result. One is that in calm conditions, the fly can be so disproportionately heavy on the end of the fine leader that its momentum carries it over and downwards as the leader straightens. The result is that it arrives on the water with a splash, alarming the fish.

When fishing into a wind, the opposite problem arises. The fly proves so bulky and offers so much resistance to the wind that the leader cannot drive it forward. As a consequence, the fly is blown back and falls some way short of the fish, often descending in a puddle of coils, sometimes behind the end of the fly line itself. Again the result is no rise to the fly, this time because the trout has not seen it.

The third and most frustrating problem when a fine leader is used is that even if all goes well and the fly is delivered and the fish absorbs it, the nylon proves too weak to set the hook. The result is either a pricked fish or, worse, a break on the strike.

The answer to all of these problems is to tie mayfly imitations, as well as imitations of other large insects like the daddies and the damsels, to leaders not only of appropriate strength but, crucially, of appropriate diameter. A bulky fly needs a bulky leader to deliver it accurately and it takes a strong leader to set a big hook. Because strength alone is not a solution the superfine, super-strong and too often super-brittle materials that some manufacturers offer, should be avoided. A tapered nylon leader ending in 6lbs breaking strain nylon with a diameter of .25mm is, I find, perfect for the job, most of the time.

Another cause of grief at mayfly time can crop up late in the evening after a heavy hatch, but it is more commonly experienced during the last few days of the fortnight itself. It is manifested in two ways, in each case because the fish have become selective.

First, at the end of the day's hatch, trout will sometimes switch from eating the newly hatched fly to the dead or dying spinner, presumably because the spinner, which has laid its eggs and then become trapped in the surface film, can be taken with less effort. Anyone who misses this change in feeding behaviour, misses out. Next, at the end of the fortnight, the fish simply become more and more sated and less willing to move to intercept a fly. Then, observation of which stage of fly they are taking – spinner or dun – needs to be allied to casting accuracy.

There are times, late in the fortnight, when the best fishing is not to be had with the mayfly at all.

On waters where dense mayfly hatches occur, trout see an awful lot of food and more anglers than at any other time. Fish that survive the first onslaughts can not only become sated with the big fly but more cautious as well. Then, quite often, they will choose to feed early – and mostly on the small flies that late spring brings. On hard-fished waters, therefore, it often pays late in the hatch to get to the water early and to seek out those quietly feeding, tucked-away fish that are more willing to look at small olives than anything else.

Even then, the odd fish can surprise. Two of the most

interesting trout I ever took during hatches of mayfly were not feeding on Ephemera danica at all. One was totally preoccupied with a heavy and simultaneous hatch of the tiny Iron Blue and the other, to my total astonishment, was taking floating snails – facts I learned because each fish eventually made a mistake.

It pays to keep both eyes open at mayfly time, for all that the seemingly obvious seems to tell us. If we do not, and if we fail to use leaders that will bring a fooled fish to the net, we are inviting – and deserve – disappointment.

The Lady Gives it a Go

I HAPPENED to be talking to a colleague at The Times one day when I mentioned that for the first time in 25 years, my wife had expressed an interest in fishing. She had been out for the day with me many times, I said, but only for the company and the chance to spend a day by the water. She loved rivers and lakes, but had never actually picked up a rod.

There was a pause. 'You mean that the wife of the Fishing Correspondent of The Times has never been fishing? Not once?'. Not actually fishing, no, I said. 'And that suddenly, after 25 years, she's decided to give it a go?' That's right, I replied. It was our silver wedding anniversary that had prompted the thought and now here she was, out of the blue, planning to give it a go. Another pause. 'Good heavens. I think that's extraordinary. You should write a piece on it when she does.'

And so, soon after the big day, I did.

* * *

I CANNOT remember quite how the subject came up, but in some conversation or other my wife said she would like to find out what fly fishing is like. To say that it came as a bombshell would be to overstate the power of bombs, even large ones.

After 25 years of tapping her temple at my friends and me; of tolerating our skilful exaggerations and excuses for returning late; of side-stepping line and avoiding tackle; of putting up with wriggly things in boxes and disagreeable aromas from the car, here she was expressing interest herself, for the first time.

The operative word is interest. My wife, like many another, had been to the river with me countless times, but not to fish. She loved being by the water, but mostly she just sat in a chair and read, or went for walks. Now, suddenly, this.

There were good reasons, she said. Curiosity had seeped in through the pores. After 25 years of contact with my enthusiasm she had become 'contaminated but not infected'. Now that the last of our daughters had left home, she had time to see if she liked it: she'd give it a go, just once. Our silver wedding seemed an appropriate occasion.

There are plenty of ways to start fly fishing. There is the do-it-yourself route that I followed. There are professional fishing instructors everywhere. There are hotels that own fishing rights and many that run residential fly-fishing courses. And, of course, in my wife's case I could teach her. I finally rejected the latter – 25 years of marriage seemed too much to take risks with – but I did want to do things properly. I decided that she should either lose interest in comfort or catch the bug in style. If the lady was going to fish after all these years, it should be somewhere exotic. The River Test, in Hampshire, leapt to mind.

A few days later I called Bernard Aldrich, the keeper at Broadlands. I had known Bernard on and off for years and knew of his teaching prowess. Would he be willing to do the honours. 'Delighted', he said. 'And we'll do it here.' I booked us into an hotel near Romsey.

Now my wife had heard about the Test. I mean, which fly-fisher's wife has not? This is the river on which Frederic Halford and George Selwyn Marryat pioneered imitative dry fly fishing over a century ago. It is the most famous trout river in the world. Whole libraries have been written about it. Many a man would give his right arm to fish it – a few, possibly more. Such men would have questions on everything – on the water and the fish, on tackle and techniques, on flies and leaders, you name it. Would there, my wife wanted to know, be any toilets on the banks?

Conscience niggled between arranging the trip and actually going. If my wife hadn't picked up a rod before she got there, half Bernard's time would be spent teaching her to cast, leaving little time for actual fishing. I would have to show her the preliminaries, myself. We went out onto the lawn with a rod. Look, I said, you do this and this and this, making what I hoped would look a series of dazzling passes. I gave her the rod. 'You mean like this?' she asked, and made a series of extraordinary first-time casts herself. They were not perfect casts but they were remarkable for a beginner and they got better as Broadlands approached.

We had chosen the wrong weekend. A gale was blasting in from the west. There were occasional flecks of rain and only intermittent sun. The river, after a wild, wet week, was rollicking down. The mayfly was up but the water was cold. There were no rising fish to be seen. I set my wife up with an 8ft rod – 8ft 6ins would have been better but the wind was too strong – and watched as Bernard took over.

We all know how tricky flyline can be. Under calm conditions, in the hands of an expert, a cast can be made to cut the air with surgical precision. In the hands of a beginner when the weather is rough, it can look like a bowl of spaghetti thrown at the wind. In no time, with Bernard to guide her, the lady was putting out a better line in such conditions than any beginner I had seen. Occasionally her cast was damaged by a sudden gust, but mostly it held high and straight. I saw her in a new light. Here was not only Earth Mother, Healer of Sick Children, Dealer-with of Spiders and Best Friend, but intimidatingly confident Fisher Wife.

Eventually, with Fisher Wife holding the rod and Bernard walking upstream beside her pointing to this and that, I went off to find water of my own. When I returned 90 minutes later, the pair of them were waiting. My wife was wearing an expression I knew of old – half amusement, half challenge – and the pitch of her voice was familiar. It was slightly over-solicitous, just a little loaded.

'Got anything, then?'

'No. Haven't seen a bloody thing.'

'Excellent,' she cried, exuding the sympathy my family has always shown when I've suffered some fishy come-uppance. She pounced on the grass and leapt up. 'I got this!' A 2lbs brown trout, expertly caught under the gills on her crooked forefinger, was thrust forward for admiration and my inner defeat.

'I got it myself. Ask Bernard. On a nymph. Killed it myself, as well.'

Bernard nodded and beamed as though he had given birth which, in a way, I suppose he had.

Later – by which time, mercifully, I had evened the score – we stopped for lunch. Food filled and drinks mellowed. Fisher Wife spared me nothing, recounting the story of her triumph in minute detail, milking it in a way that seemed strangely familiar. She gave me the heart-stopping take bit, the fighting with savage fury episode, the last-minute drama with the rod wrenched around to breaking point, etc etc. It was a virtuoso performance from one so new to the game and brought murmurs of fatherly appreciation from Bernard, though not from me.

That evening, back at the hotel, the lady repeated her performance for the other guests, adding – shamelessly, I thought – an extra half pound to the fish's weight, when four ounces would have been more appropriate for a beginner. Everyone was enthralled. The hotel manager, who had weighed the fish and who was hovering nearby, raised a Jeevesian eyebrow, but said nothing.

'Look here,' I whispered later. 'That fish. That was blatant exaggeration. I know exactly how much it weighed, to the ounce.'

She looked me in the eye and smiled. 'I know you do,' she said. 'But you're such a good teacher. I learned ages ago that in fishing, the truth is far too rare a commodity to be used all the time.'

I looked at her first in horror, then in amazement, finally in relief. Here was an angler as to the manner born. The next 25 years looked safe.

Fred Buller

Anglers can make names for themselves in their own time by catching big fish, by advancing tackle and technique or by establishing themselves as columnists in newspapers and magazines (in the rarest of cases, by all three). But the angler who wants to make his mark on history had better write a book. It is books that show us where we were and how we got here and the best of them, along with the names of their authors, gleam like beacons down the years.

The vast majority of books have not gleamed. They have been the regurgitations and the also-rans and they have rightly been forgotten. The exceptions are works that, through the insights and diligence of their authors, have in some way moved the sport on for the rest of us; or else that, through sheer literary merit, thrill and beguile us now as they thrilled and beguiled us then.

It is a rare book that stands outside these categories or that embodies something of the qualities of each. One of my friends, over a long life, has produced several.

*   *   *

Thanks to much of his writing and to his early books in particular, Fred Buller is widely regarded as a pike fishing specialist. That is a long way from the truth. Though he has been fascinated by pike since childhood, Buller's interest in the fish is not as an angling target at all, but as an animal: as an engrossing creature of extraordinary appearance, associated with man for millennia.

If he were asked to categorise himself, he would say he is an all-round angler with a special interest in pike. But then, the inference of that isn't entirely right, either, because Buller has many special interests. He is certainly Britain's – and one of the world's – leading pike authorities. He is Britain's greatest living angling historian. He is hugely knowledgeable on big salmon and fly fishing for salmon is his favourite pursuit. More importantly, he is the author of some of the most valuable, stimulating and idiosyncratic books ever to appear on the sport and at the time I am writing this (mid-2007) he has three more books in the pipeline, two of them finished texts, one of them on the verge of publication.

The fact that, at the age of 80, Buller has three books in train gives some indication of his extraordinary energy. The fact that one of them is on the biggest Atlantic salmon ever caught anywhere and that another is entitled *Images of Fish and Fishermen in English Medieval Church Wall Paintings* gives some indication of his range of focus.

Buller's energy is fuelled by an unbounded curiosity – especially about the origins of angling and about the esoteric in angling. This curiosity is sustained by an almost pathological unwillingness not to file away any angling fact that he finds remotely interesting. It is the consequential steady accumulation of randomly acquired data, allied to an ability to identify connections and patterns amid the seemingly unconnected, that has brought to light much that might have been lost to the sport and given us his extraordinary body of work.

Frederick (Henry Ernest) Buller was born in Fulham, London,

on October 12, 1926. His parents moved to Kingsbury, Middlesex when Fred was three and it was there that he was brought up and educated. By the age of five he was catching sticklebacks, roach and gudgeon from the nearby River Brent. Thanks to a family connection in Blandford, Dorset he was, from the age of seven, able to expand and hone his skills on the dace, perch, roach, chub and trout of the Stour. He banked his first pike when he was nine. By his teens he was, like many dedicated boys at that age, quite expert.

Buller's passion for fish and fishing led him, at the age of 17, to leave grammar school for a job at what is now the Freshwater Biological Association (FBA), based on Windermere. The three years that followed were to set Buller's compass for life. He met and worked under some of the great biologists of the day, among them E.B. Worthington, who headed the FBA at that time, and Winifred Frost and Margaret Brown, authors of the much-praised study, The Trout. He learned about biology and fisheries research – and acquired a research worker's attitude to order and precision. He bought his first shotgun.

In 1945, when military service beckoned, he volunteered for the Fleet Air Arm and trained as a map-maker, a job that entailed flying, photography and the building of maps from aerial photographs. On demobilisation in 1947 he rented premises in Edgware and started a tackle business.

It thrived. Buller acquired the first British agency for Barbour clothing, began to wholesale fishing and shooting books, then moved into guns and gun-making. He employed his own gunsmiths and aimed at the very top of the market.

In the early 1980s, Buller bought the famous London gun-making firm of Frederick Beesley. Subsequently he acquired

Watson Brothers and then Charles Hellis and Sons. Hellis, Beesley and Watson as the new business was called, made bespoke shot-guns – some of them costing up to £84,000 a pair at turn-of-the-millennium money – for wealthy, private clients. In 1988, Buller moved his business to Amersham, in Buckinghamshire, where it currently still exists, now owned and run by his son, Bruce.

For all his gun-making knowledge and prominence – he was at one time chairman of the Gun Trades Association – it is for his contribution to an-gling literature that Buller is best known. It is a contribution that was enriched by the company he kept.

Through his tackle business he met Fred J. Taylor, who worked as a salesman for John Goddard's tackle manufacturing company, Efgeeco. Through Taylor, who in later years was to become a prolific author and broadcaster on angling, he met some of the best-known anglers of the time including, crucially, Richard Walker and Hugh Falkus.

The group around Walker and Buller – Falkus, in the main, ploughed his own, distant furrow – included at various times not only Fred Taylor but his expert angling brother, Ken; Leslie Moncrieff, a design engineer and champion sea-caster; Peter Thomas (who, Walker always said, was a better fisherman than he himself was); Peter Stone (another future author and specimen-hunter), Maurice Ingham and others. There has never been a time in history when such a creative and articulate group of anglers has come together, pooling knowledge and enriching one another's output. Through its deeds and writings this group, with Walker at its centre, was to change the face of angling for ever – above all by introducing science and logic to displace myth and potion.

It was with Buller at the helm that the Moncrieff Rod

Development Company was formed in 1963. Walker and Fred Taylor soon joined and the group developed, from first principles, a range of innovative rod designs for sea, coarse and game fishing, which Hardy Bros manufactured and marketed. It was the Moncrieff Rod Development Company that helped to design the first rods to be made from carbon fibre. Walker designed the Farnborough carbon fibre trout fly rod, the biggest-selling fly rod in Hardy's history. Buller still owns one of the first rods ever to be made of the new material – an experimental carbon spinning rod.

Buller had already dipped his feet in ink with articles for *Angling Times* and *Creel* when his first book, the slender *Fred Buller's Book of Rigs and Tackle* appeared in 1966, complete with contributions from Walker and Taylor. (Another book featuring Buller with his friends, this time including Falkus, would appear as *Successful Angling* in 1977).

It was, though, his other books that made Buller's name. They are all, in their way, extraordinary. Name a Buller book, look at its contents and style and you will know instantly that no-one else could have written it (possibly would have thought of writing it – maybe, even, would have wanted to write it). It is, with each, as though where others could have seen only the marble block, Buller could see the finished artwork deep inside.

The first of these major books – and the most famous – is *Pike*, which appeared in 1971 (revised and published as *Pike and the Pike Angler* in 1981). He wrote it at the request of Richard Walker, who had been asked to compile a library of fishing books, each dealing with a single fish species.

Walker well knew Buller's extraordinary knowledge of pike. Buller had been imprinted with the image of the first pike he saw in close-up, a fish of two or three pounds shown to him by another boy when he was aged about eight. His imagination had been set on fire with tales of a monster pike told to him by an adult angler he met a couple of years later. He had fished extensively for pike since – and at the time that Walker met him, Buller had long been engaged on a quest for a monster. Buller, Walker knew, had read everything he could find on the subject. No-one knew more.

When *Pike* came out it carried all the Buller hallmarks that were to become familiar. It was painstakingly researched. It was comprehensive and authoritative. It was methodically organised and vividly illustrated. It was full of fascinating, by-the-by detail. It was also written in the lucid and curiously conversational style that is Buller's own.

There were few questions that a layman could have asked about pike that were not either answered or in some way addressed in this book. There were introductions to pike evolution, pike anatomy and pike behaviour; information on pike tackle and when, where and how to catch pike; lists of the biggest pike ever known; notes – shock-horror for many today – on 'pike for the table'. *Pike* was not merely an angling book, it was a text book.

In his foreword to it, Walker recounts Buller's greatest angling loss. It occurred during a piking expedition on Loch Lomond in August, 1967. Buller and Peter Thomas were in one boat, Walker and Ken Taylor were in another. Buller put up a roach dead bait which he fished in shallow water close by. A monstrous fish was soon hooked and battle began. Before a knot gave way and the great creature escaped, it swam within six feet of Walker and, in the clear water, Walker had an excellent view of it. 'It frightened me', he said. He estimated its length at five feet and its back at 10 inches across. His immediate assessment, and that of Ken Taylor, was that the fish had to weigh better than 50lbs. Some years later, after he had worked out a formula for calculating pike weights with considerable accuracy, Walker revised his estimate to 'about 65 pounds'. At that weight, the fish would have been a world record. Forty years on, Buller says he still wakes up in the night, thinking about it.

A quite different kind of book followed, this time written with Hugh Falkus. Falkus and Buller's *Freshwater Fishing*, first published in 1975 and much enlarged in 1988, was the start of a collaboration between the two that was to last until Falkus' death in 1996. These two strong personalities had a relationship that was full of warmth, mutual respect and professionalism punctuated – Falkus was notoriously volatile – by volcanic eruptions. The secret of the partnership's durability appeared to be that no matter what the subject of the row and no matter how vehement the argument, no reference was ever made to it again, by either man, even if they met or spoke the next day.

Freshwater Fishing – the second edition especially – is in my view the finest general work of angling scholarship yet written (though I do need to add a caveat, here: Buller and Falkus asked me to write a brief contribution on trout rise forms for this edition, which the finished book now contains). *Freshwater Fishing* is packed to the fin-tips with information on everything from bleak to barbel, ruffe to roach, trout to tench, sticklebacks to sturgeon. Each fish's natural history is discussed. So is how to find it, how to catch it, how, if appropriate, to cook it. For this complex book, as for all his others, Buller designed every one of the 500-odd pages – and drew all the pin-sharp illustrations himself – to ensure that each piece of text had the relevant drawing or photograph close by it and not, as is so often the case, several dislocating pages distant.

More pike books followed including, in 1979, the wonderfully titled *The Domesday Book of Mammoth Pike*. This work expanded the big-fish list included in *Pike* by documenting the largest known specimens (i.e. fish of 35lbs and over) caught anywhere in the world in the previous 200-plus years.

There was an air of inevitability about *The Domesday Book*. Buller conducts a voluminous correspondence and, after *Pike*, so many readers sent him notes on other known big fish and offered him clues on additional – hitherto undocumented – whoppers, that the original list grew almost organically. Buller went to immense lengths to find anything that could verify the capture of each fish and to obtain photographs of it or of the person who caught it. He travelled widely to photograph the scenes of many of the dramas described, giving to every story, wherever he could, a sense of place.

Buller reckoned at the time that fewer than 300 pike of 35lbs and more had been caught in the previous three centuries and recorded 240 of them in *The Domesday Book*. Remarkable though this feat was, Buller's estimate proved decidedly conservative: with *More Mammoth Pike*, published in 2005, Buller added 131 new fish to the list and few can now doubt that more will eventually swim into view. Each fish is placed in numerical order of size (from 92lbs down) with details of weight, length, girth, location, name of captor, date caught, method used, source of information and notes on supporting visual evidence (eg photographs and the like). Many case histories are supplemented by anecdotes and garnished with the fruits of detective work by the author. In one among several striking investigations, Buller shows how Alfred Jardine, the great Victorian pike angler, must have inflated the weight of a pike caught in 1879, from 35lbs to 37lbs, in order falsely to claim the species record and 'hold' it for many years.

Buller has used a similar overall formula for *The Domesday Book of Giant Salmon*, the first of the three works yet to come.

Angling – the Solitary Vice (2000), a collection of pieces published in various specialist and private journals, gives a useful insight into more of Buller's 'special interests'. Here, there are essays on sturgeon (he saw an image of a sturgeon in a 15th century church wall painting and went to Canada to catch one); on a 4th century engraving of a salmon angler; on the earliest fishing reel (he went to China to research reels); on the lamprey (written after catching a trout with a sea lamprey clamped to its side); on fishing in Ireland (Buller had a house in Mayo that, for three decades, he used as his base there – and that he allowed his friends to use as a base when on jaunts in the west of Ireland) as well as an essay on angling in Russia (Buller fished in Russia for pike). There is, in addition, an important essay on the earliest hooks and the earliest fly (i.e. the fly used by the Macedonians and described in *De Animalium Natura*, around the year AD 200, by the Roman writer Claudius Aelianus).

The work that Buller regards as his most important is *Dame Juliana – The Angling Treatyse and its Mysteries*, which appeared in 2001. This work, another collaboration with Falkus though finished with the help of Malcolm Greenhalgh following Falkus' death – put the earliest book on angling in the English language under minute scrutiny.

It had two aims. One, to bring the importance and originality of that first work – the *Treatyse of Fysshynge wyth an Angle*, published in 1496 – to the modern reader, by making the ancient text read-able and comprehensible. The second was to examine whether or not the book really was written by Dame Juliana Berners, reputed Abbess of Sopwell Priory, near St. Albans, in Hertfordshire, to whom history has long ascribed it.

Before deciding to give the Dame the claim to fame (by default, because there is no alternative named candidate), Buller and Falkus produce evidence to suggest that the Treatyse's famous frontispiece – it shows a medieval angler fishing a small river with an exotic building in the background – was no mere flight of some illustrator's fancy but a scene from real life. Specifically, they suggest, it could be a view across the River Ver, in Hertfordshire, with Sopwell Priory in the distance.

The ancient text and the differing views on authorship are de-scribed under the heading 'The Dame and the Treatyse' elsewhere in these pages and there is little point in repeating them here. However, the scholarship and industry Buller and Falkus invested in the Mysteries can be glimpsed from a few points of detail.

The first is that, in an attempt to show that the frontispiece re-ally could depict the River Ver with Sopwell Priory in the back-ground, the two men sought permission from the local authority to fell a stretch of woodland scrub alongside the Ver that blocked the view beyond. They were granted permission and, at their own expense, put a team of men to work – eventually being rewarded with a view of the site where Sopwell Priory once stood: it was di-rectly behind the spot on the banks of the Ver where, they suggest, the ancient angler might once have been depicted.

Buller and Falkus went to other extraordinary lengths. To make the ancient text more accessible, they reproduced in the book a simultaneous, line-by-line translation into modern English. To bring its descriptions of fish and fishing to life, they had tackle made up to replicate that described in the 15th century text. They had artificial flies tied to represent ancient dressings described in a section on fly fishing. They published authoritative attempts to relate descriptions of natural flies described in the original book to the natural flies we know today. From conception to completion, Dame Juliana – the Angling Treatyse and its Mysteries took 30 years exactly to make. It will, quite separately from the contribution it makes to angling scholarship, remain a curiosity of angling literature in its own right.

Throughout all this activity, Fred Buller has continued to fish, to shoot – and to press ahead on other long-term, overlapping projects that may, at some point, appear in print. He has made his mark on angling not because of the great fish he has caught, though there have been a few. Nor has he, like some of his friends, made great advances in tactics and technique, though unquestionably he has added detail here and there. What Buller has done is to rescue, unearth, hoard, digest, analyse, interpret and package, passing on to the rest of us aspects of a heritage that would otherwise have been lost. It is a unique – and uniquely valuable – contribution.

Getting Stocking Levels Right

ALTHOUGH I like to fish for wild trout and am passionately interested in conserving them, I am not a wild trout purist. The idea one sometimes hears expressed – that no water containing wild trout should be stocked – is simply not realistic. The demand for fly fishing is so great, the pressure on waters so relentless, that wild populations alone could not sustain them. To make large numbers of rivers unavailable because some wild fish might be present, would leave so little fishing that the numbers that could be catered for, would collapse.

Exactly what kind of stocking might be needed will depend, of course, on individual waters and the opinions of those who fish and manage them. Three factors will be in the mix: the frequency of stocking, the numbers to be stocked and the sizes stocked. On waters where some wild fish survive, the last two especially can prove contentious.

* * *

THE possibility of catching a big fish, not necessarily big in absolute terms but big for the water from which it is taken, is one of the great buzzes of angling. While some big fish are caught by luck, plenty more are taken by skill and so to catch a whopper puts a feather in the cap. It has always been so.

In recent years, however, size alone has interested some anglers and a few stillwater fisheries have catered exclusively for them. At one point there was an outcry against the consequences, when a handful of fishery owners used huge stock fish to manipulate the old record fish lists: they reared fish already bigger than the existing record when put into the water. When these farm-reared porkers were banked – which they usually were within hours – the fishery owner claimed the wild-fish record and waxed fat on the publicity that resulted. Before long, this manipulation was ended because the record lists were reorganised specifically to exclude it. Today, the fact that some waters are stocked with 20-pounders and above is neither here nor there. Ponds are self-contained and nothing else and no-one else is affected.

Rivers, though, are different. It is not just that what is done on one reach can affect other reaches. Large numbers of rivers that offer trout fishing have a small head of wild fish remaining and there has to be an interest in preserving them.

Enter the problems, especially on rivers where the sizes of fish stocked are grossly disproportionate to those of the wild fish around them.

No-one puts 20-pounders into rivers but fish approaching double figures do go in, sometimes. When big, farm-bred fish are put into a river holding wild fish, first they harass and agitate the wild stock, then they instinctively seek out the best feeding places. Because they have the muscle and teeth to do so, they drive away the wild fish already occupying these lies and the displaced fish drive away the smaller wild fish holding the next-best lies. It is a domino effect that works all down the wild fish population. It results in many fish being driven to lies that cannot sustain them. These fish lose condition. Some of them die. The natural stock is eroded.

There are other consequences. Big, hungry stock fish in a river that cannot sustain them will also die if they are not quickly caught – but not before, in their mounting hunger, they have eaten whatever they can get their jaws on, small wild fish not excluded. In winter, when the native fish and the stocked fish move onto the spawning beds, the stock fish add to the churn on the gravels and often dig out the eggs of wild fish there before them. More insidiously, stocked trout sometimes mate with wild trout, weakening the genetic integrity of wild fish populations.

For these reasons and others, stocking decisions on rivers need much thought. In the case of a democratically run club, much will depend on two points. The first is the value the membership places on its wild-fish heritage. The second is what it decides it wants from its fishing, not just in the short-term but the long. While stocking with huge fish may create localised disasters, requiring memberships to fish for tiny fish all day, every day, would lead to boredom and simply drive people from the water. Compromise will be required, all around.

Some other kinds of fishing can be boring. Waters so heavily stocked that a fish dare not leap out of them for fear of not getting back in, take away all challenge. Waters where the numbers stocked are so niggardly that little sport can be expected no matter how great the effort, are a turn-off. Waters that are stocked with fish all the same size, whether half a pound or ten times that weight, remove the element of surprise.

A successful stocking policy needs to meet three criteria. First, it should offer the possibility of sport to the average rod, but not the certainty: that is, the number stocked should be neither suffocating nor miserly. Second, it should offer variety, in that an angler would never quite know what was going to poke up its nose or grab his fly next. So a range of fish sizes should be put in, these sizes not wildly out of keeping with the fish the river supports naturally.

The third point is an extension of the second. The ideal stocking policy would offer the chance of a once-a-season or a twice-a-season corker to a small number of rods. These would not be gargantuan fish but beyond the general run, adding a frisson to the season for the few who caught them.

Such a mix would, I suspect, keep most (though naturally not all) anglers happy. In sustaining interest it would help to sustain numbers. It would ensure that the needs of wild fish are factored into the stocking equation and it would keep our sport anchored in the real world, where it belongs. Some clubs and owners seem to get it all right – but alas, surprisingly few.

Stalking Fish on Lakes

WHY *do we go fishing? There can be lots of reasons but one of them, certainly, is to catch fish. How do we catch a fish? Easily stated, less easily done. We catch a fish by getting it to take our artificial fly (or lure or spinner or bait) into its mouth, by striking when it has done so and then by bringing it safely to the net.*

Self-evidently, in this process, a trout fisherman needs to bring fly and fish into close proximity – and the fish needs to suspect little, when he does so. Obvious? Of course. Generally accepted? Almost certainly. But on the bank, the behaviour of some can suggest otherwise.

* * *

AN ARTICLE in which I described stalking and catching one of the biggest brown trout of my life, attracted a lot of interest from readers. Several wrote in with stories of their own best fish. Some wanted to hear more about the technique of targeting individual fish with weighted nymphs – the successful tactic, for me.

Their reaction came to mind a little later, when I found myself driving past one of the best-known stillwater trout fisheries in England. Although this fishery is famous for the size and quality of the fish with which it is stocked it is, in most other ways, typical of the specialist, man-made commercial trout lakes that have made fly fishing as accessible as it is.

A feature of many such fisheries is that their water is clear: so clear that, on a calm day, individual fish can be seen and hence stalked. They offer a form of fishing that makes its own high demands and which, in its tensions, frustrations and excitements, can turn what might have become a day of aimless, speculative casting into a locked-on hunt.

The water I chanced upon lends itself to this fishing style and, passing it for the first time, I pulled over. I crept to within a few yards of the nearest angler and asked him how things were going. Not well, he said. He was standing by the water's edge, rummaging through his spools of nylon and boxes of flies. He'd had nothing. He didn't know whether it was his fly, his leader, his line or what. Either way, he was getting frustrated.

How to tell him? Even from where I was, crouching low on the bank, it was obvious that were he to cast until Domesday, he would catch nothing the way things were. And this in spite of the fact that – this being the water it was – trout as big as submarines would be gliding through the weedbeds at his feet.

My friend's problem was that he was ignoring the two basic rules for stalking fish in clear waters. The first is that the angler cannot afford to make his presence known. The second is that if he wants a fish to take his fly, the fish must see it, first.

It might seem odd that such things need to be said, yet they do. Indeed, fishery owners rely on such basics being ignored, to get their costings right. So do the consistently successful anglers, who need someone to subsidise the fish they take away or else ticket prices would soar.

My friend on the bankside was on a small lake almost devoid of cover, yet he was standing right on the water's edge. He was maybe 6ft tall and the bank was maybe two feet above the lake's surface. It was obvious that, from the position of the fish in gin-clear water, he would be about as invisible as a chimney-stack on a cliff-top. His casting movements would attract more attention, the rhythmic flash from his gloss-varnished rod heliographing his presence to fish miles away.

The flashing rod problem can be cured by applying a thin layer of matt varnish – a finger-tip smear is enough – over the high gloss that manufacturers put on all their rods because anglers foolishly demand it. The need to keep physically out of sight requires attention to a lot of detail.

Polarising glasses are often worn to cut out surface reflections and enable fish to be more easily seen – but the sun can flash even more effectively off glass than it can off varnish and so the lenses should be shaded with a brimmed hat or a hand. Bright clothes are out. Sudden movements should be avoided. Standing up – at least until the near water has been explored – is a no-no. The water should be scanned from far back, approached in a crouch, the last few yards often on hands and knees. Many casts will be made from a kneeling position.

Once an unalarmed fish has been targeted and the angler is in a position to cast, the need is to get the fly – almost always, in this style of fishing, a nymph – quickly to a place where the fish can see and take it.

Large trout cruising several feet down in lakes are usually re-luctant to investigate anything far above their heads and so the nymph must be got down to the fish. Which means using a nymph with weight in it. Experienced stalkers carry nymphs with varying amounts of lead or copper wire under the dressing, giving each fly a known sinking-rate. Exactly which weight of fly to choose depends on the circumstances of a given time, among them the depth of the fish in the water, the speed at which it is travelling and the thickness of – and hence the resistance offered by – the leader when sinking. When taken with factors like wind-drift and surface movement – as, for example, near inlets or outlets – such circumstances will dictate the distance in front of the fish to which the fly must be cast, if target and sinking nymph are to coincide, deep down.

To see, for the first time, all of this come together in the hands of an expert can be to witness what looks like sorcery: a long period of stillness and silence, then a single cast made and a fish instantly hooked. It looks so uncannily simple.

But of course, there is a rider. It is illuminated by the story of the tourist who stopped a New Yorker in the street. 'Excuse me,' she asked, 'but can you tell me how I get to Carnegie Hall?'

'Lady', came the reply, 'you gotta practise'.

Giving Logic a Chance

IF there is one thing we anglers are good at it is complaining about our luck, by which we mean the absence of it, by which we mean the absence of fish.

Luck is always going to play a part in angling, but it need not be a central part. In angling, as in other activities, we can make much of our own luck by pruning out chance. To do that means thinking logically about what we are trying to achieve every time we put up a rod and take it to the water.

The process does not begin with myth and folklore, as much behaviour might suggest (take tail of newt and eye of toad), with personal convenience (I'll fish over there because it's near the car park), or even with what someone who has just caught a fish tells us (exactly how many fish has he caught today and how many last week, when he was in a different place in different conditions?).

The process begins with the fish. It means thinking about the fish's needs and behaviour and focusing everything we do on them: our approach to the water, our choice of tackle, our tactics, the kinds of flies, lures and baits we use. It means learning to give the fish not only what they want but when, where and how they want it.

* * *

IT is astonishing how many of us ignore the obvious when we take up fishing. It is as if, when we put our tackle into the car and drive off, we leave our critical faculties behind. We seem not to make the connection between whatever success we achieve elsewhere in our lives and the thought and experience that contribute towards it. This is as true of scientists, politicians, businessmen and lawyers as it is of everyone else. When faced with a stretch of river or lake, intelligent minds often go blank. We tackle up, fish as we have always fished – too often, where no fish could possibly be – and then complain that we have caught nothing.

Maybe it is because we put so much energy and mental effort into our everyday lives: maybe because, when we go fishing, we just want to switch off and dissolve mental stress away. I do not know but if it is, our expressions of frustration are an odd way of showing it.

The study of fish and how they live and react to changing circumstances – flood and drought, high temperatures and low, gluts of food and the lean times – is a fascinating study in its own right: a study so absorbing that, once begun, it not only provides an escape from stress but absolutely guarantees better results.

Let us look at the process involved. It is very basic and it is launched by the kind of questioning that, in other situations, we would all likely embark upon immediately. It begins with the needs of the quarry – let us say it is a trout – as it goes about its business in the water.

Question: what does any trout need if it is to stay alive and thrive? Answer: it needs to have an adequate supply of food, a comfortable place from which this food can be accessed with the minimum effort and it needs to stay away from harm and the threat of harm. Question: what, broadly speaking, could an awareness of these needs tell us about the likely whereabouts of trout in rivers? What, broadly speaking, could it suggest about the likely whereabouts of trout in lakes?

We are beside a river. Does the stretch of water in front of us have bends in it, or is it more or less straight? Are there places where the banks pinch in (and so where the water will be deeper) and places where the river is unusually wide (where we can expect to find shallows)? Where is the main push of the current, which carries most of a river trout's food, in each place? What, taken together, do these things tell us about where on this reach, most food is likely to be concentrated by the water? Now look again. Where, in or near the places likely to hold most food, are the places a fish could lie with least expenditure of effort? Among these potential lies, which are the ones that could give a fish a sense of security or give it a bolt-hole if danger threatened – deep water, say, or a weedbed, or a sunken log or overhanging trees?

And so the options are narrowed.

Now we are beside a lake. Here, we know that there is no current and that, like most creatures, trout will avoid extremes of heat and cold. Do the contours of the banks – are they steeply sloping? – give any clue to where the deeper water (the water least affected by surface temperatures) might be? Do the contours of the banks – are they low-lying and do they enter the water at a shallow angle? – give a clue to where the shallow water (the water that will heat up and cool most) might lie? How hot or cold has it been of late? Is it a windy day or is it still – and if windy, to which bank is the wind pushing the surface water and the food drifting in it? Are there, in this seemingly bland sheet of water, discernible or known features that might concentrate food and be attractive to fish – say shallows amid deeps, deep pockets in shallows, weedbeds, sunken trees and hedgerows, places where streams flow in or where springs well up from the bed?

Now, on this river or lake, are any fish rising? If they are rising, are the rises small and gentle or full-blooded and violent? What do these rises tell us about the way the fish making them must have been moving – ie, fast or slow? What kind of bug or fly – let us assume that these fish are not eating other fish – is in this water that could cause the fish to move in such a way? At this time of year? At this time of day? Do I have something to suggest this bug or fly? If I do, how does the likely behaviour of the natural fly prompting the response that I can see from the fish, suggest I present my artificial?

Now choose the fly. Decide how and where to fish it. Cast. Fish the artificial – static or moving and if moving, how? – in the way that best suggests the movements of the natural creature being imitated. And so on and so on. As thought follows thought and step follows step, logic and observation clarify the options and make choices simpler. They prune out chance and give every action a purpose. Catch rates increase and frustrations decline.

The sense of satisfaction soars.

Chub, Dace, Roach, Barbel

I WAS brought up on coarse fishing. That is what pretty well everyone around our way did, when I was a lad. It was not until I was in my 20s that I discovered trout and fell in love with them. For years I was obsessed with them, studied them, wrote books about them.

Years later, half a lifetime later, a chance meeting with the most famous coarse angler in the entire galaxy led to talk of chub and dace; to praise of roach and barbel; to odes to floats. And so, after a long, long absence, I decided to make their acquaintance again.

* * *

IT TOOK a few trips, of course. After so many years of travelling light – a tiny rod, a box of flies, a spool or two of nylon – naturally it took a while to get back into the swing of things. But then, how could it not? There is a world of difference between light, mobile, fly fishing for trout, wandering free as the air and the next rise, and the generality of coarse fishing.

I had done a lot of coarse fishing as a lad and, having known nothing before it, took to all that it entailed like an angler to water. But going back, adjusting again to the immobility, assembling again the clutter of tackle, dealing with the mess and goo of baits after the simplicity and aesthetics of pursuing dainty trout, took some getting used to.

It was Chris Yates who persuaded me. The most revered coarse angler in Britain, the sometime long-time holder of the carp record, told me of the great fish to be found in a particular reach of a particular river midway between our homes. There were not large numbers of fish, he said, but numbers of large fish. There was talk of 13lbs barbel, 25lbs carp, 25lbs pike, 6lbs chub and 1lb dace, all taken by members of the syndicate that had rented the water in the previous few months. Memories from my teens and early twenties stirred. Would I be interested in giving it a go again? Seriously? Yes, indeed.

And so, one crisp day in March found me tottering and tripping over the meadows, burdened by all of it. I had brought out the ancient, wonderful Wallis Wizard rod I had once done a newspaper round to buy. I had brought out the ancient, silky-smooth Speedia centrepin reel, duly oiled. There were the old boxes of floats and weights (yes, I still have them all); the great, long-handled net; the flask and sandwiches (for me), the tins of pork luncheon meat and sweetcorn (for the fish); the metal-framed, collapsible chair.

Opposite the weir-pool, a little downstream from the falls where the water caught the light like bent glass, we had a pow-wow, discussed swims and tactics, floats and weights and drank piping tea Chris brewed in his storm-kettle. Then we fished. He used a small lead and explored the river bed by touch, I opted for the ease of the float.

That first day, as it happens, we both blanked but in the close season that followed, the bug wriggled and began to bite. Come June I was out again, in August once more, in November and December twice apiece. It is not that I was catching a lot – this water is, as Chris had warned several times, more fishing water than catching water – but I got a few and rediscovered much.

Take the fish. When trout anglers are fishing, they are utterly single-minded. Other fish become a nuisance, a distraction – even, in the minds of a shocking and blimpish few, vermin. Yet to set the trout aside, to go after coarse fish for their own sake alone, is to see each species beautiful in its different way; to recognise – no surprise, this – that each kind needs a different approach based on its special behaviour. It is to understand quickly how many fish are far more difficult to catch than the average stocked apology for *Salmo trutta*.

There may be an element of novelty involved, of course, but if I had to pick out two highlights from that first full year, both would be from coarse-fishing days.

One afternoon in August I found two great chub basking close to the surface, each one behind a dense weed bed that broke the current in heavy, deep water. Over the space of three hours, on and off, I did not make a single cast that attracted interest, though I crept through sedges six feet high crouched to half their height; although I kept the rod down, moved so slowly that I scarcely knew I was there myself, cast so gently that the free-lined bait made scarcely a ripple going in. I came away from the water nettled, cramped, frustrated and humbled – but seized with the fascination of the challenge.

The second experience was an afternoon in December, on a branch of the river close to the place that Chris and I had first tried. Immense barbel lived there. They moved about but had preferred places. They were notoriously difficult to deceive.

In the high, heavy water I forsook the float and touch-legered,

Yates-style. I used four or five swanshot maybe two feet from the hook. They gave me just enough weight to touch and hold bottom, offered just enough buoyancy on the current to allow me to trundle the bait a yard or two if I raised the rod and encouraged it.

I fished a size four hook tied directly to a 7lbs line with large chunks of pork luncheon meat as bait. A yard or two back from the water's edge I sat in my chair, absolutely still. I held the rod in my right hand, felt the line in the fingertips of my left. With the rod balancing on my crossed knees, there was no weight to fatigue and distract. The line ran straight from my fingers down to the river bed where I knew the great fish lived. I imagined them there, hugging the bottom and sensing my bait: approaching it.

Little by little, the light faded. The trees shrank back to silhouettes, the reflections left the water and it darkened to pewter. The moon came up. The river eased and slid and made soft, liquid noises. The line in my fingertips became an electrified nerve, formed a link between my imagination and the down-there unknown.

Gradually the messages coming up the line took on more meaning. I began to map out the river bed in my mind. I found myself differentiating between the grating touch-touchings of the leads tumbling over gravel and the slow silken slide as they passed over silt. I came to recognise the gathering heaviness of a weed before the line let go. Just occasionally I felt an exploratory 'pluck-pluck' that had me hair-triggered and alert, with every nerve tingling and each sinew taut. Sitting there, rooted alone in the dark, took me back to my angling roots and maybe beyond.

Of course, fishing for chub and barbel was not the whole of my year, or even the main part of it. Game fishing and fly fishing are still my great love. Yet to rediscover coarse fishing gave me excitements long forgotten. It continues to give my fishing a new kind of roundness. The baskets and boxes, the baits and the seat are easily shouldered, now.

Halford and the Dry Fly

I HAVE written before that in my view, Richard Walker was the most important known angler of all time (and if that statement is contested then who, it seems reasonable to ask, is better fitted to that crown?). Walker was not only a brilliant angler who caught specimens of many species – he was a talented engineer, an observant naturalist and an outstanding communicator.

Walker's attitude was that any fish, even the biggest and most difficult, could be caught provided it was fished for with sufficient determination, in the right way, in the right place, at the right time, with tackle capable of hooking and landing it. His work led to a deeper understanding of fish of many species, to huge advances in technique, to tackle developments of many kinds – and to specimen-hunting as it is currently practised. By the time of his death in 1985, almost single-handedly, Walker had dragged coarse angling out of the dark ages into the light.

Game fishing does not have a Richard Walker, someone who made that kind of all-embracing contribution; but it does have its great figures in both salmon fishing and trout fishing. Dry fly fishing for trout is dominated by one name, above all.

*　*　*

A READER OF The Times once asked me to settle a dispute he was having with a friend. Who, he wanted to know, had been the most important figure in the history of dry fly fishing? He gave me no indication of either his own opinion or that of his friend. My judgement would be accepted as final.

What surprised me about the question was that there could be any dispute. There is only one contender: Frederic Michael Halford, born 1844, died 1914 and author of *Dry Fly Fishing in Theory and Practice*. Halford's name is revered in the four corners of the angling world. No-one before him or since has had remotely his impact on that branch of the sport. If the answer to the question posed is clear-cut, however, the background is not. Behind Halford, little-known, little-sung and author of nothing, stands George Selwyn Marryat.

Halford, a sometime businessman and Marryat, a one-time soldier, were both comfortably raised in a time when fly fishing was in creative ferment. In 1836 Alfred Ronalds had shown the importance of considering the world from the trout's underwater point of view – and discussed the significance of reflection and refraction for the first time. In 1841 G.P.R. Pulman had shown the value of fishing with a dry fly on the surface. In 1857 W.C. Stewart had demonstrated the value of the upstream as opposed to the downstream cast, which enabled a floating fly to drift to a fish naturally, instead of dragging across the current. In the lifetimes of the two men split cane rods, silk lines and hooks with eyes were all developed.

There seems little doubt that when it came to fishing, Marryat was a better performer than Halford: indeed, contemporary opinion has Marryat as the finest fly fisher of his day. It seems likely he was also the more creative of the two. However in angling, perhaps to an extent not true in other sports, it is not performance that defines greatness and that leads to immortality, but books: especially the extent to which a book advances thinking on the sport and influences its future development.

It is here that Halford comes into his own. While Marryat published nothing, Halford published several books, two of them seminal. His first, in 1886, was *Floating Flies and How to Dress Them*. It systematised the means by which many aquatic flies could be imitated successfully with furs, feathers and silks. *Dry Fly Fishing in Theory and Practice*, published in 1889, was the second. This book drew together all the diverse aspects of dry fly fishing in use or being worked upon at the time, related them one to another and laid them out as a coherent and purposeful fishing strategy. Essential entomology, artificial flies, how, when and where to cast, fish feeding behaviour, hooking, playing and landing of the quarry and much else are all there, for the most part presented as validly for today as for the time in which they were written.

So while Halford did not invent the dry fly or dry fly fishing and certainly did not work alone, he it was who undertook the labour of setting everything down so that the rest of us could have it: who, through these two books and especially through the second, passed on the essentials on which this lyrical and beautiful branch of the sport is now practised, worldwide.

The puzzle is this. Marryat taught Halford much of what he knew and worked intimately with Halford in researching the material that formed the basis of both books – yet he declined any connection with either. When Halford suggested that he had been so much a part of the work on the first that his name should share the title page, Marryat declined. When the second book was finished, Marryat would accept only the dedication of it to him, by Halford. No-one knows why. There have been theories about this and suggestions of that: but it is all conjecture.

The two men were introduced to one another in the spring of 1879 by Francis Francis, the greatest of the Victorian all-rounders. By that stage Marryat was already recognised as a brilliant fly fisher and a master fly-tyer. Indeed, Marryat is known to have worked with another famous figure of the time, H.S. Hall, not only on the refinement of the eyed hook but on the creation of fly designs that would float longer than the conventional dressings of the day.

After their introduction, Halford and Marryat met frequently, formed a close friendship and years of intense collaboration on fly-fishing matters began. They laid open the stomachs of trout so they could see what insects the fish preferred to eat from all those available to them in and on the water. They caught living examples of the same insects and reared and studied them. They developed dry fly patterns to imitate these insects and dressed them on the new, light hooks. Later, they studied rods, lines, and all else relevant to delivering their new flies to the fish, even against a wind.

When *Dry Fly Fishing in Theory and Practice* eventually came out, it carried one of the most fulsome dedications that can have appeared in any book. Addressing Marryat, Halford said: 'If these pages... contain anything that is useful, anything that is new, anything that is instructive (then it) is due to the innumerable hints you have been good enough to convey to me'.

Halford – the great, later the somewhat imperialistic Halford – signed it 'your faithful pupil'.

No doubt there about Halford the Communicator's view of his debt to Marryat the Decliner – and hence about the debt owed to Marryat by every fly fisher since. Yet still Marryat's precise contribution is not known because he wrote nothing of it and no-one else did, either.

All we can say for certain is that Marryat must have been extraordinarily creative and practical; that he was a dazzling performer because everyone else said so; that he was 'full of wit and repartee' because Halford said so; and that he was somewhat idiosyncratic because he was given to wearing knickerbockers and Tam o' Shanter not only when fishing but on relatively formal occasions.

Which leaves us with the nub. While it remains a mystery that Marryat should have decided to stand aside from works to which he clearly contributed so much, that choice has had two inevitable results. The first is that it has consigned him to the shadows for ever. The second is that Halford now reigns supreme – and alone.

John Goddard

I HAVE been fortunate, over a fishing lifetime, to meet and fish with many fine anglers, quite a lot of them authors, some of them famous. A few of these men have become friends – one or two, close friends. John Goddard has been one of the latter. John and I have fished together for over 30 years and, for a period of four years, we collaborated intensely in producing The Trout and the Fly, a work in which we paid every bit as much attention to the fish under water as we did to the angler on the bank.

John has been the pre-eminent angling entomologist of his time. He is also one of the most complete all-rounders who ever lived or, at least, who ever wrote a book. His contribution to the sport as a whole has been so wide-ranging and unusual that it needs to be placed on record.

* * *

I FIRST met John Goddard in 1973. I was well into my first book, The Pursuit of Stillwater Trout and wanted to include some photographs of the natural flies I planned to mention, alongside their matching artificials, so that the reader could relate one to the other.

There was, at that time, only one source of such pictures. Even by then, Goddard had made himself famous. His Trout Fly Recognition (1966) introduced thousands of readers to the kinds of flies they were likely to find at the riverside. Trout Flies of Stillwater

(1969) did the same and more for those who fished lakes – and was perfectly timed to catch the rising tide of interest in that emerging branch of the sport.

I had begun fly fishing just a few years before and had trodden the traditional path of lucky-dip fly choice, allied to chuck-and-chance-it presentation, punctuated very occasionally – as much to my surprise as its – by a fish. Finally, frustrated that I was putting my yearned-for outings to so little use, I decided things had to change. I constructed an aquarium, devoted an entire season to the study of aquatic bugs and nymphs, tied my own imitations of them and fished the results in the ways I saw the naturals move.

My catch rate soared, I wrote to the then editor of *Trout and Salmon* magazine, Jack Thorndike, to tell him and he asked me to write a series of articles setting out my experiences. When that series was finished he asked me to write another and then another. In due course a publisher asked me to write a book along similar, though naturally extended, lines. It was for this book, *The Pursuit*, that I needed the photographs.

I wrote to John with a list of the flies I needed and he, the most generous of men, responded. By way of thanks, after a few exchanges of letters, I invited him for a day at the stillwater I was fishing at the time – Latimer Park Lakes, in Buckinghamshire – and we hit it off. Subsequently he invited me to his home, I invited him to mine and the rest, as they say, is history. Just two years later, over dinner at my home, we hatched the idea of collaborating on a book. *The Trout and the Fly* (1980) resulted.

John Goddard is, of course, best known for his entomology and his trout fishing, but he has been an all-round angler in a sense that few anglers understand it: coarse angler, trout angler, sea angler with both bait and fly and international big-game angler who represented his country several times. But it is his writings on trout and entomology that will prove his legacy.

It is probably true to say that, more than any other British writer in the 20th century, John Goddard persuaded anglers at large that a knowledge of entomology could be a huge advantage when trying to catch trout on artificial flies. He not only designed a hatch of imitative patterns himself, but adapted the dressings of others and wrote extensively on methods for fishing them. He delivered the complete fly-to-landing-net package.

Others had trodden the entomological path before him. Frederic Halford and George Selwyn Marryat had studied the fly-life of the southern chalk streams in the 1880s and 1890s and, thanks to Halford's writings, had effectively systematised dry fly fishing as a sport by the turn of that century. G.E.M. Skues later did much the same for those who had fished the chalk streams with sunken flies, by showing how nymphs could be imitated and fished. In being able to stand on their shoulders – and to a significant extent also on those of J.R. Harris, who published *An Angler's Entomology* in 1952 – Goddard was able to take anglers further, both technically and geographically.

He created, or had a hand in, many brilliant dressings. The so-called G and H Sedge, a collaborative product with an earlier fishing partner, Cliff Henry (it is tied with deer hair, which is hollow and therefore virtually unsinkable) is known the world over. His delicate, brilliantly observed PVC Nymph, was one of the first flies to incorporate plastic in its design. Scores of other dressings have stood the test of trout and time.

John Goddard was born in Vauxhall, London, on August 27,

1923 and brought up from an early age in Carshalton, Surrey. He caught his first fish, at the age of five, from the nearby River Wandle, an appropriate water given his future interests as it was from the Wandle that Halford took his own first trout on a fly, in 1868.

A brief spell as an apprenticed mechanical engineer, followed by call-up in 1942, service with the East Surrey Regiment (though not action, partly thanks to a disastrous landing as a trainee paratrooper which put him in hospital for weeks) was followed by demobilisation in 1947. For the first time, Goddard junior joined F.G. Goddard, the family's garden furniture business run by his father.

Garden furniture was not top of many shopping lists in the years following the war and, with the business struggling, the younger Goddard persuaded his father to branch out. He had pursued his interest in angling, knew something about the marketplace and proposed that he both design and commission products to meet a rising, unsatisfied demand. The family's existing workforce would make the products and a team of salesmen would sell them direct to tackle retailers, cutting out any middle men.

The strategy succeeded, not least because the first thing Goddard designed and marketed – in 1949 – was a combined angler's seat-cum-tackle-box that proved an instant hit: so much so, indeed, that it helped to launch the now-booming marketplace in angling luggage and accessories – seats, tackle hold-alls, rod cases, trolleys and the like. Efgeeco, as the new angling supplies business was called, thrived and, at its peak, employed 60 people and had over 250 products in its catalogue. Goddard went on to become long-time vice-chairman of the Tackle Trades Association and the first chairman of the Angling Foundation. He eventually sold the business to fish, travel and write (as well as play golf and bridge, his other long-term interests) in 1984.

Goddard's involvement with the tackle trade, and an interest in carp fishing especially, brought him into contact with Richard Walker, the central figure in angling at that time, and a group of brilliant and innovative anglers who surrounded Walker – among them Peter Thomas, Peter Stone, Fred Buller and Maurice Ingham. Fred J. Taylor, another member of the Walker circle and a brilliant angler and natural communicator, worked as an Efgeeco salesman for many years.

In the mid-1950s, Goddard's fishing life took the first of many new turns.

Up to that time, fly fishing for trout had been largely river-and-loch based, the privilege of the better-off or those who lived near water. With the growing realisation that reservoirs could be a source of revenue and leisure as well as water supply, more and more water companies stocked their lakes with trout and opened them to the paying public. It was a process that, almost overnight, brought fly fishing within reach of millions. The opening of Weir Wood reservoir, in West Sussex, brought it within Goddard's reach. He took it up.

In 1957 Goddard met Cliff Henry, already a skilled stillwater fly fisherman and the pair became friends. Together they fished Weir Wood, Blagdon and Chew; then Goddard and later Henry joined the ancient Piscatorial Society, based in Wiltshire and switched their attention to rivers. The water at Abbotts Barton, on the Itchen, the beat made famous by Skues and by then in the Piscatorials' portfolio, became a special focus.

Both men became fascinated with the difficulty of this gin-clear, slowly paced water. It gave the fish plenty of time to scrutinise the dressings they were offered and to find these flies wanting. Together, Goddard and Henry decided they needed to know more about the naturals they were trying to imitate – and to create better artificials. They began to collect specimens at Abbotts Barton, which Goddard photographed; then they moved further afield eventually, between 1961 and 1965, travelling to rivers all over Britain to collect, describe, photograph and imitate the natural flies they found.

(It is worth saying that even the photographic content of this project presented challenges, not least because macro photography was in its infancy and because the flies and bugs refused to keep still long enough to have their portraits taken. In the absence of written references on the former, Goddard had to develop his own combinations of lenses and lighting, from scratch. On the latter, he initially killed the flies, which proved to be unhelpful from an aesthetic point of view, then he tried anaesthetizing them, which made them too droopy. Eventually he took to placing them in a flask and heating the glass gently, which caused the flies to become just comatose enough to get the job done).

With the encouragement of Henry – and of friends who by now included David Jacques (subsequently author of *The Development of Modern Stillwater Fishing*), Oliver Kite (*Nymph Fishing in Practice*) and Dermot Wilson (*Fishing the Dry Fly*) – Goddard began to think in terms of a book. He already had some experience of writing for the coarse fishing magazines – his first article had appeared in *Anglers' World* in 1962 – and *Trout Fly Recognition* resulted.

The work found a ready market. It helped fly fishermen not

only in the cocooned world of the chalk streams, but on rivers everywhere, to identify the flies they came across and to choose and tie better representations. It included descriptions of the males and females of different species, even going into detail on the colour of eyes and the shapes of wings; on body shapes and segmentations; on legs and tails. Many naturals were shown in colour photographs that by now were better than any previously published. Goddard was elected a Fellow of the Royal Entomological Society on the back of it.

Trout Flies of Stillwater, published three years later, performed a similar service for lake fishermen but was more helpful still, this time Goddard going into detail not only on how flies and bugs might be imitated, but on how these imitations might best be fished. These two books were the first of a dozen that Goddard was to write, most of them with a fly fishing theme. The culmination of his entomological work, *Trout Flies of Britain and Europe*, appeared in 1991.

In tandem with his work on *Trout Fly Recognition* and *Trout Flies of Stillwater*, Goddard had been pursuing an interest in sea fishing that stemmed from boat trips he undertook while holidaying with his wife Eileen, in Polruan, Cornwall, in 1957. His early outings were off the Sussex coast, at Littlehampton. Later, Bernard Venables, a co-founder of *Angling Times* and author of the famous Mr Crabtree books, invited him to join a shark fishing party to Looe, in Cornwall. Goddard enjoyed the experience and shark trips to the West Country soon became an annual fixture.

In time, Goddard began writing about these trips for *Angling Times* and as a result, the Portuguese tourist authorities asked him to survey the big-game fishing off Portugal's coast. Other surveys followed, several of them undertaken with Leslie Moncrieff, a noted sea fisherman, casting champion and rod designer as well as a photographer. The publicity surrounding the two men's captures of shark, marlin and tuna effectively kick-started the angling tourism which Madeira and the Azores have enjoyed ever since. Before long, Goddard was invited to fish for England in international big-game fishing championships and subsequently he captained England's A team for several years. *Big Fish from Salt Water* was to appear in 1977.

Around that time an invitation from the Bahamas Tourist Board saw Goddard take up yet another kind of angling – fly fishing for exotic species like bonefish, sailfish, permit, snook, trevally and tarpon. He has since traveled hugely in pursuit of such fish, making numerous trips to the Seychelles, the Bahamas, Cuba, the Cayman Islands, Mexico and Belize. His pursuit of big trout has taken him many times to the United States and over a dozen times to New Zealand, often leading fishing parties for specialist travel agencies.

By the time Goddard had launched into fly fishing in the sea, he and I had begun to fish together regularly for trout, on both stillwaters and rivers. Our outings became almost weekly from 1976-on when we both began to fish the Wilderness water of the Kennet, at Kintbury in Berkshire.

The Wilderness, at that time, was probably the finest trout fishery in Britain and some brilliant anglers fished it – especially the group which gathered together on Saturdays. On Saturdays, intensive periods of fishing were separated by long lunches. Considerable quantities of wine often lubricated the sometimes highly technical, often amusing, always absorbing conversations.

We had many guests there, especially – though not only – from the United States. Nick Lyons, the most famous of America's angling publishers and essayists and author of, among other books, *Fishing Widows* and *Spring Creek*, came several times. Likewise Gary Borger, author of *Designing Trout Flies* and *Presentation*. Len Wright, who wrote *Fishing the Dry Fly as a Living Insect*, paid us a visit. So did Lefty Kreh, a dazzling caster and author – again, among other works – of *Fly Fishing in Salt Water*. So did Hoagy Carmichael Jnr, son of the famous songwriter and author of a major work on rod-building. On these occasions the company was so stimulating and the conversation such fun that we had to drag ourselves away from the fishing hut to give the trout any attention at all.

In many ways it would have been difficult, I suppose, to find two more different individuals than Goddard and myself, in both background and temperament, to collaborate on a book but, in 1980, after four years of observation, research, discussion and photography – much of the latter from under water – *The Trout and the Fly* resulted. We broadly split the work on the book, with Goddard taking prime (though not sole) responsibility for the photography, while I wrote the final text. Of course, each of us was intimately involved in the experiments and ideas that lay behind both.

We had a diversion throughout this period. In 1978 I had persuaded the BBC that what Goddard and I were doing would make an interesting television programme and during the latter part of our work a BBC television crew spent what amounted to months on the riverbank with us. It proved a fascinating – if often frustrating – experience. It also provided us both with some memorable moments.

One came in the first few days when our producer, a somewhat highly strung individual, repeatedly kicked a barbed wire fence in frustration at some happening or other then, to the amusement of everyone around, followed our gaze down to boot height to find that he had ripped his wellie in several places. A favourite of my own was when the same producer, as I was trying to drive a line into the teeth of a downstream gale for the benefit of the camera, shouted: 'No, slower, slower – move your rod more slowly', an instruction that, had I attempted to follow it, would have blasted my line behind me into the mid-Atlantic. While filming on the Itchen one day we saw something that neither John nor I had seen before – and which neither of us has seen since: a huge brown trout, a fish of maybe five or six pounds, swimming slowly upstream with a smaller trout flexing and twisting, clamped broadside in its jaws. The television crew was unable to catch the moment but John managed to snatch a few frames with a motor-driven 35mm camera before the great fish slowly turned away and was lost to sight. The dark drama of that incident – nature red in tooth and gill, day and night and mostly far from sight – has lived with us both and we talk about it still.

The Trout and the Fly attracted huge publicity when it came out. The BBC film, a 50-minute documentary, was screened at prime time in the week of publication. Also that week, *The Sunday Times Colour Magazine* ran seven pages of pictures and commentary on the work we had done. In the United States *The New York Times* ran a two-column review and later listed the book as one of its top 10 books of the year. A handwritten note of appreciation arrived from President Carter on White House notepaper and a copy of that – I don't get many letters from American Presidents – hangs framed on the wall beside me, as I write. Another letter came from Lord Home, the former Prime Minister. It is a matter of pleasure for us both that, at the time of writing and 27 years on, *The Trout and the Fly* is still in print in several countries.

If John Goddard's friends had to pick out a quality above all others to characterise him it would not be his fishing skills, remarkable though they are: it would be his undiminishing enthusiasm for fishing. I have never known an angler so single-minded and determined. Even on days when, for one reason or another it was clear that nothing much would be happening, Goddard would be first up the bank and most eager to get into the boat.

It was not unknown on the Wilderness to find that, having arranged a time to meet, John would have got there early and would, with a wide smile, be waiting with the news that 'I've found a good fish for you to try.' It was a greeting that filled his friends with a mixture of amusement and dread. We all knew that if John had found such a fish first he would already have caught it (in which case it would be almost impossible to catch again), or that he would have failed to catch it (in which case it was likely to prove impossible for us also), or it would be in an impossible position to reach. But still, from time to time, we were all suckered into trying to prove him wrong – almost always to his great amusement.

John has enjoyed prodigious energy, even into old age. In his middle years he would walk the whole of a big water like the Wilderness – it covered several miles of main Kennet and carrier – sometimes more than once on a dour day, looking for a rising or an interesting fish. He would, sometimes, settle down for hours on a particularly difficult fish, often enough returning in the dusk, grinning broadly. There are not many of his friends who, at one time or another, have not been left exhausted in his wake.

John Goddard is not a naturally outgoing man. From outward appearances, to those who do not know him, he can appear reserved and even taciturn – a perception not helped, in his later years, by poor hearing. Relaxed among his friends, however, another side shows. He can, in full flow, come close to holding court. He has an impish sense of humour and can be a creasing teller of stories, often against himself.

His angling life, in its scope as in its specialist depths, has been extraordinary.

Just Going Fishing

ASK a group of anglers why fishing is so important to them, what they get out of it, and the answers are likely to vary according to their backgrounds, their ages, their experience levels and much else though, of course, there will be common themes.

At one point, a period of enforced abstinence gave me cause to consider what had become important to me. It was not until I was back on the banks, though, that my thoughts cleared and the truth really dawned.

* * *

I HAVE confirmed something that I had long suspected. It is that after a lifetime of fishing – of plotting and hoping, casting and catching, skill-honing and study – it isn't the fishing itself that is so important to me any longer but the idea of going fishing. In fact what matters, at rock-bottom, is the simple ability to go if the mood inclines.

The year of the great foot-and-mouth outbreak – 2001 – distilled things. Like most anglers that year I was kept caged and fretting, first by floods and then the disease. The latter effectively closed the countryside. Winter dragged, spring crawled. The possibility of a wiped-out season was being widely mooted. Then, in May and out of the blue, came the announcement: rivers would be opened forthwith.

Within 24 hours I was knee-deep in buttercups and ladies' smock. Swifts and swallows were sculpting the air. A cuckoo called and a song thrush sang and a skylark's cup overflowed. Mayflies hatched. Midges scribbled messages in the lee of hedgerows. Beyond them, reflecting the sun and blue sky, the river glinted and beckoned.

It was then, while walking across the meadows and before the water had even been reached, that I felt all frustration and urgency ebb away. Once on the bank I laid the rod in the rushes, put up my little collapsible chair, took out the 8×30 binoculars that go everywhere with me, poured a cup of tea and settled back. I stayed there, absorbing it all and being absorbed, zooming in on this and that for maybe an hour and a half. The rod I had pined six months to use, stayed untouched. I even – am I really admitting this? – took out the newspaper I'd meant to catch up on at lunch time and read it through.

It was an extraordinary interlude, not some calculated heightening of longed-for action but a profound pleasure in its own right, one equal, I knew, to anything the act of fishing could offer that day. The fact that no fish were rising might have had something to do with it – except that the next trip out fish were poking their noses up and I did precisely the same. It was enough, even after six months' starvation, just to be beside the water and everything in and around it.

Anglers have long recognised this kind of thing. There are, they say, six stages in an angler's life. The first is when he just wants to 'go fishing'. Then he wants to catch something. Then he wants to catch a lot. Then he wants to catch the biggest fish. Then he wants – a subtle shift, this – to catch the most difficult fish. Then he comes out the other side and just wants to 'go fishing' again.

Over the years I've known the lot – and felt myself dipping into the last. I've known it from the beefy little gudgeon that hooked me as a lad on the Tees to the hunting and capture of great fishes abroad. For the greater part of my angling life I have been fascinated by trout especially, have spent years studying the fish and its behaviour, refining my approach and technique, even – it gives some idea of the obsession – to the extent of photographing flies' feet from underwater at night (I wanted to see how trout looking upwards could unerringly see insects on the surface in the dark when I, looking down, could see nothing).

For years no fish, not even the most awkwardly positioned and hair-triggered, was safe from my intensity. Then my attitudes started to change. The owners of some fisheries see it happening all the time. For so much a season, let us say, an angler buys the right to fish on one named day – Tuesdays, Wednesdays or whatever – each week through spring and summer. Every allotted day is jealously guarded and hungrily used. Nothing gets in the way of it because, if it is missed, there will be no fishing until the week after.

Then the same angler switches waters and, for a larger sum, buys the right to go whenever he likes, as often as he likes – and a strangeness comes over him. He does not fish more as he had intended, but less. Because there is no pressing need to go today, he will go tomorrow instead. If that is inconvenient or the forecast is bad, there is always the day after, the weekend after – or next week. On fisheries such as this, which theoretically should be busy every day, there will be whole days, whole weeks in the season, when not a soul disturbs the fish or the water they swim in.

None of this is to say that for old hands, fishing – the act of fishing – is no longer enjoyed: it is enjoyed enormously but in a different way. When, on my second outing of that plague-ridden year I did pick up a rod, I rejoiced in the crafts that enabled me to approach fish undetected, exulted in the wristy skills that placed the fly like thistledown in front of their noses, felt the deep satisfactions of holding caught fish head-on into the current until their strength returned and they swam strongly away again, wiser and free. I enjoyed the art of it all and the science of it all.

But it was all so relaxed. I did not get hung up on any fish, was pleased if I caught a particular fish but not frustrated if I failed. I took a long lunch. And I packed in early to sit talking to my friends while the light slowly ebbed and the fish went on rising and the ducks in the gloaming conversed in soft syllables.

There was something else. Whereas in my fish-hungry days I'd have remembered minute details about every trout taken no matter how many there might have been, would have talked endlessly afterwards about them with my companions, instead I talked of the fishing very little. What my friends and I talked of afterwards was not the fish but the loveliness of the valley and the quality of the light; the dangers of the mink and the threat to the water vole; the silt-pans, cracked as old tiles, that the floods had left behind in the meadows; the single white cloud that had floated across the sky like a remembered thought. Of how few mayflies there had been. Of the lateness of the ash trees and the yellow flag iris. Of politics, heaven help us.

And all of this – all of it – not after a season sated with action but after a long, enforced abstinence, a deprivation of water. I have been startled by the abruptness of the realisation and know well what it implies: that I've come through angling's first five stages and come out the other side.

There can be no going back – and I am comfortable with the thought. Mostly, I like just 'going fishing' again.

Life and Death in the Arctic

I WAS close to the Arctic Circle, in the far north-west of Hudson Bay. I had been sent there to write a piece about polar bears – to find them, to get close to them, to give some sense of the bleak and beautiful landscape in which they live. Images of life and death, animal and human, were all around. Amid them all was the Inuit boy, the one with the rod.

It was extraordinary to see him there. In that wild and cruel place, life was lived at existence level, hand quite literally to mouth. Pretty well anything that moved was food or profit, sold for its flesh or its fur. The most direct means of acquiring either, gun or net, was used. And yet there was this young boy, fishing with a rod and line for the sheer pleasure it gave him.

I had seen him out on the estuary the night before, helping to set the nets for great arctic char. I had seen him that morning, helping to bring them in: great fish, double-figure fish, slashing at the water and the mesh and the light. I had watched him gut them and hang them up to dry in the wind.

It was evening when I saw him on the river, spinning with a rod and a little silver spoon. He was utterly absorbed, studying here, casting there. A couple of modest char lay on the rocks behind him. He could have been me at that age, any young lad anywhere of that age – with this difference: most lads are not spending their waking hours fishing to live, as this lad was. For most lads, fishing is diversion. Although this boy fished for a living, he fished for diversion, as well. The harshness of life – the trapping and shooting, the skinning and cleaning – had not rendered him immune to the fact that angling is fun.

The piece that follows is not about fishing or the boy, but about the world in which that boy and the great bears live. The fact that the boy owned a fishing rod may seem to be a slender excuse to include this piece in this book, but it will have to do. Every time I think of that raw-edged place, I think of him.

* * *

WE HAVE mostly given up when the call comes. The heat of the sun and the warmth of our hope have gone. We are standing with our backs to the bows, hunched and closed off; all of us turned in on ourselves against the roar of the engine and the buffeting of the waves and a wind off the pack-ice that cuts like a knife.

I am cocooned with my thoughts and fatigue, looking down a wake that looks like white stallions rearing, like stallions beribboned with rainbows when the sun hits the spray. Then the radio shrieks and a foreign voice barks. David Tuktudjuk, our Inuit guide, eases back on the throttle, makes an understood reply and turns and translates. 'Bear. John got a bear'.

The words course through the boat like an electric charge. 'A bear. A bear. John's found a bear!' We are all at the gunwales in a flash. It is what every one of us – Americans, Canadians, Germans but mostly British – have spent long hours on the bay in the hope of hearing. We are outdoor enthusiasts and amateur photographers. We have come to Sila Lodge on Wager Bay, hard up against the Arctic Circle in Canada's North West Territories, for the wilderness experience – terrain, birds, animals, everything. The great prize, though, is a polar bear sighting. Every group ever to come here has seen at least one and most groups have seen several. This, on our first day, is our chance.

David opens the throttle again. The boat tilts and turns, the horizon lifts and lowers and the nearest pack ice begins a sedate waltz. The amazing shapes slip by again – gargoyles and castles, insects and dinosaurs, anorexic Giacomettis and rounded Henry Moores. The sun reaches its fingers through the feather-bolster clouds. Light winks and slides, bounces and slips. All eyes scan and search. Lenses as big as bazookas are trained over the side.

'There. There. In front of John's boat. It's walking left to right. See it? See it?' We do see it.

Very few people get to see a bear, any kind of bear, in the wild. Fewer still get to see a polar bear in the wild because for most of the year it lives in inaccessible places. Almost no-one, not even those who go where it can be reached, when it can be reached – which means to only a handful of places in the world, in summer – gets to see a polar bear on ice. In summer the bears follow the ice as long as they can but then the ice melts and the bears are driven onto the land. Most sightings of polar bears are made on the thawed brown earth.

Yet there he is, maybe 100 yards away, shambling steadily away through a white luminescence. He is a fur mountain, rippling: maybe, if he stood upright, 11 feet tall from tip of black nose to hardly there tail. He will weigh over half a ton. He is gigantic, the biggest and meanest non-aquatic carnivore in the world. Bigger and much meaner than the grizzly. Only last night John Wilkes, who part-owns Sila Lodge, told us that the difference between the polar bear and the grizzly was that the polar bear lacks the grizzly's sense of humour. There are, someone else said, records of polar bears attacking narwhals and Beluga whales.

It was John, in the other boat, who had made the radio call. He brings his low, narrow craft alongside and invites four of us in.

Two Americans, a nimble lady from Manchester and me scramble aboard. The slender steel boat can go places the larger boat cannot. We turn away. John threads us through the ice with the delicacy of a tapestry-worker's needle.

He tells us as we go how unusual this is. The bears follow the pack ice when it breaks up in summer because drifting ice means fish and fish means seals and seals mean fat, juicy food. Wager Bay is one of the last places the ice melts and so is a natural gathering-ground for bears. Some years maybe 200 can be in the bay. Even then, most sightings are of bears on land because the lodge can only be open for July and August and by then the ice has usually gone.

But there are some freak years. Some years, like this year, the ice has not gone. This year the long winter and unusual winds have held the ice back in every sense and have blown new ice in from Roes Wellcome Sound and Hudson Bay beyond. It is because of the numbers of bears and opportunities like this – opportunities, John says, that are unique to Wager Bay – that he opened the lodge in the first place.

We are moving closer to the bear all the time. When we are 50 yards away, the bear slides into the water. He seems bemused more than anything, maybe a little irritated; but certainly not afraid or in any way distressed. At 30 yards we can see how he is swimming. It is a heavy waddling action, all rear-end. At 20 yards we hear him grunt softly. It is half nasal, half gut, like the cough of a lion in the African dusk.

When we are 15 yards away – like the lion confronted by a safari drive, he does not seem to see people in a boat as a threat or food – the bear decides to perform. He turns his head from side to side so we can see his profile. He makes for a patch of reflected sky and swims through the clouds. He half-lifts himself onto a ledge of ice, cascading water and light before gently slipping back. The cameras go click-click-click.

After 15 minutes, when we have edged so close that I could almost have touched him, he gives us some last, memorable shots. He heads for an ice floe, seems to gather himself into himself, and then hauls himself onto it. For a moment he is high above us, massive and gleaming against the light. He looks down his long nose at us with his point-blank eyes. He shakes himself like a dog and a Catherine Wheel of spray encircles his shoulders. Then he lollops away with his coat surging along him, as though half-carried forward by the momentum of his fat.

We all know how privileged our sighting has been; how unusual it is to see a bear on ice, so close. That night in the lodge, in the glow of shared experience and much duty-free, muscles and tongues relax. There is talk of nothing else.

Next day, we learn just how privileged. The ice that 12 hours before had seemed to fill the bay has gone, the only indication of it a white line on the horizon, insubstantial as a mirage. The winds that had weeks ago blown it in, have in a trice blown it out.

The days are different after that. We spend them alternating between wildlife hikes over the tundra and excursions in the boat, looking for bears on the islands and the shore. Once, we see the effect a bear on land can have on humans caught unawares.

One night everyone is gathered in the communal hut, talking of this and that, the next moment there is a blur past the window and shouting from outside. Everyone makes a dash to peer out. A polar bear has slid down the side of the gravelled ridge where the aircraft land, into the centre of camp.

The Inuit children start to scream and clamber onto a hut roof. The bear moves towards the hut and there is more screaming and shouting. The rifles and rubber bullets are in the hut beneath the children – bears are never killed in this place, they are warned and frightened off – and the men are dispersed around camp. There is a flurry in the corner of the room, one of the camp staff finds a thunderflash, runs out and throws it. There is a loud explosion, the bear whirls and bounds away.

It is all over in moments but it is the starkest lesson – not only of the fear in which polar bears are held but of the speed at which they can move if they wish. In the safety of the boat and in the company of professionals there is a temptation to take one's safety for granted. But this is no dude ranch. This is for real. After that, no-one is allowed out of sight or shout-range of the lodge, unescorted. Every hike close to the water is accompanied by a guide with a gun.

The hikes are low-key affairs, but memorable. The statistics of the North West Territories – 1.3 million square miles, 59,000 people, nine per cent of the world's fresh water (though it looks like all of it), an average winter temperature here of minus nearly 30 Centigrade – say both something and nothing. They are so large and out of context that they can scarcely be grasped. The hikes make everything plain.

From any kind of distance the rocks and tundra seem raw and unyielding, timeless and empty – and yet they are full of life, clinging on. Dwarf birch and willow grow to ankle height. Rhododendrons come up to our laces, moss campion reaches the tops of the soles of our boots. Every day-long walk, every step taken, crushes Lilliput underfoot.

The three hikes in our week are guided by Paula Hugheson. She is joint manager of the camp, 25, half-Inuit, resourceful and engaging. She has a degree in botany from Winnipeg University. She packs a .38 revolver and has thunderflashes at her waist 'because even inland you never know, you never know.'

Paula shows us nests and birds, animal tracks and bones, tells us more about droppings than some really want to know.

We see snowgeese and oldsquaw, osprey and loons, peregrines and horned lark. There are eider ducks and ruddy turnstones everywhere. Lapland longspur and snow bunting abound.

We see animals as well, scratching their livings from the hard, barren ground. We see furtive lemmings hiding under rocks, see ground squirrels in the open as cheeky as street urchins, watch Arctic hares bouncing along like furred rubber toys. We see caribou every day, mostly in ones and twos. Because there is no hunting from the lodge the caribou know little fear and are as interested in us as we are in them. Time after time they will come up and circle us, moving with their precise, high-stepping, pony-trotting gait, throwing their crooked shadows on the ground.

We see the grave.

We are walking over a high headland that looks down over Wager Bay. The sky is wide and blue. The treeless hills roll to infinity all around. The wind rummages and slices and whips tears from our eyes. Even at boot height the tiny flowers tremble, as though fearful of being unable to cling on.

There is nothing, absolutely nothing but the wild; nothing between the row of huts which constitute the lodge encampment and the sprinkling of Inuit settlements a hundred miles away on the coast. There is no sign of humanity at all save for the old circle of stones that once held the walls of a skin tent tight and the grave between the rocks, just beyond.

It is a young man's grave, David Tuktudjuk thinks. He heard tell a young man once drowned here.

There is not much to it. Because of the hardness of the permafrost, the Inuit cannot bury their dead: in these places they simply lie the bodies on the ground and cover them with stones. Here, high on the headland overlooking the waters that claimed him, the young man's body had been covered with his kayak and the kayak had been covered by stones.

It is clear that was long ago. Over the years the wind and the ice and the animals have been at work. The kayak has collapsed, the stones have fallen in and the bones, the bones of the young man who had once lived and fished and trapped and maybe loved here, are scattered to the four winds beneath the brazen sun.

The difference of culture is impossible to miss. David, whose people have been on terms with death here for 4,000 years, is matter-of-fact. I feel a mixture of curiosity and shock. One of the group, a surgeon from London, gathers up some of the bones and comments on them briefly before placing them back with the rest. I find a stray piece of wood and instinctively lie it over them. There is some distracted small talk about the realities of the place and the price the Inuit have paid for their tenacity, then we go. For a while we talk in a lower pitch. Silences intrude.

Now, looking back, certain images stand out. There are the fishermen with their nets and the great trapped char. There are the skins of the foxes and wolves at Baker Lake settlement, pegged out on lines to dry like the weekday wash. There are the white beluga whales in the sea off Churchill, sprinkled like ice floes when we come in to land. Of course, there is the Inuit boy with the rod, fishing for pleasure as he fished to live.

Two images, though, pervade all. The first is of the polar bear on the ice high above us, embodying the terrible beauty of Canada's far north. The other is of the young man scattered on the headland, symbolising life there as fragile as the present moment; life as transient and frail as the flowers of Lilliput – and yet, like the flowers, clinging on.

A Perfect Day

THERE are some days that stand out in the mind. The day we caught the
monster, that fish we lost at the net, that time we caught next to nothing but
this or that occurred. Days lodge in the mind for all sorts of reasons and a single
event can be enough.

There is a difference, though, between a day that is remembered and a
memorable day. If a fleeting moment can make the former it takes something
more – and probably something more sustained – to make the latter.

Take the perfect day, for example.

*   *   *

IF feedback is to be believed, my column in The Times is read by almost as many non-anglers, as anglers. Even those who do not fish
seem to find some interest in or to have some curiosity about the
fishy pursuit – much of it, no doubt, born of bemusement that
anyone should want to fish at all.

If these deprived folk could experience the kind of day the rest
of us have from time to time, could know a perfect angling day
from inside rather than outside – could live it, breath it, dabble
their toes in it – they would have no doubt why angling has a following of millions. Angling – above all else, for me, fly fishing – can
seduce and absorb, utterly.

What makes a perfect day? Is it fish? Well, yes: while it is possible to have a great day on the water without a fish being banked, a perfect day's fishing requires at least some contact with the quarry.

Glorious scenery? Well, yes, that too: a great day's angling can be had in an unattractive location, but not a perfect day. Likewise the weather, the company, the character of the water, the degree of the angling challenge artfully met and much more. By definition, the perfect day needs everything and needs it in perfect proportion.

Let me take a real day, as an example.

First, let me be clear. Like most of us, I live in the real world. My local fishing is done on a wonderful river, but it is primarily a coarse-fishing river and my pleasure comes in hunting and stalking fish – mostly trout, but also chub, grayling, dace, roach and others – that are either taking flies from the surface or that can be conned into taking a nymph below it. Further afield, much of my fly fishing is on stocked trout waters, where the fish tend to be of uniform size and – usually – to offer an indifferent challenge.

But every now and then, like most reading this, I get invitations to fish other waters. My perfect day was on a water I fished as a guest: the upper reaches of a pristine stream. The only fish in it were naturally spawned brown trout and grayling.

There was, that day, in that valley where the willows and alders grew, no wind. The sun, other than when it forgot itself behind small, drifting clouds, shone all day without ever becoming too hot. The river was gin clear and shallow and wide: so clear and shallow that every stone on the bottom might have been picked out and scrubbed; so wide that between its greensleeved banks, the water could only be covered by wading.

Flies hatched intermittently from the moment we arrived to the moment we packed up. Swifts arched and swallows skimmed. Kingfishers put blue splinters in the eye. From time to time, water voles busied themselves along the banks. Here and there, water crowfoot curled its daisy-chains over the surface, orchestrating the drowned music of the currents.

More to the point, fish dimpled.

Now these were not ordinary fish. These were fish that, in their shallow, gin-clear, evenly paced water, were accustomed to the attentions of anglers. They had disdain written into their genes, contempt threaded through their tissues, deep cynicism etched behind their eyes. They scrutinised every fly cast to them and analysed its drift before, almost always, turning away. They were educated fish. They were famously difficult fish.

There was something else about them: being wild and plentiful, they were small. The average trout in that water weighed maybe six ounces. A pound fish was a corker. So, in terms of absolute size, even though this was trophy fishing, these were not trophy specimens. They would have held no appeal to the chest-beaters and the medallion men, but they held immense appeal to the lovers of delicacy and challenge. They offered fishing at its most demanding and refined.

Under normal circumstances, I would have tackled such fish with my conventional light-work outfit: an 8ft 6in, four-weight rod and a leader that ended in a 3lbs breaking-strain point.

There were two buts. The first was that I had fished this water once before and the fish had rejected such crudeness comprehensively. The second was that I had recently acquired an 8ft 3-weight, a wand so light that I could hardly feel it in my hand. So instead I put this up with a 3-weight line – the lightest I had ever fished with – and attached to that a 10ft leader with a 1.5lbs breaking-strain point. I do not know what a human hair breaks at, but this leader was very little thicker and could not have been much stronger.

I slid into the river so softly that I scarcely knew I was there and began. For a while, casting was a problem. On a leader so fine even the minute, home-tied smudge of brown I had on the end wanted to turn over abruptly and plop onto the water. But little by little, it came. After a while, cast after cast was floating to the surface like thistledown.

And then that perfect day began. The fish saw the fly but not its gossamer leader, saw the natural way it floated and not its drag. All sounds faded away and the world closed in. I became cocooned in a world of green-hazed light, winking water, flickering flies, precise casts and dimpling rises, with fish after deceived fish being brought to hand before being released to shrug more wisely away.

Between morning and afternoon, a long lunch on a bench under a willow with my pal, the binoculars to hand. Sandwiches and a good cheese, a bottle of white that had been cooling in the water, soft conversation and some laughter, wildlife intimately observed. In the afternoon and early evening, more of the same kind of fishing, then 30 minutes on the bench again as the sun went down and the bats came out and late fish still sipped and rolled.

In that soft gathering dusk a day of sublime delicacy and in-volvement, a day absorbed into the river and its beauty and its life, came to a natural end. Peace reigned, inside and out. Non-angler, know why we do it.

Making Fishing Too Easy

ANGLING *changes all the time. Typically change is internal, generated by our-selves. Tackle improves in effectiveness, techniques offering greater efficiency or convenience evolve, fashions in preferred species come and go. It is all natural and, in many senses, revitalising.*

Other change comes from outside, sometimes imposed, sometimes not. Imposed changes – to close seasons, to fish size limits, to whether or not we can use split shot and the like – may prove short-term inconveniences but in the main are quickly accommodated. Other forms of change, not imposed but not avoidable ei-ther, can prove more problematic.

* * *

THE decision in the latter part of the last century to stock trout into the new generation of big reservoirs – Chew Valley in the west country, Grafham and Rutland Water in the midlands, Kielder in the north among others – transformed trout fishing.

It brought fly fishing, hitherto the preserve of the well-off and those living in the right places, within reach of all who wanted it. It fuelled a demand that through the 1970s and 1980s saw small, specially created trout lakes breaking out like an aquatic rash across the countryside. Today, fly fishing is greatly expanded be-cause of these developments and pretty well everyone involved – angler, fishery owner and tackle dealer alike – has benefited.

Over the same period, something similar happened in coarse fishing, but the results may prove less benign.

A burgeoning interest in fishing for carp began it in the late 1980s. The ending, in the mid-1990s, of the close season on still-waters and hence the coming of year-round angling on most places except rivers, accelerated it. Now, commercial coarse fisheries – old lakes, disused gravel pits, specially dug and stocked holes in the ground – are doing business in their hundreds. Each week, hundreds of thousands of coarse fishermen pay hefty sums to fish them.

Competition between these fisheries has led to many attractions – waterside parking, refreshment facilities, tackle shops, bait supplies and all else – being introduced to draw in custom. More to the point, very large carp are now routinely stocked to attract those wanting to catch them and the stocking of smaller species at great densities has become commonplace.

On the big-fish waters the result is instant whoppers. Elsewhere, the result is more fish competing for the available food and so becoming easier to catch. It has all given the many anglers who fish them – though just as many disdain them because of their artificiality – the kinds of results that, in a natural setting, they could never hope to achieve.

Now here's the rub. Unlike trout fishing, which has been through this cycle and come out the better for it, coarse fishing is in the middle of it and appears to be threatened by two long-term problems. One is the impact of commercial waters on the numbers fishing rivers, the second is the possible impact on angling numbers as a whole.

Much river fishing involves walking, often considerable distances. On many reaches the fish can be unevenly spread and difficult to find. When found, these fish have appetites attuned to what a natural environment can provide and when they eat it is with a wild fish's caution. Variations in flow can make tackle control difficult and bites tricky to spot. Consistent success on rivers comes hard-won: it takes effort and knowledge and tactical skills – and it cannot be guaranteed.

Now signs are emerging that easily reached, customer-friendly and instantly gratifying stillwaters are taking anglers away from rivers – and from clubs which have river waters. Even the biggest clubs are not immune to the impact. In the 1970s, the vast Birmingham Anglers Association had over 1,000 fishing clubs, most of them offering river fishing, affiliated to it. Thirty-five years later the number was 250. A lot of clubs, a Birmingham official said at the time, had fallen out through natural attrition and other causes but the commercials had sucked thousands of one-time individual members – and many affiliated clubs – away.

'Lots of youngsters today have never used a conventional rod and reel or fished a shallow, fast-flowing stream', he was reported as saying. 'Small commercials are all they know. All they have to do is ship out their pole and catch a carp. It makes it very easy.'

This apparent drift from rivers to stillwaters may in due course be exacerbated by a fall in angling's numbers.

One of angling's appeals is its sheer unpredictability. In natural situations, the angler rarely knows when a bite is coming, often not what species and size of fish may result. When a net-full of fish is taken or a whopper is landed, the elation and sense of achievement are natural and real. The blanks and frustrations that surround such days are what validates them. Disappointment and frustration are normally as much part of an angler's baggage as floats and bait.

Heavily stocked commercial fisheries, with their guarantees of success, do away with all of this. Over time, it seems reasonable to ask, if there are no blank days and problems to be overcome – what then? If landing a hundred roach or several dozen bream becomes an everyday event, or if monsters are regularly landed not because they are hard-won but because only monsters are stocked in that place, whence comes the sense of achievement and how can interest be sustained? Just as occasional success thrills, glut surely deadens.

It is against this background that the long-term inflow of young entrants to the sport – its very lifeblood – seems threatened. More and more, young people are being introduced to angling through the commercial fisheries because early success is deemed vital in attracting them. But young people have naturally short attention spans and today have a myriad other attractions to wink and seduce. Muddy old angling, out in the sticks and offering fish that will bite if they are merely asked, may seem to hold little in the way of challenge and excitement. It is not difficult to see angling becoming less something to be explored and mastered over a lifetime than to be transiently experienced on the way to the next thrill.

And so it could be that, over time, potential recruits brought in through the commercial route will steadily turn away, bored. If they do, then rivers will suffer still more, trout fishing will lose a traditional source of recruits and angling's overall numbers – the sport's greatest single strength – will go into further decline.

None of this is yet certain, but there are straws in the wind.

Yes, commercial trout fisheries proved a benefit to angling. Commercial coarse fisheries may not prove the same.

Morality Tale

DON'T you get fed up with them? Morality tales, I mean. The way the goodie always seems to get the baddie, the way nice guy always gets the girl, the way the bully always gets his come-uppance on the last page but one?

Story-tellers and the media love this kind of thing. You would think they were the self-appointed keepers of our moral welfare; as though it were their job to keep our eyes on the horizon where the sun is lifting and not on the mud that is squelching underfoot.

I once had a perfect example of it while driving to the river. A story came on the radio about a small boy catching a 32lbs carp from a lake one afternoon when, in the same place that morning, a group of international competition anglers fishing a practice session had failed to get even a nibble. On what was admittedly a quiet day, the national news managed to turn these two mildly interesting, juxtaposed events into a David-and-Goliath, well-isn't-life-just-like-that story when the chances of it happening again were millions-to-one against.

It set me thinking. I remembered a morality tale of my own.

* * *

LET me say straight away that I know this is going to sound ridiculous. It all seems so hackneyed and cliched, so outrageously improbable from beginning to end that I hesitate to tell it at all; yet the drama I once saw unfolding between two young anglers was worthy of a Hollywood film.

It was some years ago. The first lad, the one I saw getting off the bus where the path leads to the river, looked like a caricature of a Victorian waif. He was about 12 years old, thin and pale. His shirt collar was ragged. His trousers were a size too big and – yes – they were tied up with string. One of those safety pins you see on kilts held a ragged hole in his pullover, closed. He clutched a fishing rod in one hand. There was an old plastic bag, presumably containing his bits and pieces of tackle, in the other .

The rod was one of those little 'Catchem' toy rods that I thought had long since disappeared: a seven-foot, solid glass job with a wooden handle and a cheap little plastic, fixed-spool reel. The whole outfit looked pathetic but it was amazing, knowing the story, that his mother had managed to buy it at all.

I'd seen the lad before, of course – his family was well-known in our part of town. The lad had still been a baby when his father died. Against all odds the mother, a remarkable woman, had brought up seven children alone. She took what she was due from the social services but declined all charity. She went out cleaning. She took in ironing. She took in laundry. She worked from morning till night. All the children, when they were old enough, worked about the house or did odd jobs for money, which helped. The lad with the rod did a paper round each morning and evening. Someone said the money he earned put the only meat on the table the family ever saw. The whole family saga could have come straight out of Dickens.

I knew the other lad by sight, too, the one backing out of the big BMW as the poor lad was climbing down from the bus. His family lived not far from me and the lad was as unpopular with the local youngsters as his parents were with their neighbours. His father was a nasty piece of work, one of those self-made men who are bumptious and loud and always flashing their money about. His wife was notorious for her spending. Their only child was a snooty little brat, indulged and rude. I know it's hindsight, but if anyone deserved their come-uppance, it was this lot, the father and son especially.

I was not surprised when the rich, spoiled lad backed out of the car with a glistening Hardy rod scarcely out of its wrappers and a brand-new tackle box that rattled with gear. I was not surprised, either, at his reaction when he backed into the pale-faced lad and the cheap little rod clashed with his own.

'Hey, you, watch where you're going', the little so-and-so said. He loomed over the poor lad though they were much the same age and he jutted his podgy face forward. 'Just you watch it, or...' Then he saw the poor lad's rod and he actually burst out laughing. 'What d'you call that?', he jeered. 'Hey, Dad, look at this kid's fishing rod. It's one of those cheapos the newsagent used to sell. They're b—y useless. Bet he's a b—y useless fisherman, too.'

I saw the poor lad flush. 'All right, son', the lad's brass-necked dad called through the car's open window. 'Not everyone can be as lucky as you. His rod's useless but yours is a belter. And you've had coaching.' Then – imagine it, loud enough for the poor lad to hear him – 'Show him how it's done, son. Show him who's boss.' I was furious. How could he? How could anyone? I was half towards the car to say something when it pulled away with an upholstered whoosh.

The damage was done, of course. I saw the thin, pale-faced lad look down at his rod and then half-turn to me. His face crumpled.

His wide eyes were suddenly blurred. I was beside myself with fury. I thought of saying something, first to him, then to the spoiled brat, but as quickly decided against it. Better say nothing to either. I was alone with the two lads and the path to the river was long and secluded. I knew, even in those days, how things could look.

You'd have thought the rich kid knew how helpless I felt. In a flash he was barging past me and barging past the poor kid. 'Out of the way, cheapo', he said. 'What a stupid rod. What a useless fisherman.' And then he swaggered on towards the river, his fine rod flashing and his tackle box clunking.

I'm not really sure what happened next, except that the pale-faced kid got his top-ring caught in a bush and had to reach up to get it out. Then, with the little rod held high and aloft I saw him pause and stare at it. It was as though he was really looking at it – really seeing it – for the first time. I saw the lad stiffen and straighten and lift his head. 'Just you wait', I heard him say quietly. 'You don't need a posh rod to be a good fisherman. I'll show you, I'll show you.' His voice – there was no mistaking it – was steady and strong. His eyes had turned cold as steel. He held the little rod high, for all the world like Excalibur. A beam of sunlight flashed from a rod-ring. It sounds preposterous I know but something, something I could not define, was suddenly in the air. The lad lengthened his step. I lengthened mine.

Most of the best places were taken when we got to the water and fate, deliberately it seemed, placed the two lads side by side.

They both tackled up. The spoiled, rich kid set up his glistening, three-piece trotting rod and one of those incredible Stream Runner reels. The poor, pale-faced lad checked his reel and his cheap little wooden-handled rod. The rich lad opened a tackle box that gleamed like a shopping mall and selected one of those Superzoom, Easy-cast floats. The poor lad groped in the jumble of his plastic bag and got out – you could hardly have made it up – a little, home-made float, a bit of shaped cork with half a drinking straw stuck through it. And so it went, with visual cliché piling on visual cliché, all the time the rich lad smirking at the poor lad and making snide asides, the poor lad saying nothing and keeping himself to himself, doing what he had to do.

Standing there, looking on from a distance, I could feel that something-in-the-air growing that I could not place. Then, suddenly, it clicked. What I had was an overpowering sense of déjà vu. This was exactly like a thousand Hollywood westerns. There was the rich lad and the poor lad, the braggart and the underdog, the good and – as it were – the bad and the ugly. These two boys, in that bay on the river, were playing out their own High Noon.

I thought of the rich lad's dad bragging and of his flashy car, then of his wife in her fineries, flouncing down the road. I thought of the poor lad's mum and the way she must have scrimped and scraped to buy him the rod – the little glass rod that looked so pathetic and that the rich kid had said was useless. I thought, too, of the way the rich kid had said the poor kid was probably a useless fisherman and of the steel that seemed to enter the other's young soul. I found myself half expecting the tension to reach all around and the anglers either side to gather close and watch; to make a silent half-circle as the two lads cast out. Maybe a single, distant bell would toll.

The rich kid cast first and his float landed barely a foot from the side – an omen, I knew, of what was to come. Then the poor lad cast and his float sailed high and straight, far out into the river. The demolition began. Three barbel, seven good chub, two cracking roach, a big grayling, a big trout and dace beyond number. They came one after another, with scarcely a minute between them. Yes, the little rod was useless and the pale-faced kid turned out to be useless, too. He couldn't even read the swim.

The rich kid fished him clean out of sight.

Size and Relative Size

ANYONE who has lived a life knows that everything relates to everything else and that, out of context, most things are rendered meaningless. This is as true in angling as in anything else and it is as true for fish as for fisherman. It is especially true of fish sizes.

* * *

IN ABSOLUTE terms, an eight-ounce trout is a small fish, but place that fish in the context of an acidic highland lochan or a rushing mountain stream and it may well prove a corker. In absolute terms, a five-pound trout is a thumper, but if it is farm-bred and taken from a water in which 10-pounders are mostly stocked then it will be seen as relatively small.

Territorial fish like trout know their places in the size and pecking order only too well. The importance of size – relative size – is written into their genes, whispered into their heads when they are still curled up in their eggs and blind. It is borne in upon them when, as tiny fry hatching out in the spring, they try to find lies for themselves among the gravels and stones of the stream bed. Although emerging at much the same size, some are more innately aggressive and stronger than others and these fish adopt behaviour or postures that ensure dominance. They win for themselves the lies that offer the greatest amount of food and safety for the least expenditure of effort and maximise their own potential at the expense of their neighbours.

What counts beneath the surface is jaws and teeth and energy. Every dreaming pond is its own Serengeti, every bright brook its own red-tinged Zambezi. In the real world, in spite of what Hollywood cartoons might suggest, cheekie-chappie little trout do not snap at big fish and harass them aside. They stay clear.

Anglers know all about relative size, too. Recognition of it is what enables them to fish for seemingly tiny fish one day and apparent monsters the next, with equal absorption. Sights and expectations are automatically adjusted to the water concerned. Success, other than for a tiny minority, is not always about catching fish that thud the scales down. More often, it will be about achieving the best possible result in the circumstances of the day and if that means banking an eight-ounce trout instead of a five-pounder, then so be it.

Beginners, who are naturally fish-hungry at first and then size-hungry, eventually come to appreciate this. Indeed, with a few years behind them, anglers discover that challenge is what really appeals and that challenge need have nothing to do with size, at all. Often enough, it will mean extracting the most awkwardly placed fish that can be found, almost regardless of its size: the fish that, because of some line-snagging, fly-skating quirk in the current or the presence of trees and the like makes the task of getting a fly to it in a natural way, all but impossible. At other times, though – and inevitably – the challenge will involve a whopper.

Experienced anglers know that the kinds of lies that produce big adult fish are the same as those that produce big little fish: the places that offer the best returns in food and safety for the least energy output. An old hand can recognise them and, when he is walking a river, he can look out for them and concentrate his efforts on them. Now, the factors that have allowed a prize fish to grow big and strong prove its weakness, because they give its position away.

When he sees a potential big-fish lie, an experienced angler will not be in a hurry to move on, even if no big fish can immediately be seen. A big fish will often patrol a small area around its home lie and if it happens to be briefly absent, smaller fish will take the larger fish's place because of the advantages it offers. The moment Mr Big reappears, however – now backing tail-first downstream from some upstream jaunt, now sidling sideways across the current, now shrugging slowly upstream like some heavy-shouldered, menacing, big-time hood, the lesser fish drift back to their own positions to give him room.

Two of the more interesting opportunities I've had to use observations like this – to find a probable big-fish lie and to use the antics of lesser fish to confirm it – occurred close together, on utterly different waters. One was a tiny stream containing only small wild fish, the other a sedate river that is stocked with large trout. On both, I found what appeared to be a likely big-fish lie and melted into the undergrowth to watch it, even though no big fish was in sight.

On both, after several long minutes spent crouching and watching, an agitation among the lesser fish in what appeared to be the best place in each pool, suggested that something was unsettling them. On both, I stayed motionless and waited. On the little stream, where the fish averaged three or four ounces apiece, a 12-ounce monster shrugged into view and took a well-placed nymph at once.

On the second, the sudden migration upstream of a shoal of small grayling and the sideways, passage-clearing drift of trout between 1lb and 2lbs, indicated a much larger presence drawing near. I tensed, glued my eyes to the water downstream and then, slowly, along a channel between two weed beds, a huge fish, heart-stopping in its bulk, mooched into view. This time a rather heavier nymph proved the medicine. I flicked it three or four yards upstream so that it had time to sink as it drifted downstream on the current. By the time fish and fly coincided, the nymph was right in front of the monster's nose. All that eight-pounder had to do was open and close its mouth as though stifling a yawn – and it was on.

On both of those occasions, I was fortunate that things worked out. Of course, they might not have: I might have misread the water or the behaviour of the smaller fish, as I have done many times before. I might have crouched there all day, for nothing. But as it happens, this time I did not. So does size – absolute size – matter? Well, yes, it certainly can at first. But later on it is relative size that becomes important: relative size and challenge, especially.

Reet Queer Trout

THERE is not an angler alive who has not experienced the bizarre inconsistencies of fish. Their behaviour changes week by week, day by day, hour by hour, minute by minute. Now they will do this, now they will not do this. Now they will do that, now they will not do that. Often, there seems no rhyme or reason to any of it. Learning to cope with it is, in part, what angling is about. It is just the way fishing is.

* * *

A GLORIOUS day found me fishing an idyllic, spring-fed lake with an experienced, fly-fishing pal. The lake was that rarest of trout waters, the home of a long-established population of large, wild fish.

The sun was up. Not a breath of air disturbed the surface. The water was as clear as thought. Every frond of the lush weed, every stone and piece of marl on the bottom, could be seen as if picked clean with a scalpel. We saw hints and winks of fish, the occasional slow-oiling rise. Conditions were perfect for delicate, long-leader nymph fishing. We had a quiet morning but, with the water's owner on the oars, an extraordinary afternoon.

From around three o'clock the fish simply went crazy: wonderful trout of between 1lb and 5lbs snatching the flies, running away with the lines, wrenching down the rod-tops, one after another. We stopped counting, but I guessed that by the time things went quiet around 6pm we had netted and released 30, maybe more.

Yes, I know it wasn't politically correct. Yes, I know the done thing would have been to stop after half a dozen apiece. Yes, I know the mullahs and ayatollahs will be demanding our heads and wanting to know what kind of angler could want to catch as many as that.

Well, that day, I'm afraid, my pal and I did. We both recognised the experience for what it was: a one-off, a day to be set in the scales against all the blanks and the singles and the losses and the break-offs and the soakings and angling's myriad other frustrations. We exulted in our good fortune and went on enjoying it as long as it lasted, chortling like schoolboys. Later, our host looked back through the books. Our bag was a record for the water, which had been in his family's hands for generations.

Which was all very nice. I mention it, however, for another reason. The following day the owner, tethered to the oars while ghillying for us, returned to the water with another friend, naturally hoping for some of our luck for himself. And what did the two of them get? Zilch, nada, rien: a blank, under apparently identical conditions, for two anglers, one of whom knew the water, the lies and the fish better than any other alive.

I cannot explain the behaviour of the trout on either day. Certainly on the day my pal and I fished, our result was not the product of extraordinary skill: the fish were too abandoned for us to feel that, appealing though such an idea might be. On the day our host fished and blanked, the reason was certainly not that we had caught or alarmed all the fish because the lake was large enough to have been mostly untouched. It was an extraordinary contrast, extreme and inexplicable – to us, at least.

A Yorkshireman I once knew would have responded in the way he responded to any angling imponderable put to him. He would listen attentively to all the details and nod. Then, no matter what improbable behaviour had been recounted, would say: 'Aye, lad, there's nowt so queer as fish.' And then, after a pause, 'and they can get a lot more queerer than that, tha knows.'

I'd discovered just how much more queerer, early on. The first trout I caught on a fly came off Lough Sheelin, in Ireland and it weighed 3lbs 7oz. It was an extraordinary first fish for anyone to catch, a blind fluke. The following day my companion took his own first trout on a fly. A driving wind and torrential rain made casting almost impossible. The boat was pitching and rolling on huge waves. His fish snatched his fly when the wind destroyed his backcast and hurled it onto the water behind him. It was a stunner – 4lbs exactly.

Bizarre things have happened many times since. In the early 1980s I was fishing Rutland water from a boat. It was a baking day. The sun blazed. The fish must have been poaching in their own juices. My companion and I saw nothing, caught nothing and anticipated nothing. Eventually we moored up in a bay for lunch. In desultory mid-conversation, I lobbed the crust from a sandwich overboard. At once a back broke the surface and in a single, porpoising roll a vast brown trout took down the bread, leaving only a series of rings ebbing on the flat-calm surface. It was the only fish we saw, all day.

One boat-fishing scenario crops up time after time when two anglers of equal skill are out together. Trout will take one angler's fly relentlessly while leaving the other, fished just feet away, un-touched. After a while the unsuccessful angler will put up the same flies as his pal and fish those – but it makes no difference. The man who is getting the fish begins to see the funny side of things and starts to chuckle. He bites off his apparently infallible fly and offers it to his companion – but goes on catching with something different when still his friend catches nothing. A few more chuck-les, part-tinged with embarrassment. By now the man facing the whitewash is seeing the attractions of homicide. He feels a bit silly but accepts an invitation to swap places in the boat. Finally he even agrees to swap rods – neither move, naturally, making a difference. Silence and tension mount. Friendship becomes temporarily strained. And then, bingo – the following day the situation is re-peated – or completely reversed – again for no apparent reason.

The most extreme variation on this theme happened to an-other boat-fishing pal of mine. He caught trout after trout, his companion, nothing. Eventually, they got to the seat-swapping stage. No sooner was he in the seat his companion had just left, my friend told me, than a trout leapt clean out of the water and landed flapping at his feet.

Do I believe it? Yes I do, because I know the man concerned. I also know that anyone who spends as much time on the water as a keen angler sees lots of unusual things, some of them extraordi-nary, a few scarcely credible.

It all puts the behaviour of the fish on that wild-trout lake into perspective. Thirty giving themselves up to newcomers one day and none succumbing to the local expert the next? A four-pounder snatching a fly when it touches the water on the back cast? A lone sandwich-chomper? Yes, even a fish leaping into the boat at one end to rub in the salt for the chap at the other?

Of course. Why would we question any of it? Trout are reet queer, tha knows.

My Way with Carp

EVERYONE knows about carp – about their strength and intelligence, I mean. Everyone knows you have to do weight training and press-ups before taking them on. Everyone knows that most of them have got Ph Ds. Everyone knows that lots of anglers have devoted their lives to finding new ways of fooling them.

But all of that counts for nought, for some of us. Some of us are neither troubled nor intimidated by any of it. We go about carp fishing in our own way and still we get results. I use the winter madness method.

* * *

THERE is a lot of twaddle talked about carp. Most people think carp fishing requires skill and cunning. Fortunes have been made and countless books have been written, pushing the same propaganda. H.T. Sheringham knew better. The great writer and humorist, writing early last century, pinned his faith in luck.

'Cultivate your luck', he wrote. 'Prop it up with omens and signs of good purport. Watch out for magpies in your path... Throw salt over your shoulder. Touch wood with the forefinger of your right hand when you are not doing anything else. Be on friendly terms with a black cat. Walk around ladders... Perform all other such rites as you know or hear of. These things are important in carp fishing.'

On the other hand there is the winter madness method. Here you put carp completely from your mind for a lifetime, then stumble across several meadows in a howling gale and driving rain, burdened with bags and baskets, rods and nets, chairs and groundbaits. You fill your wellie at that place where the bank gets as slippery as a skid-pan, lunge for a branch to save yourself from going right in and then watch the little thread of bubbles your thermos flask leaves behind when it somehow launches itself from your back-pack and falls into deep water. Next you assemble what gear you haven't left at home, heave a bait out into the murky night and, as the wind rummages about you and the rain drives down, you fall to wondering why you are fishing in the dead of winter when you could be in a warm, well-lit room having your teeth extracted without anaesthetic.

Each to his own, of course, but that is my way. The only time I tried it, on a river near my home, it worked a treat.

I'd been out all day, was fishless and cold in the gathering gloom, when the madness came over me. Though a warm hearth and a hot meal beckoned, I decided I would not pack in yet. I would drive to the other side of the valley, lug my gear across the squelching meadows and try the little sidestream where someone had apparently taken a big chub the week before. It seemed reason enough at the time.

Thirty minutes later, squinting up into the last of the light, I was running a half-ounce ledger-lead up the line and struggling to tie on a size 10 hook. A piece of bread flake from the centre of a large, white loaf was eventually pinched aboard and swung out. I clicked on the bale-arm, wound in until I could feel the line running down to the lead as tight as a drawn nerve and settled down to wait. The rain pattered and drummed on the back of my hood. A heron loomed out of the dusk and wheeled away, startled. More lights on the distant hillside came on.

Tweak-tweak. It was an oddly distant sensation, the merest enquiry at the bait, signalled up the line. I paused, felt it again and struck. In no time, a bemused little chub had visited the bank and was back in the water. Another piece of bread flake and another cast. Settle again. Tweak-tweak. A small trout this time, anticipating its open-season by the better part of a month. It comes in and goes back as fast as the chub. Two in two casts, both small. If I get a third bite and it's a tiddler, I'll knock off. Definitely.

Tweak-tweak. I begin to lift the rod – and suddenly it's hit by a sandbag. There is a huge swirl and, as the line is ripped out and the reel spool whirs fast enough to melt, a great bow-wave catches the light and reaches up the banks on either side of the narrow little stream.

It is 10 minutes before I feel a weakening, see the rolling and the lunging; sense victory. I am backing down the bank towards my distant net when I get clear sight of her. A carp, a big, wild, beautifully scaled common carp, massively broad and deep. I crouch down, set the rod-butt into my midriff and lean back. The rod handle creaks beneath my grip. The fish shrugs and wallows towards my reaching net. There is no hope of lifting her one-handed. When she's in the net I drop the rod, grasp the net rim with both hands and heave. The weight, for someone who mostly pursues trout with a fly, is incredible.

On the bank, with the shrouds peeled aside and the last light upon her, she seems even bigger than I'd originally thought. How big? Not big by the standards of the carp aficionados or the hand-reared porkers stocked in commercial fisheries – but big for a real carp, a wild carp, a river carp. Big enough for me. I lift her into the mesh weighing-sling and hook the spring-balance through two of the loops. The torch beam lights the little arrow jiggling and bouncing while the fish settles. I squint, register the weight and squint again. Fantastic: 17lbs exactly.

I shield my camera from the rain and snatch a couple of quick shots. Each time, for one-sixtieth of a second, she gleams up out of the dark like beaten gold. Each time I register the lit beads of rain on the grass, on the rod – and beam at my own delight. A minute later, the biggest fish I have caught from an English river in a lifetime is taking deep gulps of oxygen, sweeping my holding hands aside and heading back into the suddenly warm night.

That evening I fall to thinking about the absurdity of such a fish taken in such conditions at such a time of year, with so little expectation – and remember Sheringham's comments about luck. I reach up to the bookshelf and check the size of his own biggest carp, a fish he wrote up in 1911. It weighed 16lbs 5oz. Brilliant. Nearly three-quarters of a pound lighter than mine. Magpies and ladders and black cats nil, winter madness and astonishment one.

Need, Ego and Addiction

ANGLERS quite often describe their sport as addictive. We use the term as keen golfers might use it, or chess enthusiasts or gardeners. We use it to describe an utterly absorbing counterpoint to our working lives and domestic responsibilities: an activity to which we could devote far more time than is usually available.

That is, most of us do. For a few, angling can become addictive in a literal, clinical sense: it can induce a physical and psychological craving, like alcohol or drugs. It can, when need becomes entangled with ego, become a life-orientating compulsion that is out of proportion to all else – and it can lead to disaster.

A glance into the pressurised, hot-house world of carp fishing might suggest that this is where most addicts will be found. Trout fishing, though, also has its psychological victims and it is from trout fishing that the most extreme story of need, ego and addiction has come. It led to a man's life and reputation being publicly destroyed. To spare him further pain here I have changed his name and location - but that is all.

* * *

THERE have been no sadder developments in angling in modern times than the withdrawal by its holder of a long-standing, officially recognised record for the rainbow trout. The reason, he said, was because he did not really catch the fish at all: he found it lying dead in the water, slipped his net under it when no-one was looking – and claimed it as his own.

The revelation attracted huge publicity. It was at once a tragedy and a liberation for the angler concerned. The affair caused him to live a lie for years. It cost him, he said, both his marriage and his sport. It also demonstrated how even angling's sleepy hollow is prey to human frailty and exploitation – and showed the near-impossibility of vetting any record claim in a totally watertight way.

In April, 1995, Peter Black, of Greydon, in Hampshire, claimed the record for an artificially reared rainbow trout with a fish weighing 36lbs 14oz – a monster of a fish, six or seven times the size of the average salmon seen on the fishmonger's slab. It came from Dever Springs fishery, a renowned – even notorious – big-fish water not far from his home. The fish appeared to fulfil all the criteria set by the British Record Fish Committee (BRFC) when assessing a record claim.

In July, 2003 Black, apparently worn down by stress and by conscience, wrote to the BRFC saying he had lied about the fish. 'I am very sorry and deeply regret what I have done but I cannot live a lie any more as it has destroyed my marriage and it has very nearly destroyed me. As a result I have given up fishing altogether... Now I can sleep at night knowing I have nothing to hide ... I only hope people will respect me for coming clean and telling the truth.'

Black went further in interviews. According to one newspaper, he said he realised the fish could not have been dead long when he saw it lying in the margins. He netted it out and 'in a moment of madness', told two anglers who passed by that he had caught it. Before he knew what had happened, he claimed, the fish had been weighed, the press had been called and the bandwagon was under way. 'Since then, my life has been hell. This is the only way I can repair what I have done.'

Another newspaper reported that Black's teenage hobby had 'flourished into a blind addiction.' It quoted him as saying 'I was just so ambitious. That record got me recognised. I was completely oblivious to what was happening in my family and now my wife is filing for divorce.'

Few could take pleasure from such a story. Many will feel that in declaring the truth, Black deserves the peace of mind he obviously craved. There is not an angler on the planet – or any other human being – who has not in his time exaggerated and if Black's exaggeration was greater than most then so, heaven help us, was the price he had to pay.

The BRFC came in for some stick in the affair, but absolutely no blame attached to the committee. The Black case simply proved what all of us knew: that no set of rules ultimately depending on the integrity of a chain of human beings – often needy and sometimes gullible human beings – can be foolproof.

The rules governing record fish claims are about as tight as they can be in the real world. They include a need of verification of place, date and time of capture, method used, verification of species – many a fish submitted as a pure specimen of one species has been shown to be a hybrid – plus witnesses to the recorded weight, the accuracy of the scales used and all else.

Black's case was supported by the two anglers who saw him with the fish in his net and who can have had no cause to doubt his claim that he had just caught it. The fishery owner had bred the fish and so knew the monster was in his water. Under the circumstances, confirmation of this 'record' by the BRFC must have seemed more straightforward than most. The fact that a monster trout should not only come from this fishery but actually be expected from it, must have been a clincher.

It was also simply part of a progression. For years, a small group of fishery owners had vied with one another to stock ever-larger fish because of the publicity – and hence the business – that monster fish attracted. Over time, these fisheries became the focus of a tiny minority of the angling population that is interested only in absolute weight.

The fact that to the majority of anglers there might seem little sense of achievement in catching a huge fish from a water in which only huge fish have been stocked, was neither here nor there. Nor was the fact that to many it seemed as though those involved – both fishery owners and anglers – had lost touch with what real angling is about. The point is that such a market existed and that the then owner of Dever Springs was a leader among those who set out to cater for it.

The sizes of stock fish grew relentlessly. Before long a 20lbs trout had been reared and caught, then a 25-pounder. A 30-pounder was the next logical step – and so Black's monstrous fish became an inevitability.

This entire movement – which said more about a fish-breeder's ability to rear porkers than an angler's ability to catch them, and which eventually led to the record lists having to be re-defined to take account of them – did angling no good either in its commercialism or in its rejection of traditional sporting values.

In particular, it subsequently seems, it did Peter Black no good. His story was of a tragedy waiting to happen.

Grafham – and Alex Behrendt

FEW – or, at least, few who have travelled much – would disagree that Britain has some of the finest trout fishing in the world. There is scarcely an angler who wants it who cannot find fly fishing within reach of his backcast.

Once upon a time, such riches would have seemed impossible. Trout waters had existed only where God had poured them. Fly fishing was the province of the well-heeled and the geographically blessed. Then, in the space of a few years, two quite separate events changed the landscape for good. One was the opening in 1966 of Grafham Water, in Cambridgeshire, as a public trout fishery. The other was the decision of a remarkable former German prisoner-of-war to stay on in England and to create a small, stillwater trout fishery near Romsey, in Hampshire.

Grafham launched a movement that effectively brought to the heart of England the equivalent of Scotland's lochs and Ireland's loughs: vast sheets of water, teeming with trout, that were available to the public from boat and bank. Alex Behrendt pioneered the development of the small, purpose-built trout waters that now gleam and glitter in the countryside like scattered coins.

Together, they brought the mountain to Mohammed. They made fly fishing available to Everyman. In the process they saw off much of the snobbery that had marked game fishing for too long. Grafham, first.

* * *

GRAFHAM was not the first water supply reservoir to be stocked with trout and made available to the public. Lake Vyrnwy, in Wales, had opened in 1891. Blagdon, in the west country, had opened in 1901. Chew Valley Lake, near Blagdon, followed suit in 1956. What made Grafham, in the Midlands, so special was its size and location, the quality of the fishing it offered – and the timing.

Up to the mid-1960s, trout fishing was beyond most anglers' reach. The chalk streams of the south were beyond their pockets. The teeming waters of Wales, Scotland and Ireland were far removed from the great centres of population. Grafham opened in the heart of England as the motorway system was being developed and as more and more people were gaining access to cars. Its 1,500 acres were within reach of millions.

The lake had been stocked with half-pound trout 18 months before opening. In the summer of 1966, visiting anglers could not believe what they found. Pretty well wherever they cast their flies, tight-muscled and ferocious fish leapt on them. The smallest, gorged on the sticklebacks and snails that had quickly colonized the water, had reached 3lbs. Four-pounders and five-pounders were little more than average. Six-pounders were common. Chew, itself a big lake, had opened with a fanfare and fine fishing, but not on this scale. And Chew was more remote.

The sport Grafham offered was, by any measure, astonishing. It was accessible and it was cheap. The publicity that resulted was huge and anglers who had never fly fished before – among them, me – converged on the new water. Demand outstripped supply.

Other water authorities saw what was happening and followed suit. Soon, the 3,100-acre Rutland Water opened close by. So did Draycote, near Rugby. More huge, new reservoirs were opened to trout fishing in Kent, Essex and Northumberland. As the resource expanded, so did the numbers wanting to enjoy it.

Most of the newcomers came from the ranks of coarse fishing and they included many of coarse fishing's finest brains. They brought insight and free-thinking to a branch of angling long burdened by tradition. A period of technical innovation unequalled since the 1880s and 1890s, was soon under way. New tackle and techniques to meet the specific challenges posed by large, lowland and in many places deep new waters, appeared.

Before long, drogues were slowing the drift of a boat in a strong wind, enabling water to be fished more thoroughly. Clamp-on rudders that could cause a free-drifting boat to run diagonally across the waves instead of straight downwind, had a similar effect. The first lead-cored lines emerged and suddenly fish in the deeps could be reached and caught. Rods designed to handle such lines were brought to market. Carbon fibre put other rod technologies into the ark, overnight.

Though most developments concentrated on boat fishing techniques, others gave attention elsewhere and soon the first nymph fishermen appeared on the banks. Their use of imitative patterns cast on long, disturbance-free leaders brought a delicacy back to fly fishing on lakes that some of the new techniques had seemed to take away.

It was while all these developments were taking place on big waters that Alex Behrendt, in Hampshire, was creating a separate and quite distinct layer to the market.

Behrendt, a former German infantryman, had spent the last months of the Second World War in a prison camp near Romsey, in Hampshire and, on his release, had decided not to return home.

He had married a local woman who worked at the camp and was intent on using his knowledge of fish-farming, his pre-war profession in Germany, to make a business.

Behrendt knew that the British did not share his countrymen's taste for carp; that they were, however, keen on angling; and that trout fishing was mostly costly or inaccessible. That was why, with the help of his wife, he bought two overgrown ponds in tangled woodland outside Romsey; spent a couple of years working on them and stocking them with trout – and then invited anglers to come and catch them on a fly.

With that single, seemingly unexceptional act, Behrendt significantly changed the face of British angling. Behrendt and his Two Lakes fishery became the catalyst for a boom in a new kind of trout fishing: fly fishing on man-made small waters. Anglers had fished ponds and lakes for coarse fish for centuries but, in the late 1940s, fishing for trout was still largely confined to the rivers and lakes of the north and west.

By stocking his first two lakes with trout and digging more on the same site, by working out how to attract anglers from a distance and make a profit, Alex Behrendt found a way to make high-quality fly fishing available not simply to the well-to-do, but to those of modest means; not just in the north and west but wherever the right holes could be dug in the right ground.

Over the years others saw what he was doing and followed suit – often with the help of courses that he himself ran. Man-made trout fisheries broke out like an aquatic rash across the English landscape. Today they are everywhere, catering for hundreds of thousands of fly fishermen. It is a multi-million pound business. By-the-by it has taken pressure off rivers and their wild-trout stocks, adding an environmental benefit to all else.

Behrendt's childhood would have made a sub-plot for Dr Zhivago. He was born in Dnepropetrovsk, south of Chernobyl, in 1910, the son of a German father and a Polish mother. Four years later, on the outbreak of war between Russia and Germany, Behrendt's father, as a German, was sent to Siberia. He was not imprisoned but, with other Germans, was required to live in a small, policed region of Turkestan. Somehow, his wife obtained permission to join him with their young son and daughter.

In 1918, with the war over and Russia now in political turmoil, the Behrendt family headed back to Germany across the wastelands of Siberia. They made the 2,000-mile trek on foot, by horse-drawn sleigh and later by horse and cart, across Russia and northern Europe by way of Moscow, to a small town south-east of Gdansk. It was 1920 before they arrived.

In Germany, Behrendt's father set up a carp farm and it was there that his son learned his trade, travelling extensively through Europe to gain wider experience. In 1942, now conscripted into the Wehrmacht, the younger Behrendt found himself back in Russia and at the front. He was wounded by a grenade and evacuated. On recovering, he was sent to Italy where he was eventually captured and shipped to England. He spent the next 18 months as a land worker in the prison camp near Romsey.

It was in the camp that what would have made the story for a second novel, occurred. Behrendt met Katherine Armstrong, a local woman who helped in the canteen there, part-time. They became friends. On his release, the two decided to make their relationship permanent – and so began the astonishing marriage of a former German army corporal and the widow of a British Royal

Navy captain who had been lost in the war. They were to be together for 50 happy, though childless, years.

With £1,250 provided by his wife, the two bought a 33-acre plot of woodland overgrown with laurels and brambles, that had on it two unkempt ponds. A further £250 bought a converted, single-decker bus, which was to serve as home while Behrendt worked on his fishery.

His first thoughts had been to stock with coarse fish like carp and tench. Then he met Alfred Lunn, keeper to the Houghton Club, on the nearby Test. Lunn advised Behrendt that if he wanted to make money he should set his cap at those who had it – trout fishermen. And so, far from major centres of population, sandwiched between the Itchen and the Test, the two most famous trout streams in the world, and realising that he would have to provide superlative sport if he were to attract business there, 'Two Lakes' was designed as a fly-only trout water.

Over the years, with Katherine helping him all the way, Behrendt continued to dig and hew, channel and landscape. The fishing he provided for home-reared, fully finned, hard-fighting rainbow trout in increasingly beautiful surroundings, began to attract the clientele he sought. It was a single-minded, hard slog – but by the 1960s politicians and captains of industry, scientists and national newspaper editors, generals and admirals were all beating a path to the corporal's door. The little site outside Romsey first became the best-known, small stillwater fishery in Britain – and later the best-known in the world. The bus became a house, the two lakes became eight.

Over four decades, Behrendt pioneered virtually every aspect of the modern, small-water trout business, from the types of location and water quality required, to the densities at which fish could best be reared and stocked and the limitations on methods for catching them. The marketplace around him boomed, but not everyone got it right.

One key to Behrendt's success was the rules he established and his attitude towards them. Only rules that worked to the benefit of fish, fisherman and owner alike were to be adopted. Once established, they should be communicated to the anglers immediately – and adhered to. There should be no exceptions. None. Few among his distinguished customers doubted that he meant it. Some were to find out personally. 'Clever Dicks' – rule-benders – were quickly shown the gate.

This is not to say that Behrendt was rigid or humourless, simply that he had a clear vision of what he wanted to do and was determined to achieve it. Indeed, Behrendt was courteous and engaging and had a wry sense of humour. One story, reported by a Two Lakes member, passed into legend.

Mr X was fishing one of the lakes when he hooked a large trout. The trout made a searing run down the middle of the lake and Mr X was obliged to follow it – which he did until a large tree on the very edge of the bank, blocked his way. What to do? The trout was continuing its furious progress, the hook-hold or leader might give way if pressure were applied in an attempt to turn it and desperate measures seemed to be called for.

Mr X made up his mind. He tried to pass the rod around the tree with one hand and reach it on the other side with the other hand. In the process he somehow lost his balance, teetered briefly on the brink – and fell bodily into the water, a total immersion. A few minutes later the hapless angler, rod recovered but fish lost, was dripping and squelching his way back to the car park. Behrendt, his German accent still noticeable, suddenly appeared from the opposite direction and took in the situation at a glance. He looked the forlorn angler up and down, put on a mock-stern face and shook his head. 'No vading'.

Behrendt founded the annual Two Lakes Fishery Management Conferences in 1969 and they ran for 18 years. Like everything else he touched they became internationally recognised, attracting speakers and often hundreds of delegates each year from Europe, the United States, Asia and the Far East. In 1977, much helped by Katherine, he wrote the Bible on his subject, *The Management of Angling Waters*.

The Behrendts retired in 1988 and sold the fishery and the land, retaining a plot near their old house, on which they had built a bungalow. When Katherine died in 1990, Alex was heartbroken. Soon it became apparent that the new purchasers of the fishery could not repeat his success. Behrendt had not only owned the business, he had been the business – the brains and the magnet. Without him it went down and down. Eventually, the new owner abandoned it altogether and nature began to reclaim the land.

Behrendt declined to move and stayed on in the bungalow with his loyal housekeeper, Esther Stone. As the long years passed he saw the lakes dry up one by one and the rushes and the brambles grow back over all he had created. Then, on October 16, 2005 he, too, died in circumstances that might have reminded some of Miss Havisham at home. The comparison, though, would have been wholly inappropriate. Unlike Dicken's famous character, Behrendt showed no bitterness to the end – and left a legacy for millions behind him.

Pig Eats Rod

IF THERE is one thing we British are known for, it is our love of animals. Speaking personally, when it comes to our furred and feathered friends, I am Francis of Assisi himself.

But I am also an angler – and long experience has shown that animals and angling do not mix. When we are out by the water and some four-footed creature approaches, or some large bird zooms down, or if some whinging speck busies itself about our ear, it is almost always bad news.

* * *

IT WAS a particular pleasure to hear from friends of a misfortune that befell a well-known and notoriously boastful angler. Apparently his rod, an expensive American affair, his pride and joy, was eaten by a pig.

I am not in a position to say what carbon fibre tastes like preferring, as many of us do, more conventional fare. But clearly the pig enjoyed the stuff because it consumed the lot – not merely biting the rod but chewing and swallowing it, bit by bit, from the tip down.

The incident happened while the man in question, a quite noxious individual, was staying at a farm, fishing the nearby river. He had left the rod in the farm porch overnight and when he went down next morning, he found the pig snuffling and salivating over the cork handle, all that remained.

The incident has cast new light on pigs, showing them to have a sense of humour and justice not otherwise to be guessed at. But then, anglers who spend a lot of time in the countryside have learned not to be surprised by its creatures.

A little-known quality of the cow, for example, is its rasping tongue. Many years ago on the Kennet, in Berkshire, a friend of mine rolled up in a spanking new car, resplendent in its metallic silver paint. Alas he knew little about the behaviour of cows, still less about their tongues – and so, to avoid the heat of the day, he parked in the shade of a great chestnut tree in an open field, right by the river. He remarked, if I remember aright, how wonderfully pastoral the view was – the river sliding, the birds singing, the fields green and flower-strewn. God was in his heaven and the lowing herd was winding slowly o'er the far side of the lea. We moved off upriver, casting lightly as we went.

When we returned that evening it was to a car which, had it had four legs instead of wheels, would have made a passable representation of a Dalmatian dog. Its paint, in patches, had been licked clean through to the dark undercoat, the resulting somewhat haphazard design nicely complemented by two broken wing mirrors and a dent in the nearside wing.

Elsewhere bulls charge, geese honk, bees swarm, dogs snap and snarl, mink steal our fish and horses are famously unpredictable.

I do not know much about goats, but I do know they are stupid and ungrateful, both facts I learned to my cost some years ago while fishing the Wiltshire Avon, as guest of a club that has water there.

I found myself walking beside a fence that marked the boundary of one of the many splendid homes of Sting, the singer. A small goat – apparently the great man collected or bred exotic species at that time – had managed to get its horns trapped in some wire mesh nailed to the inside of the fence, presumably to stop the animals trying to squeeze beneath the bars. The creature was tugging this way and that, uttering pitiful bleats. Other goats were standing around and looking on, doing absolutely nothing.

I determined, instinctively, to set an example. I clambered over the fence, threw my leg over the animal's back cow-poke style, gripped its horns firmly and with much tugging and heaving I worked them free. I straightened, paused for breath and then bent down to pick up the fly box that had fallen from my jacket amid all the action. At once the beast I had just freed ran forward and butted me in the bum. It was not a severe butt, but it was not a token butt, either. I have never helped another goat since.

Few creatures are nastier than swans. Swans disguise their true nature beneath a haughty demeanour and a high-prowed grace. They are fiercely territorial and bad-tempered. When they have their young with them they are all hisses and menace. When they are preening themselves or pretending to lie coiled up and asleep, they always have one eye open, following you like the end of a gun barrel. It is a given among anglers that a swan can break a leg with one blow of its wings and so anglers always give them a wide berth – often having to sacrifice good water in the process.

Mercifully, we have H.T. Sheringham to turn to for advice in matters fauna as in so much else. Sheringham knew everything there is to know about the hazards of the countryside and, in 1925, he set some of them out in *Fishing, its Cause, Cure and Treatment*.

A wise general reaction to danger, Sheringham says, is some 'fast running.' If he is caught out in a storm an angler should not worry about thunder, 'which is all bark and no bite', but should take lightning more seriously. If in the open and he senses a lightning bolt coming, Sheringham advises the angler to take avoiding action – for example, by hiding under water 'to escape notice'. Alternatively he can 'duck his head when a flash comes' or, failing that, he can 'consult an electrician'.

On the matter of creatures he suggests that 'for dogs, stones are the specific', that all bullocks really require is 'deference' and he reminds us that 'while all snakes are not adders ... all adders are snakes', which is helpful. Sheringham is particularly good on bulls. There are, he says, three ways of bringing a bull under control: '(1) beating him with an iron bar until he repents of his sins; (2) taking him by the horns and wrestling with him until you have him at your mercy; (3) twisting his tail until he is calm'.

Of pigs, however, Sheringham says nothing. Unlike my friends and me. We are full of praise for pigs. Pigs are great. They have a sense of humour and they bring home the bacon: pigs like the carbon-muncher anyway.

Sex in Angling

ONCE upon a time, the angling press was a refuge for the innocent. It seemed, in this sordid old world, so benign and wholesome. Deep into Specimen Bleak or Gudgeon Monthly, life's tawdriness simply faded away. In particular, in the angling press, we could get away from the commercialised sex that, even then, seemed to be everywhere else we turned. Well, not any more. At least, not in the newspapers I get to read.

* * *

MOST of us have heard about the psychiatrist who keeps making abstract doodles on a piece of paper and, when he asks his patient what each reminds him of, the patient says 'sex'. After a while, the psychiatrist puts the papers away. 'An easy diagnosis', he says. 'You're a sex maniac'.

'What do you mean?' comes the indignant response – 'it's you who keeps drawing the dirty pictures'.

I know how each of them feels. Sometimes, when I open the angling press these days, all I seem to see is sex, sex and more sex. An edition that *Angling Times*, the sport's tabloid weekly, brought out to mark the opening of a new coarse-fishing season on rivers, is typical of the kind of thing I mean. But before I get into what distressed me so much about this issue, let me make plain what did not: I'm not having anyone thinking I'm a prude.

First, I can cope with the 18-stone, shaven-headed lovely on Page 3, the chap showing off part of a massive catch of bream taken on – I quote – 'Frenzied Hemp and Tails-Up Boilies', for all that he's clad only in an earring, a gold necklace, wellies and heavy-duty fishing overalls.

I am dismayed but not shocked to see a brazen television show host – you know, that chap who fronts the 'Who Wants To Be' series – posing in a wet T-shirt with his arms around as lovely a 13olbs catfish as you'd see in any of the Sunday tabloids.

I'm appalled but not complaining about the filth that must be festering under headlines like 'Your Tackle on Test' or 'The Session of a Lifetime'. And naturally I discount the piece headed 'Long, Slim and Beautifully Presented' that I read on the natural assumption that it was yet another article about me, only to find that it was actually about floats.

No, what troubles me is the way this paper has begun to reduce real, beautiful sex – the sex that should be part of a long-term, loving relationship – to raw, commitment-free mechanics. Dr Paul Garner, the paper's so-called 'Fish Doctor', was the main culprit in the issue I'm referring to. He devoted an entire, drooling page to pheromones.

You don't have to have smoked behind the bike sheds to know what pheromones are: even kids, these days, know they're those undetectable smells and things we all give off, the ones, it's alleged, that give certain individuals of the opposite sex, the hots. They seep from our pores, drift off into the ether, attach to and spread from anything we touch.

Talk of pheromones *per se* is not new in angling, of course. Professor Peter Behan, a distinguished Glasgow neurologist, once published a treatise in which he suggested the reason women have caught so many of the biggest salmon and the fact that these fish have been male or – you'll forgive this, 'cocks' – is because these grizzled old, big-kyped brutes were in some way attracted by the pheromones women anglers leak into the water or whatever.

Mercifully, I thought, for someone prepared to fantasise like this in public, Professor Behan did not detail exactly how women leaked their pheromones into the water and nor did he deal with the apparent sexual proclivities of the hen fish women catch. Even the good professor baulked at a discussion of, as it were, female-on-female action. But talk of pheromones in angling, he certainly did.

So it's not pheromone-talk as pheromone-talk that's distasteful. What shocks about Dr Garner's outburst is his willingness to go that bit too far, his determination to say anything to grab 15 minutes of attention. Dr Garner is no sooner into pheromones than he's talking openly about – brace yourself – tubercles. Yes.

Opposite his own picture he has a picture of a big male bream covered in them – you know, those little raised white spots that look a bit like goose-bumps. They're all over the fish's head and shoulders. Dr Garner theorises that tubercles in male bream produce sex pheromones that attract females and paints, between the lines, a somewhat unedifying picture of lady bream nudging one another and saying things like 'Cor – get a load of the tubercles on that!'

The sex pheromones given off by tubercles and the like, he suggests, can also tell male fish a lot about their rivals. It seems that male bream become highly aggressive when spawning. 'Each male continuously patrols and fights off other males that try to enter his territory', the Fish Doctor says. Much fighting and damage is avoided, apparently, because 'the fish are able to tell the size and strength of their opponent from his pheromones', along with much else. The man is David Attenborough going on about dung and urine, all over again. If you listened to him, you'd think it was the Serengeti down there.

I'll not go into the details of Dr Garner's piece in case the children or the servants get to see this. All I will say is that there are smells and tubercles all over the place, not to mention references to pain and fear and certain other topics that smack of S and M. It's all so sad – and so far removed from the kind of thing the founding fathers of Angling Times, great men like Bernard Venables and Richard Walker, had in mind when they launched the paper all those years ago.

At the same time, I don't want to rubbish the whole publication. There is still lots of good, solid fishing advice to be had in Angling Times and it is being promoted in some interesting ways. One of them is via the reader information service that the paper, for some reason, buries among the small ads at the back.

The advertisement that caught my eye when I pored over this section – I was looking through it for a new roach pole at the time, as I recall – had a rather busty young woman with large, pouting lips as its central feature. Presumably this young woman is a red-hot angler who is offering fishermen advice, over the telephone because the caption has her saying 'Don't Talk, Just Listen', over a premium-rated number that shows her advice does not come cheap.

Sadly, for all the value to anglers of this brave new venture – and for all the joy of seeing good, straight advice on how to get 'em out amid so much that shocks – this young woman's service seems doomed to fail. I don't care how hot an angler she is and how many whoppers she's had on the bank – I don't see anyone paying premium rates to listen in silence while she goes on about her big 'uns and her handling technique.

I mean, for a couple of quid we can get all that information, better and more cheaply, from Mr Crabtree Goes Fishing. And with Crabtree we get pictures, as well.

Skues and the Nymph

THERE have been relatively few giants in angling. There have been many brilliant performers, but performers are different. Vast numbers of fine performers have left behind little but a reputation for sharp eyes, deft hands and the ability to capitalise on tactics and techniques developed by others, just occasionally by themselves.

Likewise there have been countless clamourers and tweakers – men who have claimed a breakthrough because they have wound five turns of silk around a fly's head instead of four or who, in such and such conditions, shot their floats this way instead of that.

A giant is another kind of being. A giant has achieved his status because of the fundamental nature and relevance of his contribution. He is a man who, by dint of insight and work and intelligence (and often by his ability to communicate, though not always) tells us all something we did not know and moves the sport forward.

A man could easily be a giant in historical terms without himself having been a great practitioner, though most giants have been pretty good with a rod. G.E.M. Skues certainly was.

*   *   *

AT THE request of a reader, I once wrote about the man I consider to have been the most important single figure in the history of dry fly fishing. The ink was no sooner dry on that piece – to be seen elsewhere in this book – than two readers asked who I considered to be the most important figure in nymph fishing.

Given that it was then exactly 50 years since the death of my nominee, it seemed as good a time as any to name him. I had about as much difficulty in identifying George Edward Mackenzie Skues as the father of nymph fishing as I had in identifying Frederic Halford as the man who did most to give us the means of fishing imitations of winged flies, on the top.

Skues made his reputation in a lifetime of experiment and observation on the Abbots Barton beat of the Itchen, outside Winchester. Halford carried out his researches, in collaboration with others, on the upper Test near Stockbridge. Both relatively small, wonderfully clear rivers, were flowing laboratories for the study of aquatic life.

Halford, in two brilliant books, showed us not only exactly which winged insects trout eat and how they might be imitated in dressings designed to float – but set out a methodology for fishing them that was more scientific, effective and aesthetically pleasing than anything available before. Broadly speaking, he made the case for casts to be made upstream, to precisely targeted individual fish feeding at the surface, with representations of the bugs they happened to be eating at the time. The difference between this and the traditional, random fly fishing carried out up to that time, was the difference between the rifle and the blunderbuss.

Skues proposed a similarly precise approach, with artificial nymphs, to fish feeding under the surface – again a huge advance on the traditional, current-dragging, downstream casts using sunken flies, used to that point. What is more, though we do not know Halford's precise personal contribution to the development of the dry fly method (because he worked with a collaborator) we do know how much Skues contributed to the development of nymph fishing. He contributed 100 per cent.

Halford and Skues knew one another. They first met in 1891 when Skues was invited to the Itchen as a guest. Halford, who had already made his name, happened to be on the water at the same time and was not shy in advising what flies should be used. Skues, notoriously independent, went his own way – and fished the great man's socks off.

It was because Skues found that Halford's dry flies often failed to catch underwater feeders that he began his own researches. Little by little he developed and tested practical alternatives based on meticulous study of the fish and the way it fed, below the surface.

Though Skues' respect for Halford's contribution never wavered – he described Halford's 1889 book *Dry Fly Fishing in Theory and Practice* as 'the greatest work that has ever seen the light on the subject of angling for trout' – he became increasingly frustrated by Halford's failure to acknowledge the value of the artificial nymph and he had no time at all for many of Halford's slavish followers.

These individuals were so taken with the beauty and precision of the new dry-fly approach that they took it up like a religion then turned it into a cult. While Halford argued that the dry fly was superior to the wet because it was more effective, his followers took things further. They decided the dry fly was superior in every conceivable way. First it became 'more sporting', then the only 'proper' way to fish. In a matter of years, sub-surface fishing on many classic chalk stream beats was debarred – as it still is on some today.

It was into these changing times that Skues sowed the ideas he had been developing. In 1910 he published *Minor Tactics of the Chalk Stream*, the first work to talk about fishing wet flies and nymphs in the same kinds of terms that Halford used for the dry fly. Then, in 1921, Skues published *The Way of a Trout with a Fly*.

This work, in the eyes of many, is the greatest work on fly fishing for chalk stream trout to have appeared in the 20th century. It was a veritable tour de force. In it, Skues addressed fish behaviour, optics and fish vision, sub-surface entomology, fly and nymph design, the different ways trout take different flies, fishing technique and much else. On the way, and naturally, the book put nymph fishing centre-stage. Halford's protagonists railed against Skues as though at a heretic, absurdly likening his precise approach with the nymph to the only kind of sub-surface fishing they knew – random, downstream casting. Right up to his death at the age of 90, Skues had to fight skirmishes against the backwoodsmen, on the nymph's behalf.

For all that, the advances and insights Skues single-handedly made and set out for posterity, now stand with the greatest contributions ever made to fly fishing. Collectively they stand with the recognition in 1836 that the reflection and refraction of light are important when considering how the trout in water might perceive the angler on the bank. They stand with the observation in 1841 that flies floating on the surface sometimes had the edge on the traditional dressings that sank. They stand with the promotion, in 1857, of the free-drifting upstream cast over the traditional current-dragging cast downstream. They also stand comparison with the mighty works that Halford, with help, handed on.

There is no doubt that the independent and iconoclastic Skues could not have made his contribution without having the benefit of all these others: every innovator stands on the shoulders of those who have gone before. But he is the founder of the modern school of nymph fishing, bar none. Like Halford in that different way, he stands alone.

Staying Silent and Still

ONE of the commonest defence mechanisms in nature is the ability to stand or lie absolutely still. When still, a camouflaged creature dissolves into its background. Without movement, there is less to attract the eye, even in the open. This is as true at the waterside as it is anywhere else - and the experienced angler knows it.

* * *

IT IS often like this. Fly fishing is often a matter of just waiting and watching. Well, waiting and watching and keeping silent and still. I learned long ago that if I wait and watch and stay silent and still long enough in the countryside, something is likely to happen.

That is why I am here, thigh deep in the river, waiting and watching as the evening closes in. There is no sign of a fish and only a sprinkling of flies; yet there is something in the air, some low-voltage prickle that keeps me here, that has me expectant and alert at the end of a long day. It has been an astonishingly thin day for late May unless you count the two small fish before lunch and the incident under the willow tree – which as it happens, I do. The incident under the willow tree especially.

That was about an hour ago. I was wading near the island when the heavens opened and I made for the bank to shelter under the tree. I was able to sit on the bank, back against the tree, with my feet on an old post sticking up from the bed, a foot or two out. I had been there quite a while, simply waiting and watching, when I noticed the trout – a brown trout, of course, this being kept as a brown trout stream. It was maybe a foot long. It was riding the slowed water in front of the post, right under my feet.

I don't know how long the fish had been there by the time I saw it, but clearly because of my stillness it had accepted me as another part of the bank and the water under my feet as just another natural lie. It was so close I could have touched it. I could have counted its every scale and spot. I watched the way it kept tilting its eyes, scanning for this and suddenly noticing that. I saw its mouth gleam as it took tit-bits from the current. One joyous lunge for a mayfly sent the water flying up, the splash on my Polaroids somehow cementing our bond.

When the rain stopped and I eventually moved and the trout saw me and bolted, I was left with that extraordinary sense of connection with the outdoors that so absorbs me. For 10 privileged minutes I had shared the life of that shy creature; had been closer to a trout behaving naturally, seen more of it for longer, than many an angler gets to see. If the day had ended then, I would have been content.

But the day had not ended then. Nor is it over now. That faint electric current – is it in the air or in me? – keeps telling me so. And so I am in the water again, waiting and watching again, silent and still; searching the water for omens and signs.

It is a known experience. Upstream, the river seems to be sliding towards me, not flowing. All around me it is orchestrating the water crowfoot, making the long fronds curl and sway as if to a languorous waltz. A cuckoo is calling. An alder fly pirouettes and curtsies around the prow of my wader. Every small sound and sight, every crinkling and easing of the water, makes the silence deeper and the stillness more profound.

A sudden tug at my eyes. There, there, by the edge of that weedbed, a movement. A rise? Probably not. Probably too small. Probably a submerged frond of weed reaching up and touching the surface from beneath. Even as I lengthen line and cast I know I am doing it more to relieve my inaction than anything else. The line goes out, the leader unfurls and the fly alights as softly as a maiden's kiss. Perfect. There is a pause, then the tiniest movement. I enquire with the rod, expecting nothing.

The suddenness of it, the awful power and shock of it, take me completely by surprise. It is a huge fish, impossible to hold. Before I know where I am the rod has been wrenched down, the loose line has been ripped from my fingers and the reel is giving line in repeated, short bursts. I see the surging waves and the cartwheeling leaps, feel the terror of the water-lashings, know the leaden dread of the weed on my line.

The world zooms in. Time collapses. Images and incidents pile one on another. An age later, maybe at some point when I sense a change in the battle, I realise how much my sprained rod-wrist is hurting and that one of my waders is awash. I am 20 yards downstream from the place where I began, backing towards the bank, surging and stumbling, soaked chest-high. The fish makes another desperate dive, I put my left hand up the rod to take some of the strain from my wrist, the rod winces and creaks and holds – and it is over. The fish hesitates and wobbles, is sliding towards the net at last, is over the net, is heaving and thrashing, deep in the bottom. I lift.

On the bank, far from the water's edge, I put down the net and peel back the shrouds. She is a fin-perfect rainbow trout, stunning and immense. She is fully two feet long; as sleek and lovely as a salmon fresh in from the sea. What is it about some fish that gives them a strength beyond the mortal? Where – puzzling thought – did a rainbow come from in this brown-trout stream?

I decide to keep her. I lie her out on the grass, surround her with meadow flowers and take out my camera. Click. Then I pack up because my cup is brimming. I know that I cannot repeat an experience like that, know I cannot improve on the day. What a fish. What a fight. Such a fascinating communion with the trout under the tree. What rewards have come again from watching and waiting. What surprises can pop up if I stay silent and still.

Strike Indicators

I ONCE *found myself having lunch with a successful businessman and, a propos something or other, mentioned the subject of ethics. He looked at me with mock incredulity and leaned over the table. 'Ethics? Ethics? That's a county in southern England, isn't it?'*

In angling, 'ethics' is the name of a deep, dark pit full of hissing and biting things. It is the subject above all subjects that sensible commentators give a wide berth, or else turn over with a long stick while their head is averted, for fear of what might lie beneath. Alas, some writers are less than sensible. I am one of them.

* * *

I ONCE received an invitation to fish a beautiful trout stream. It was one of those upmarket rivers that have fishing huts along their banks. On the floor of the hut where I was a guest, I found two small, obviously buoyant, brightly coloured plastic pads, each about the size of a fingernail.

They were, of course, strike indicators. Strike indicators originated in America and their purpose was to give a visible indication of a take when a weighted nymph was fished through fast, turbulent water. Of late, strike indicators have found their way to Britain and they are being used in situations far removed from those originally intended. In one typical circumstance they are being used to fish weighted nymphs on very ordinary streams –

including, if my fishing hut find was anything to go by, even the slowest, shallowest and most sedate.

Normally, when an angler fishes a sunken nymph on streams like this, he has to watch the end of the leader. If the leader hesitates or twitches or is pulled down, the angler strikes because such movement often indicates a take. Seeing these movements is a learned skill, much improved by practice. It takes much concentration but it can be acquired by anyone whose sight is good enough to follow a floating fly. To use a highly visible strike indicator that obviously disappears, completely de-skills this fascinating way of fishing – or so it seems to me.

The indicator is also being used on stillwaters. The weighted nymph is cast out and it sinks. When it has submerged the length of leader between it and the floating indicator, the indicator buoys it up and the nymph is left to drift and dangle from it. In other words, the indicator is used as a float and when a fish takes, the bite is again made obvious.

By varying the length of leader between the indicator and the nymph, the nymph can be float-fished at a predetermined depth for as long as required – again taking out the skill that such fishing normally requires.

My question is about the extent to which such practices are consistent with the sport of fly fishing as most people know it. Enter the hissing and biting things. How is fly fishing to be defined and by whom? What is its fundamental ethic?

At one time, fly fishing was simply the fooling of fish on feathered confections, on hooks attached to horsehair. Then fly designs got better and flies that imitated natural insects emerged. New fly-tying materials were developed. Flotants were formulated.

Lead and copper wire were used to make flies sink faster and deeper.

Horsehair lines gave way to silk, which gave way to modern, synthetic lines that can be designed to float all day or to sink at pretty well any rate to any depth required. Hazel and hickory rods gave way to greenheart, greenheart gave way to split cane, split cane has almost completely given way to carbon fibre.

In the main, this steady evolution had been welcomed. Many developments have taken the drudgery out of fly-fishing mechanics and made the angler more effective. At each stage, as always, a few have felt the new advances were not for them, and have quite properly gone their own way.

And so again the question: where is fly fishing, 'traditional' fly fishing, in all of this? The sport has frequently been moved forward by technology, there are no written rules and there is, mercifully, no prescriptive governing body to enforce them, even if there were. Everything is left to the instincts and sense of fair play of the individual and the lines that individual fishery owners care to draw. If we do not like what we see on a given water, we can vote with our feet. Few of us would have it otherwise.

And yet to many, the idea of float-fishing a nymph on a small stillwater or on a smooth, slowly paced stream as a means of removing all demand from the process, is a shift of the goalposts.

Those who use such devices will certainly claim that the strike indicator used in the ways described is merely another example of incremental change. What is the essential difference, they will argue, between watching a length of floating leader for signs of a take and – as many do – attaching a dry fly to a leader and watching that to make the take more obvious? What is the difference between watching a floating dry fly for indications of a take and an indicator designed specifically for the job?

The problem with such a view is that it enables pretty well anything to be justified. If we are fishing an artificial fly, why not a real fly? If we are using a fish-imitating lure, why not a real little fish, instead? Fewer will argue the latter case than the former, but I have seen it done, and quite seriously. The difficulty is that it is shades of grey that are at issue, not blacks and whites – and shades of grey can be difficult to distinguish from one another. A shade from one end of the spectrum, however, is very different from a shade at the other end: not black and white, perhaps, but maybe not far off.

The introduction of things like strike indicators cannot be stopped and the sport would be diminished if they could. There are, quite rightly, as many views on what fair fly fishing is as there are fly fishers who fish and every view is as validly held as the next.

At the same time, many will feel that fly fishing as it has traditionally been regarded, is being changed by the anything-goes attitude; that its long-accepted values are being nibbled away, little by little, increment by increment. I am among them.

Swans

I CANNOT get excited about swans. Well, let me rephrase that: I can and frequently do get excited about swans, but not because they are large and stately and beautiful, though they can be said to be all of these things. I get excited about swans because, as their numbers increase to levels that many of our rivers cannot possibly sustain, I see in close-up, like many of us, the devastating damage they can do.

The public, of course, does not see this damage. The public sees only the graceful and photogenic bird – and woe betide anyone who draws attention to any problem with it. This is true even if he happens to be a keeper watching his life's work being unravelled before his eyes.

* * *

FROM time to time, the national media has a field day at anglers' expense. An increasingly popular subject – and the focus of one major kerfuffle – is swans. Swans eat vast amounts of water plants like ranunculus, the beautiful, water-waltzing, oxygen-producing plant that is the basis of the food chain on which much river life depends.

Swan populations are growing and, in some circumstances, the birds are gathering in unimaginable numbers: sometimes 100 and even more crammed into maybe a couple of hundred yards of water. Of course, swans cannot help being swans, but when such armadas of reaching necks and tugging beaks get to work, they can reduce once-green and vital reaches of river to something close to moonscapes. And as the plants go so does the life-support system for aquatic insects and fish – eventually impacting some mammals and even some birds.

And the reason the press got hot under the collar? Some anglers vocalised their concern for what was happening on some rivers – a 'concern' that, when it appeared in print, somehow magically became 'anger': anglers were 'angry' about swans.

A couple of river keepers, clearly anxious and seeing the streams to which they had devoted their lives being stripped bare, suggested that maybe swan numbers should be controlled. One way of doing it, they said, would be to remove some eggs from some nests on the hardest-pressed reaches. 'Removing eggs' became characterised as 'a cull'. Now 'angry anglers' wanted to 'cull' swans – with all the lethal public relations overtones which that term carries. The issue of swan damage to rivers and river life became the issue of anglers wanting to slaughter swans.

What tosh.

Of course, deep down, most newspapers that took up the story achieved a balance. They mentioned that bodies like the Environment Agency and English Nature had registered concern about swans as well. They reported that Ministers were 'aware' of an issue and that officials were studying it. But because these are swans and the public is the public, official debate about them has been conducted *sotto voce*. The fact that anglers registered concern out loud meant that they got the focus, the headlines and the heat.

So let's stand back a bit. There really is a problem with swans: not all swans on all rivers, but some swans on some rivers that are already in terminal decline for a package of other reasons. Which rivers? Mostly they are among the chalk streams of southern and eastern England, world-renowned eco-systems which, because of their rarity and beauty and because of the plant, insect and fish life they support, have the highest levels of protection that European and British law can afford them. What protection? Protection that, on the evidence, is worse than laughable.

I have highlighted the fragility of these eco-systems many times over the years – as I have the domino-effect when one factor (or creature) gets out of kilter with the rest.

The fundamental problems are abstraction and diffuse pollution. Many rivers are being relentlessly abstracted to provide water for burgeoning new housing schemes – and as their levels fall, so available space for all the life in them, declines. Lower water velocities take a special toll of plants like ranunculus, which need fast water to thrive. In addition, they cause suspended silts to settle out, clogging the gravels in which some fish spawn and covering the stones on which specialised creatures live.

Chemical pollution from intensive farming and elements of the human wastes resulting from increased housing all end up in rivers. Insecticides kill more of the remaining aquatic flies, fertilisers promote suffocating growths of algae and hormones and hormone-mimicking chemicals have begun to change the sexual characteristics of fish.

All of this is out of sight and mind of most urban dwellers. One result of it has been that the wild brown trout, the iconic river species and once commonplace, is now becoming a rarity. Research conducted by angling biologists and statisticians has begun to quantify a crash in aquatic fly life that no-one else had even suspected.

Overlay on this crushing environmental stress the great concentrations of cormorants now roosting inland to feed on fresh-water fish, add the way swans are making life easier for them by reducing the plant life that gives fish some refuge and we pretty well have a full house. Or, to put it another way, an empty river.

If we were to surrender the comforts that underlie these pressures – our entirely natural wish for more houses, better sanitation, cheap and bug-free food – then flows might get back to normal, plant life would bloom again and the problem currently posed by a booming swan population on the worst-stricken rivers could be more easily accommodated. But it looks like being a long wait.

Who can be surprised then, that anglers, the eyes and ears of the waterside, should ring the alarm bell when yet another problem, one infinitely more localised and potentially more controllable than the rest, is added to the pile? And if it is not to be anglers who speak up for rivers, then who? The house-building industry? The farming lobby? The water companies? The hawk-eyed and naturally hair-triggered Royal Society for the Protection of Birds of which, incidentally, I am a member?

The fact is that anglers and angling are not calling for a cull of anything. They know that the swan issue is being officially researched and that they, like everyone else, must await the outcome. But the price of that waiting will be the further destruction of habitats on some rivers that may never get a chance to recover.

Anyone who sees the countryside – our entirely man-created and man-managed countryside – in the round, should know about this and be concerned about this. That is what anglers – concerned but not angry, seeking awareness but not a slaughter – are increasingly trying to say.

Tench on a Fly

OPPORTUNISM is a great thing. It is one of the qualities that distinguishes the expert from the inexpert. As a generalisation, the average angler takes a limited set of tactics to the water and hopes to find conditions to suit them. If he does, he is in business. If he does not, a blank or meagre result beckons.

The expert angler is different. He is consistently successful because he knows his quarry and how conditions affect it. He is less hostage to circumstance because, through thought and understanding, he can adjust his approach to conditions as he finds them. His awareness gives him, as it were, a kind of infinite flexibility.

I would not claim to have expert status in anything and my friends, I suspect, would disclaim the same for themselves. We all, though, keep our eyes wide open. If we do see an opportunity – especially an opportunity to try something different – we take it.

* * *

TWO fish, above all, symbolise drowsing summer. Once the slumbering waters and mist-wreathed dawns have arrived, it is carp and tench that are most in mind. I have fished very little for carp, but a friend and I have found a fascinating way of catching tench. We have not just caught a couple by accident in this way, but a great many, over time. The fish came to artificial nymphs, fished as though to trout.

The day we first tried it, we had set out to catch rudd. We knew the lake near John's home was full of rudd because John had seen them rising. Rudd are known for their willingness to take the dry fly. That was what we planned when we went. Then chance intervened.

As we were tackling up, a brief patch of clear sky on that dull day lit the water at our feet. Far down in the gloomy deeps beneath the steeply sloping banks, we saw shadows. They were short, tench-shaped shadows; big-finned, spade-tailed, dark and substantial. We could not ignore such an intriguing opportunity. We forsook the rudd and tackled *Tinca tinca*, instead.

We used the same light rods and light lines that we had brought for the rudd dimpling the surface and, for all the difficulty in seeing into the water once the cloud had returned, we opted to try to catch our tench by sight. We went back to John's house, tied up some small, highly visible white nymphs, variously weighted – and then set about the task of persuading the bottom-feeding tench that it might well be a trout.

We flicked the nymphs out directly under our rod-points and glued our eyes. The white nymphs slowly sank. They grew fainter. When, for all our concentration we eventually lost sight of them, we lifted and flicked them out again.

From time to time as we followed our nymphs down we would see, on the periphery of our vision, a large shape beginning to materialise not far from the nymph. We quickly learned that to take our eyes off the nymph and look at the shape was fatal. When we tried to focus on the shape, we could rarely see it. When we tried to look back at the nymph, we could not find it. Every cast became a battle of wills. The only chance was to concentrate on the white points of failing light as the nymphs sank and wait until the shape, the shadow, the maybe-fish, came right up to them.

Mostly, a fish heading towards a nymph went right on by. Sometimes, a shape would hesitate with the point of light right in front of it, as though it had come up against an invisible wall, before turning away. Sometimes, there would be a blink of soft light as the fish opened its mouth – the tench may be green and wonderfully camouflaged, but the inside of its mouth is not – and sucked the flies in. Then we struck. In this way, by dint of concentration intense enough to begin a headache, I took ten tench to 4lbs in two hours before lunch. John took a similar number.

Two elements of this episode surprised us. The first was that tench could be caught by design, one after another, on artificial nymphs. We could find nothing in the literature about it, even though one or two specialist writers had reported tench occasionally sipping in midge pupae from the underside of the surface film.

The second surprise was the sheer speed with which tench can suck in a nymph and eject it. Time after time we saw the huge, round, protrusible lips gleam. Time after time, we struck and missed. The fish were as fast as roach or dace in flowing water. We hit, perhaps, one offer in five or six clearly seen takes, at point-blank range, which demonstrates not only how woefully inadequate our reflexes were but also just how many tench were willing to take the artificial. That experience, when followed by others, has convinced us that nymph fishing is a viable and novel way of catching these powerful fish, but probably only under the circumstances we found.

It is quite clear that to fish blind – to cast out and hope to see a take from an unseen fish register on the floating line – would be hopelessly to limit the chance of success: any tench could take and eject the nymph 100 times without giving any indication on the leader to even the most hawk-eyed angler. Likewise, the water will need to be clear so that the fish's mouth can be seen. The fish will need to be very close to the bank, so that the instant the rod is lifted, the strike is immediately transmitted to the hook. And so on.

Of course, it is not only tench among the coarse fish that will succumb to a nymph. On their day, most coarse fish will take one, the pike, bream and carp not excluded. None, though, seems as willing to take as the tench. In drowsing summer, when the sun is up and the fish are proving difficult, it is another small wrinkle worth knowing.

The Arte of Angling

THE extraordinary story of how the world's rarest fishing book – a work that had survived unknown for almost four centuries in Britain and that ended up being surreptitiously exported to the United States wrapped in old newspapers tied with string – is well-known among bibliophiles but by very few others.

It is one of the most fascinating to come from the shadowed world of the collector – and it sheds light on the passions and money that pursue the rarest, the most original and the most aesthetically pleasing books that angling has produced in over 500 years.

It also sheds light on the scholarship to be found there – and on the big international business that old fishing books have become.

* * *

MANY hundreds of anglers in Britain, and many thousands overseas, collect old books on their sport. Christies, Sothebys, Phillips, Bonhams and others all hold sales at which individual works can fetch from tens of pounds to tens of thousands. The appropriately wallet-sized The Arte of Angling, a single copy of which turned up in 1954 and which is now in the library of Princeton University, New Jersey, was not allowed to get near to any of them.

The angling book best-known to non-fishermen – and the one many imagine was the first – is Izaak Walton's The Compleat Angler, published in 1653. Chronologically, however, Walton comes way down the line. The first work to appear in English was the *Treatyse of Fysshynge wyth an Angle*, printed in 1496. Five works had long been known to have come between the *Treatyse* and *The Compleat Angler*. In each case the author of one cribbed from the works of those who had gone before him. Izaak Walton did likewise, sometimes acknowledging his sources, sometimes not – and like everyone else he copied some of the errors his predecessors made, as a result.

Since Walton, books have come in a flood. No-one knows the number of titles to date, not least because there is no clear agreement on how an angling book should be defined, but the score is well into five figures. They have been collected for hundreds of years. Today there are dealers who trade in little else, even publishers who exist entirely by reprinting old angling classics in collectors' editions. It was one of the latter who, in 2000, brought out the only facsimile of *The Arte of Angling* to appear in Britain, the land that spawned it.

Not every angling book is collectable, of course. Fishing, like every field, produces its dross and most titles come and go like flotsam on the tide. Among the most sought-after titles are first editions by historically important fishermen, special editions of books that show how fishing flies can be tied and that have examples of finished flies set into deep-cut mounts within them – and very early and scarce titles. The first editions of the *Treatyse* and *The Compleat Angler* – the first because of its uniqueness and scarcity, the second because it is the best-known angling book in the world by far – are in classes of their own.

Two certainties are that if ever *The Arte of Angling* came onto the market again, the seller could name his price and that whatever the American Karl Otto von Kienbusch paid for the book in 1954 – the actual sum has never been disclosed – he got one of the all-time bargains.

Von Kienbusch, who collected arms and armour as well as angling books, wrote later that he was on one of his regular buying trips to Britain when the book was shown to him by a specialist London bookseller, since identified as Edgar Chalmers Hallam. 'I nearly fell off my chair', von Kienbusch said. Hallam had previously shown the book to the British Museum, but had been disappointed with the price it offered him. Von Kienbusch immediately made the dealer an offer worth three times what the British Museum had said it could pay – and the deal was clinched.

Both men clearly understood how contentious any deal involving the export of a national heirloom would be. The book was delivered to von Kienbusch at London Airport a few days later, just before his flight back to the United States was due to leave. A parcel 'wrapped in a rather dilapidated piece of newspaper tied with string' was exchanged for American Express cheques for the agreed amount – and that was that.

Back home, von Kienbusch himself funded one facsimile printing before presenting the original book to the library of his old university, Princeton, in 1956. The university printed another facsimile in 1958. The book has not been published in facsimile form in the US since – and it had never been printed in facsimile outside the US, until the UK edition appeared.

Among the many mysteries surrounding the book – not the least of them how it came to survive unknown for almost 400 years – was that of authorship. The first few pages were missing and the name of the writer – if it had originally been on them – was lost.

Painstaking detective work by Professor G.E. Bentley, of Princeton, had by 1958 led to the creation of a profile of the probable author based on clues in the text. However, Professor Bentley was unable to come up with a name that fitted his picture in all respects. Professor Thomas Harrison, of the University of Texas, took up the chase and in October, 1960 he provided one: he identified the likely author as William Samuel, Vicar of Godmanchester, on the River Ouse in Huntingdonshire, who died in 1580.

Among other points that caused a stir was the realisation that Izaak Walton clearly knew about *The Arte of Angling* – and that he appeared to have cribbed from it, without attribution, in his own book. More to the point Walton was, up to the discovery of *The Arte of Angling*, believed to be the first writer to use dialogue between an angler and someone showing an interest in angling, to convey his message. It turned out that Samuel had used the device 76 years before him – and that Walton had even taken the names that Samuel had given to his two key characters in *The Arte of Angling* – Piscator and Viator – for his own key characters in *The Compleat Angler*.

That said, there is a world of difference between the two books. *The Arte of Angling* is a somewhat no-nonsense dialogue between Piscator (the fisherman) and Viator (his pupil). It deals with coarse fishing (for pike, perch, roach, dace, chub, carp, ruffe, gudgeon and bream); with tackle, baits and tactics; and it refers here and there to the kinds of qualities a good angler needs, among them knowledge, hope, patience, humility, fortitude and piety – exactly the kinds of qualities we naturally all recognise aplenty in ourselves, today.

In *The Compleat Angler*, Walton added nothing that was new to angling knowledge and was fanciful in what he did add. However, to quote von Kienbusch, 'what makes his book unique is the charm of its style and the picture it paints of Walton the man – simple, honest, wise, compassionate, God-fearing, lover of nature and of fellow men, revelling in the innocent joys of his favourite sport.' It is these qualities that have made *The Compleat Angler* Britain's most regularly reprinted book after the Bible and *Pilgrim's Progress*. For certain, no-one reads Walton to improve his chances of winning the National Federation of Anglers' Division 1 Cup.

There is a wry point worth making and it is this: in *The Arte of Angling*, Samuel gives the first mention in angling literature to the fishing widow. Samuel has his world-weary wife Cisley telling Viator that she wished her husband had never taken angling up in the first place and then – having listened to Piscator and Viator going on and on about fishing over dinner, she says: 'You men say that women be talkative, but here is such number of words about nothing, as passeth' (i.e. all understanding).

Plenty of anglers – and not only those who read or collect old books – have heard that sentiment somewhere before.

Reading the Rise

ANY *fly fisher starting off without help will find himself challenged. Even with some experience, trout can prove difficult. There are times when not a fish is showing and the water seems to be devoid of life. At other times, fish will be rising everywhere and we cannot catch them. If anything, the second is the worse of the two. The fish are so near and yet so far. Then, the more they splash and roll, the wilder-eyed we get and the more frustrated we become.*

Observation and a little thought, though, can work wonders.

* * *

THE one route to consistent success in angling is the route that provides consistent success in all forms of hunting: a knowledge of the quarry and an ability to translate its observed behaviour into appropriate technique.

In the case of feeding trout, whether in river or lake, 'observed behaviour' means the creation of rise-forms and 'appropriate technique' means presenting the fish with something like the creature it is expecting to see – where, when and how it expects to see it.

By and large, anglers have not been well-served with information on rise-forms. Almost always we have been presented with a list of separate facts or one-off circumstances which we have had to be commit to memory individually because there has been no clear linkage between them. Now the trout will cause the water to 'bulge', now its back will show, now it will do something else. When it is 'bulging', do this; when it is head-and-tailing, do that. Knowledge has been communicated all right, but rarely understanding.

The problem of interpreting rise-forms becomes very much simpler once the behaviour of the fish, and the resulting rise-form, is seen as a simple process of cause-and-effect.

The trout, like any other creature in the wild, does not expend energy uselessly. It moves quickly only when it needs to, otherwise it moves slowly. There are a few exceptions, such as competitive feeding when a small amount of a particularly stimulating food-form appears, but such exceptions merely prove the rule.

As a general consequence it can be said that a feeding fish will only move quickly when pursuing something which itself is moving quickly and that it will move slowly upon, say, a snail. In other words there is a direct relationship between the movement of the fish and the movement of the creature it is attempting to catch and eat.

There is also, of course, a direct relationship between the speed of the trout and the force with which it displaces the water around it. If the trout is moving quickly, then the water will be displaced violently; if it is moving slowly, then the water will be displaced only gently. So we can now see linkage between the movement of the creature the trout is intent on eating and the displacement of water (the rise-form) which is entailed in its capture.

And so, by using our powers of observation and deduction, we can set aside the entomological roulette we have played hitherto and put behind us our speculation at the vice. Provided we are prepared to learn a little about the creatures which trout eat (and especially where they live and how they move) we can look at the rise-form and relate it to the speed and manner of movement of the trout. Having done that, we can relate the movement of the trout to the speeds of movement of the small group of insects around at that time – and their approximate positions in the water. Now we know not only which artificials we should be giving a wetting but where we should be fishing them and how they should be moved.

'Boils' or swirls close to the surface but not breaking it are clearly the product of a fish moving quickly just below the surface – most likely to fast-moving or awkwardly moving nymphs and pupae a foot or so down. Sedge and midge pupae and olive nymphs all fall into these categories, but the time of year and the time of day can narrow the range of possibilities.

Movements which break the surface violently are likely to be to large, live insects like adult sedges or mayflies on the surface or to sedge pupae and mayfly nymphs hatching in or swimming immediately beneath the surface: the momentum of the enthusiastic fish simply carries it through the surface to create the disturbance that the angler can see. Gentler movements at the surface in which the fish's neb shows are likely to be to small duns or terrestrials – and so is head-and-tailing when the neb shows, too.

Head-and-tailing in which the fish's mouth does not break the surface is certainly to creatures which are trapped immediately beneath the surface film (why else would only the back of the fish show?). On lakes, the most common insects which cause this kind of rise-form are midge pupae hanging below the surface film, waiting to hatch. On rivers, the answer is likely to be inert olive nymphs also preparing to hatch or, on some rivers in the late evening or early morning, the dead spinners of some species of olives drifting down beneath the surface film after their underwater egg-laying odysseys are over.

A fish which is taking in flies with an audible sipping noise – always accompanied by a tiny, pinpoint movement of water – is one that is taking dead or dying flies trapped in the surface film and there is absolutely no need to consider a fly under any other circumstances. (We know the fly is in the surface film because the sipping noise is clearly a sharp intake of air – and it is only at the surface that the air is. We also know that the fly is trapped and cannot get away because the leisurely, confident movement of a fish that will move quickly if it has to, has told us so).

All the above observations on rise-forms are true for both rivers and stillwaters, except that on rivers the turbulence and current can make rise-forms in general more difficult to see. (There is a side-issue here: fish on rivers are carried downstream by the current as they lift to intercept flies, so they actually lie upstream of the place where the rise-form is seen. This downstream drift, the extent of it dependent on the trout's initial depth and the current's speed, need to be taken into account when the cast is made).

On lakes, the presence of a fish can be deduced even when no such distinct rises can be seen or noises heard.

In flat calms, the appearance of a contortion in an otherwise steady reflection in the surface can be a sign of a fish swimming just beneath the film, or the residue of a deep-down 'boil' caused when a fish has taken a nymph or pupa. So, too, can the appearance of unsteady dark patches in an area of water reflecting light or winking light patches appearing in a water area that is reflecting shade.

Even in rippled water on lakes, the presence of feeding fish can be detected without sounds or clear rise-forms. Typically, small oases or calm patches will appear in the ripple, indicating that a fish has turned violently a little way down and sent an upthrust of water to the surface that has flattened or stunned the wavelets. Also in rippled water, cross-ripple patterns will sometimes appear, suggesting that the back of a fish has broken the surface, unseen.

And that's about it.

I do not want to imply from the above that this is all a clinical business, with rise-forms capable of being divined with a mathematical precision measurable in microns. It is not. On the day, with wind in the face, water on the move and reflections doing their stuff, it can all be a lot less apparent than it is from the pages of a book being turned in an armchair.

But the principle of reading rise-forms is sound and experience confirms it. The approach is capable of providing anyone faced with difficult rising fish that most satisfying of starting points, an intelligent basis for action.

The Boatman

THE Norwegian name for it is harling – the tactic of trolling big flies behind a boat on a river, usually in heavy water where bank fishing is impossible.

Two or three rods are used. They sit in rests that hold them like outriggers over the sides and the stern. The angler sits in the stern seat, where he can reach the rods and the boatman sits in the middle. The boatman pulls upstream just hard enough with each stroke to hold station on the current. Because he steadily pulls more strongly on one oar than the other the boat not only holds its place against the flow but moves little by little across the river. When the distant bank is reached the process is repeated a little downstream and so the river is scanned from side to side as the trailing flies search the water.

That is the gist of it. That, anyway, is how Kjell Sellaeg did it – and how he mesmerised me.

* * *

THE best piece of boatmanship I have ever seen was on the Namsen River, in Norway.

The Namsen, in its lower reaches, has to be seen to be believed. It is up to 150 yards across and up to 50 feet deep. It drains a huge mountain plateau north-east of Trondheim. Because much of its flow comes from melting snow, it never falls too low to fish: indeed, if you are a fly fisherman it is only late in the season – August – that much of it becomes fishable at all.

Most of the fishing on the Namsen is not done with flies. Most fish on the Namsen are caught on spinners and worms and monsters are often among them. Thirty pounders are – or were – relatively common, 40-pounders were not infrequently caught, 50 pounders were taken every year and 60-pounders put in an appearance from time to time. The Namsen is still one of the few places you can go to catch a monster if you are not overly fussed how you get it.

Which, of course, most of us are. When I went, I wanted any monster I caught to come to a fly. Modesty prevents me from revealing how large a salmon I had in mind for this ambition, but it was not small.

My week had not started well. I had arrived late at my hotel to be told that the river was too high for bank fishing and that if I wanted to use a fly I would have to go harling. A boat and boatman had been booked for me. I should go to the river right away.

Well, there was a boat waiting, but not a boatman. Ten minutes. Fifteen minutes. Twenty minutes. Thirty. I was about to head back frustrated when Torbjorn Tufte, a Norwegian outdoors writer, drove up with Synove, his wife. They were in the same hotel for the week, knew the river well and were taking their own boat out. Would I like to join them?

It was a kind offer but I could see that, with three adults in their boat, plus their black labrador, plus three big fly rods and all their gear, things would be just too tight. I was in the act of declining when a young man came over from a nearby car and spoke to Torbjorn in Norwegian. Apparently he had guessed my predicament, was a keen fisherman and often went harling. He was not a professional boatman but he loved being on the river. Would

I like him to take me out?

First Torbjorn nodded, then I nodded. Yes, indeed I would, I said. Thank you. We introduced ourselves to one another, shook hands – and so I met Kjell Sellaeg. Synove offered me her spare rod to supplement the one I had with me and Kjell retrieved a spinning rod from his car. In no time the two of us were heading upstream, with Kjell on the oars making for the start of our beat.

We did not talk much: Kjell's English was an effort for him and my Norwegian was non-existent. We communicated as much as we could with as few words as we could find, orchestrated by gestures. Everything was kept simple. 'Yes, my first time'. 'Two – one fish 20 kilos.' 'See the rock?' 'Good place.' 'Yes.' 'No.' 'I think so.'

At the top of the beat, we set the rods. Synove's rod went out from one side carrying an intermediate line and my rod went out from the other side carrying a sinker. The intermediate fished a Collie Dog, the sinker fished a heavy Waddington and I plopped Kjell's orange and yellow plug out on a short line from his spinning rod between them. By 8pm, with 24 hours of daylight ahead of us, we were ready. Our downstream drop began.

To either side, low hills undulated along the skyline, hazed and sombre. Pine woods serrated the middle-distance. Long, russet-roofed farms and outbuildings freckled the wide valley floor. Just opposite our starting place, immediately to our left, the austere, clean spike of a church pricked up at low, leaden clouds.

The river was deep and the surface, unruffled. Every stone on the banks, every rock we slid past, was ground and polished by water and ice. There was no wind. A few sedges flew low over the surface; a few midges scribbled patterns on the cooling air.

When Kjell moved the oars, there was no bump or click or

groan from the rowlocks – there was scarcely any sound at all. When he dipped them, the blades seemed to melt edge-on into the reflected sky. Every measured haul brought puddles of light welling upwards, each reaching back described its thin, dripping arc.

The water eased and burbled beneath our feet. Tiny vortices purled downstream from our keel. A thin wake spread. The sky fused to the land. We were in the womb of the river.

One might imagine that for an angler used to reading the water for likely lies and casting to them, for someone used to the action and mobility and involvement of bank fishing, harling might seem boring – a kind of proxy-fishing; fishing at one re-moved. Well, fishing at one-removed it might have been, but boring it was not. That evening, in that place, with that remarkable man, proved to be the most fascinating fishing experience I have had in a boat.

Some oarsmen I fished with that week, simply rowed. Kjell fished bodily with the entire boat, positioning the flies precisely, hanging them perfectly across every inch of the river, from side to side and back again.

I began to take markers from the bank and saw that, over the entire width of that huge water, each new crossing was no more than a few feet downstream from the crossing before. We were not quartering the river, we were paring it, shaving it. No lie was over-looked, no possibility left unexplored. There can scarcely have been a fish in the water that was not shown the lures. Kjell was – there is no better word for it – deadly.

At one point, far downstream, we saw a rock as big as a house. Most of it was under water but the smooth, domed top broke the surface and shrugged aside a wide, rippling V. It was a certain lie, there were probably several fish in it, but Kjell was not to be hurried. His pace and rhythm did not alter. All the water down to it was covered as methodically as the rest, from side-to-side, top and bottom, narrow strip by narrow strip.

When we were 35 yards above it, what amounted to a performance began. First, Kjell held the boat so that the Collie Dog alone drifted across the face of the rock in one direction, then in the other. Then he did likewise with the sinker. Next, he took us upstream and a few yards to one side. Now Kjell made three or four heavy strokes broadside to the river, abruptly put our nose upstream and hauled a couple of times more. Behind us the current pushed a big curve in the lines and one after another, at different depths, the lures swept quickly across the upstream side of the rock in a classic, sweeping, induced-take presentation. 'Kjell, that was fantastic.' 'Sometimes it works. I try something else. Bring in the sinker.'

The sinker aboard, Kjell pulled us upstream again. This time he let the boat slip further downstream than before, hanging the Collie Dog first in the current sweeping down the left of the rock, then in the current sweeping down the right. No response. 'Bring the intermediate in. Put out the sinker.' Now he took the boat away from the rock, pulled upstream yet again and repeated the entire process with the Waddington. 'Bring in the sinker'. Another pull upstream (all of this attention, mark you, to a single rock, just one potential lie) and we repeated the process with the plug, first to the left, then to the right. We knew there had to be fish there. You could have stubbed your toe on our tension. You could have filleted the silence with a knife. Not a nibble.

'How can they resist them all, Kjell? How can they resist them?' I turned around in my seat, speaking softly. He smiled. 'I don't know. I don't know'. He was half-whispering, too.

More scans, more silence and another big rock, not as big as the first. 'I show you something. Reel in the wobbler'. We approached the second rock from directly upstream with just the flylines out and searched the water in front of it as carefully as before. Then Kjell took the boat upstream, angled us slightly on the current and let us drift slowly back. I looked on fascinated as first the Collie Dog was positioned in the current down one side of the rock and then the deep Waddington was positioned down the other. Now, with a line either side of the rock, Kjell dropped us stern-first downstream with infinite care, feeding the two flies at the same time down both sides of the V that the rock made in the current. He made them hang and tease every inch of the way. It was fascinating to watch.

There was a near-inevitability about it, when it happened.

Further downstream, fish began to show – one here, one there, their backs lifting briefly through the surface like subliminal thoughts. Then we heard an almighty slap behind us, as though someone had thrown in a pig and great waves ebbed out. A few minutes later we heard another slap and saw more waves. The tension mounted.

In mid-river, a single tiny turbulence betrayed a rock near the surface. It was almost nothing, the merest crinkle in the smooth, deep water but a lie it unquestionably was. Not for the first time, as we approached it and to Kjell's amusement, I urged a fish to take. 'Come on, fish', I said out loud, 'come on fish.'

As the last syllables were uttered and I heard Kjell's amused

chuckle, a salmon showed its back and disappeared. The intermediate began to lift, straighten – and the rod went around. The reel
screamed and a salmon jumped. Yes! I lifted into the fish and then
passed first one of the rods back to Kjell, then the other. Somehow,
he wound in the lines while dropping us downstream and landing me on a shingle bank.

It was not a big fish for the Namsen and certainly not my monster, but I could see it was lightly hooked and I played it gently.
Close in, we could see the Collie Dog clicked into a loop of skin on
the rim of its lower jaw. Kjell sank the net, I waited until the fish
wobbled and then I began to walk slowly backwards. The fish
rolled onto its side and slid over the net.

It was a beautiful fish, lean and vibrant, silver tinged with lilac,
13lbs exactly. I grabbed Kjell's hand and pumped it up and down.
'Wonderful. Wonderful. Thank you. Thank you.' And then, because I knew the truth full well – 'but it is your fish.'

'No, no. It is your fish. It is your fish. You have the rod. You play
it well.' We agreed with gestures that we should call it a shared fish,
but it was more than that – it was a whole-team effort. Kjell had
put the fish on the line, I had landed it using Synove's rod and my
reel and the Collie Dog had come from a box lent to me by a friend
at home.

In the Norwegian way, Kjell made a bed of birch twigs and
green leaves and ceremoniously laid the fish out on it. It looked a
princely thing. It might have been in a long boat, ready for burial.
I photographed the fish, Kjell photographed me, I photographed
Kjell.

Two hours later, around midnight and with nothing more to
show, we decided to go in. Torbjorn and Synove, newly arrived

from their own fishing, joined us side by side for the row back downstream to the cars. Torbjorn was on his oars, Kjell was on ours, the two men rowing gently in a smooth, cohesive rhythm, their blades interlocking without ever touching. The water crinkled softly beneath each bow. The merged Vs of our wakes faintly spread.

On the last bend, Torbjorn's boat was full against the light, in three-quarter's silhouette. He was in the middle, gently pulling. Synove sat in the stern, stock still and looking downstream, their Labrador sat in the bow, stock-still and looking ahead. For a moment I felt cast back to an ancient world. Kjell and I might have been escort to some barge of state, with the King of Fishes laid on his altar between us.

The Dame and the Treatyse

THERE is not much new in angling. The sport is so ancient, its literature so long and rich that few can be surprised: some of the finest brains of centuries have contributed to our current levels of knowledge, each writer, with the passing of time, standing on the shoulders of those who have gone before. Each step, every subtle shift and nuance, has been documented.

A single book proved the well-spring of all. It set out, over half a millennium ago, one writer's extraordinary grasp of the essentials not only of coarse fishing, but of game fishing. The book is as mysterious in its origins as it is fascinating in content. It is our seminal work.

* * *

IT IS now over 500 years since the *Treatyse of Fysshynge wyth an Angle*, the first book on angling in the English language, was printed – and yet, when that mould-breaking anniversary came around, scarcely anyone noticed. We saw an article here, a letter published there but beyond that, nothing. It would take anglers themselves, to do it.

The news that angling has a literature that predates Walton's *The Compleat Angler* by a century and a half, indeed has anything worth calling a literature at all, will surprise no-one inside the sport, but many outside. Many non-fishermen still regard anglers as inanimate objects crouched beneath green umbrellas, ritually drowning worms. They see fishing as a sport based largely on luck or the nearness of rain and requiring a full frontal lobotomy to enjoy.

Of course, it is not true and it could not be true: angling could not be the most popular participant sport in much of the western world, if it were so uninteresting. Angling has always fascinated millions. Among them it has attracted writers and – there is something in the metaphysical nature of the sport that makes it happen – it has caused literary springs to well in those who have shown no other inclination to write.

Since the *Treatyse of Fysshynge wyth an Angle* appeared in 1496 the rich, broad stream of angling literature has been in full spate. Izaak Walton's Arcadian hymn may be the most famous fishing book but it was far from being the first and it comes nowhere in terms of technical contribution. It was the already-ancient little treatise that started it all.

The *Treatyse* was added to the second edition of the *Book of Hawking, Hunting and Blasing of Arms*, a four-part volume originally published in 1486. The *Treatyse* made a separate, fifth part.

Quite why Wynkyn de Worde, William Caxton's assistant and later his successor, should have devoted time on one of the earliest presses to a text on angling might seem a puzzle: to the apparently more upmarket interests of hunting and heraldry, perhaps – but fishing?

Well, it is known that de Worde was commercially minded and the odds are that if he published something, it is because he saw a market for it. Given the limited extent of education in those days and the very limited access to the printed word, the appearance of the *Treatyse* must therefore tell us something about the popularity of angling in the higher social circles, even in those long-ago times. So must the book's sales: it was reprinted 16 times in the century after first publication.

There is much else that intrigues about the Book and the Treatyse. Tradition has it that the Book was printed at St Albans, Hertfordshire and that the whole work, including the Treatyse, was written by a nun.

Both traditions are based on ambiguous publishers' notes. One, at the end of the Book, refers to 'Seynt albons', which has long been taken to refer to the city. The other, at the end of the hunting section, refers to a work by Dame Julyans Barnes or Bernes, long taken as a reference to a Dame Juliana Berners, alleged abbess of a Sopwell Priory, not far from the city.

The late Jack Heddon, a well-known angling historian, showed that there was a St Albans House in the precincts of Westminster Abbey, close to the place where both Caxton and de Worde worked. Heddon's view was that 'Seynt albons' refers to the house and not, as so long assumed, the city. What is more, on the basis of references in ancient literature, he took the view that whatever the Dame might have written about hunting, the tradition that she wrote the whole Book – and therefore the Treatyse as part of the Book – is make-believe.

Fred Buller, another distinguished angling writer and historian, has long supported the traditional view of the Dame as author of the Treatyse – and also the idea of a Hertfordshire connection. So did the late Hugh Falkus, with whom Buller conducted much fascinating research on the ground in that county.

Buller and Falkus subsequently set out the case for their view, alongside Heddon's, in Dame Juliana – *The Angling Treatyse and its*

Mysteries, a work published in 2001 and discussed elsewhere in these pages. While much of the book's argument is based on fact, a touch of romance underscores their conclusion: 'Until the authorship of the *Treatyse* is proved to lie elsewhere, we believe that fairness, if not gallantry, demands that our legendary 15th century Diana, possible prioress of Sopwell in the County of Hertfordshire, be left with the credit'.

Whatever puzzles surround the *Treatyse*, there can be no doubting the book's value and significance. Its scope and sophistication are, quite simply, staggering. Both qualities were recognised by subsequent writers, who plagiarised it mercilessly.

The fact that so many authors have used the *Treatyse* as a source will surprise no-one who has actually read it. The *Treatyse* covers not only coarse fishing and game fishing but offers practical and surprisingly accurate advice on where to fish, when to fish, how to fish and what to fish for. There is advice on how to make rods and hooks and tackles. There are separate references to float fishing, ledgering, drift-fishing, dapping and fly fishing.

The merits of many different fish are discussed. The remarkable tench 'heelith all manere of other fysshe that ben hurte yf they may come to hym'. The carp is a dainty fish 'but there ben fewe in Englonde. And therfor I wryte the lasse of hym'. The poisonous barbel 'is a quasy meete and a peryllous for mannys body'. The grayling, however, 'is a delycyous fysshe to mannys mouthe'.

There is lots of practical advice. Anglers should avoid being seen by the fish, 'the fyrste and pryncypall poynt in anglynge'. The rod should be kept up to let its suppleness cushion the jumps and dives of a hooked fish 'soo that your lyne may susteyne and beer his lepys and his plyngys'. Fishing in an east wind should be avoided because 'that is worste For comynly neyther wynter nor somer ye fysshe woll not byte thenne'.

There are even ideas in the *Treatyse* that modern anglers have promoted as new. The reputations of some pike fishers have been built on the advocacy of using deadbaits instead of livebaits and aromatic sea fish instead of freshwater fish. The *Treatyse* clearly describes deadbaiting for pike with herrings: 'Take a codlynge hoke and take a ... fresshe heering and ... put it in at the mouth and out at the taylle ... of the fresshe heering'.

There is discussion on dyeing horsehair lines different colours to match the water being fished – an echo of another modern vogue: 'Ye must lerne to coloure your lynes of here in this wyse. Fyrste ye must take of a whyte horse taylle the lengest heere and fayrest that ye can fynde ... and euery parte ye shall colour by hymselfe in dyuers colours.' Detailed instructions for making a range of dyes follow.

Lore has it that the Victorian or Edwardian fly fishers invented the autopsy as a means of finding out what trout have been eating. The Dame – or whomever – advises 'undo the mawe and what ye fynde therein make that your bayte for it is beste'.

Undoubtedly of greatest interest to fly fishers is the fact that the *Treatyse* prints a comprehensive list of fishing flies, with instructions on how to make them and when to fish them, through the season – 'flyes wyth whyche ye shall angle to ye trought and grayllyng and dubbe lyke as ye shall now here me tell'. The 12 dressings include what appear to be representations of olive duns and spinners, mayflies, sedge flies and a hawthorn fly – all clearly based on some understanding of entomology. Every one of these dressings would, if skilfully used, catch fish beyond number today.

No-one knows just how many angling books have been written all told though the number, in the English language alone, runs into many thousands. The flow over time has been unending and is increasing. The well-spring, the source of the torrent in every sense, was the quaintly entitled *Treatyse* with the obscure origins, now published 500-plus years ago. Only anglers could have let such an anniversary pass unmarked. As with too many a bite, we simply missed it.

The Dry Fly on Lakes

FASHIONS *come and go in fly fishing faster than they do on the catwalks of Paris. Always, it seems, someone has just developed a killer-diller fly, or a new kind of line, or has produced a thingamajig that the world has been crying out for. But blink and you miss them. Here yesterday afternoon, gone this morning.*

It has always been thus, as any glance at an old fishing book or magazine will show. And yet, from the 1980s on, we have seen the emergence of a style of fishing – an old style of fishing applied in a new and controlled way – that is genuinely carrying the sport forward. It is one that is taking its place alongside traditional loch-style fishing from a drifting boat and alongside imitative nymph fishing as an essential element in the armoury of the stillwater angler. It is the dry fly.

* * *

THE dry fly has always taken some fish from the big lakes and in the hands of a few it has sometimes taken quite a lot. But until relatively recently, the dry fly on the still waters has been regarded as a minor tactic. If the floating fly took up more than five per cent of a lake fisher's season a few years ago, then he was using it more often than most.

Now, the situation for some has very nearly been reversed. So effective has the dry fly proved that many of the country's leading reservoir anglers are using it more than all other techniques put together, especially when fishing from a boat.

John Horsey, a resident professional at Chew and Blagdon lakes and a man who, at his peak, represented England in the world fly-fishing championships three years out of four, told me that the dry fly is his first line of attack in most conditions and that he takes around 80 per cent of all his reservoir trout by using it.

Even more surprising are the conditions that have proved ideal for the technique. One of them is bright sun and flat calm, even in a boat: the very conditions, indeed, that anglers fishing traditional wet-fly techniques would regard as utterly hopeless until evening, when the last rays are slanting across the water and the evening rise, if there is to be one, begins.

Just as surprising is that the dry fly scores well in the opposite weather extreme: on a dull day with a big wave in a strong wind; in conditions, indeed, that would seem to offer a travelling fish little chance of picking out a small floater in the wind-blown turmoil above it. Indeed, the only kind of day that would not have Horsey and others reaching for the dry fly first is when there is bright sun and wind together: conditions that seem to discourage many fish from coming right to the top. These were, naturally, exactly the conditions that prevailed on the day Horsey and I managed to fish together at Chew, but still we decided to give the dry fly an airing.

We concentrated on the calm lanes that appear on most lakes on a windy day – narrow pathways of flat water that run through the ripple at irregular intervals. The thicker surface film in these lanes makes it more difficult for aquatic insects to hatch and the trout often swim up and down them, mopping up the trapped and the dead. We cast teams of dry flies in sizes 14, 12 and 10 down-wind into these lanes, as we drifted.

Even though conditions were about as bad as they could get for the technique, in a session when we would otherwise likely have seen little or nothing, we boated three fish, we were each broken and we missed perhaps another half-dozen.

It was not that there was a rise: it was more that we had created our own rise. The fish, which in the great heat must have been several feet down, simply confirmed their willingness to lift right to the surface to take a floating artificial, literally out of the blue. Had they not risen to take, we would never have known they were there.

There are several basic rules for this kind of fishing. The first is that the flies must actually be floating – be in or on the surface film and not under it. The second is that their precise location should be known, whatever the conditions. The third is that the flies should not be moved – they should be cast out and left to drift freely. The fourth essential is that the leader should be as fine as possible and, as in all dry fly fishing, it should be treated to sink.

It was because of the need to use fine leaders (small flies cannot be fished naturally on thick nylon) that we were broken. Horsey was using pre-stretched ultra-fine 6lbsnylon, I was using standard 4lbsnylon. My leader did not have the strength necessary to hold a fish towing yards of sunken line, his did not have the elasticity to absorb the shock of a take.

Horsey used three flies that sat right down in the surface film, rather than on it, as many modern dry flies are designed to do. I used two flies, one a flush-floater of my own design, the other a little black fly designed to sit up high. I used the high visibility of the latter to help me locate the former and both got takes.

The importance of knowing precisely where the flies are is

because of the takes. In spite of the liverish duo that broke us clean and the couple that splashed and rolled, most takes were sublimely gentle – mere audible sips or briefly glimpsed noses poking into the air. Even in bright sun and low ripple they would have gone completely unnoticed had we not been looking directly at them. In a wave, most offers would have gone begging, and the fish with them.

It is interesting that the dry fly on lakes has taken so long to get attention, but it has. Now, refinements of it are being pushed steadily forward everywhere. Fished with concentration and attention to detail, it is bringing many fish in the traditional dog-days of summer. The greatest problem for most anglers when afloat on a calm beneath a burning sun, is in believing that it really can work.

It does.

The Falklands

WE DON'T have to travel much to know the state of the earth because television travels for us and brings it all home – sometimes in more senses than one. Over-population, over-exploitation and pollution have wreaked havoc on land, in the seas and in the air. The scale of it, the irrecoverable loss that much of it represents, is inescapable for those who do travel: now it is not conceptual and 'out there' but here and real and deeply disturbing.

There are, though, still a few pristine places left. One of them is the Falkland Islands, a place so remote and under-populated that, in the main, only the military go there. The islands have a strategic value but they are little affected by man.

When The Sunday Times asked me to go there and write about them, to convey some sense of the Falklands experience at first hand, I had a double incentive. The first was the chance to see nature, unsullied. The second was the fishing. The Falklands have some of the finest sea trout fishing in the world, if you can catch it right. Which naturally, in the main, I did not. The islands and their people, though, were remarkable. Here is what I wrote about it all.

*   *   *

CAPE HORN is 350 miles to the west. Cape Town is 4,000 miles to the east. Europe is 8,000 miles to the north, with neither a stick nor a stone in between. The Antarctic is the next stop to the south.

There are no trees. Across the harbour from the painted,

metal-clad houses, the names of ancient ships – Barracuda, Endurance, Beagle – are picked out in rocks on the low, barren hillside. The smell of peat smoke hangs on the air. Sheep nibble the coarse grass alongside Government House. A three-masted sailing barque lies grounded and rusting close in to shore.

There is in Stanley, chief town of the Falkland Islands, an overpowering sense of looking down the wrong end of the telescope at everything: at the rest of the world, at modern urban life, at time itself.

Roughly 1,200 people live in Stanley, and about 800 more in the tiny, tin-clad settlements that sprinkle East and West Falkland and a few of the smaller islands. All who live here are a long way from their cultural roots. Next door to a South American neighbour that still struts and snorts, and in the hands of a Foreign Office that is traditionally mistrusted, they feel a sense of psychological isolation added to physical distance. At the end of the 20th century the Falkland Islands are an orphan of Empire at the end of the world, hanging on.

They are hanging on quite tightly. The market for the wool produced on the islands may have declined, but the loss has been more than offset by the huge revenues pouring in from deep-sea fishing licences sold to foreign fleets. And the islanders are determined to bring in the new money and outside contacts that tourism can provide. It is the 'Falklands Experience' the islanders are selling: the wide open spaces, the clean air, the wildlife and the way of life. The first two are wonderful, the last two extraordinary.

Everywhere in the Falklands there is a liberating sense of space: rocks and mountains, moors and valleys, creeks and bays; huge skies. In the clear, unpolluted air the detail on the distant views is so sharp it might have been picked out with the points of needles. One has the sense of seeing everything with young eyes.

All the settlements are variations on a theme. There is a bumpy grass airstrip, a cluster of painted houses, a few out-buildings, sheep-pens, a shearing-shed and lights that go out at 11pm when the generator is switched off. The farms are vast and the hours are hard and long. It is a homesteading life, a kind of permanent pioneering; but it is a free existence, lived at another pace. Parallels with the American mid-West of over a century ago abound, except that sheep have replaced cattle and, to some extent at least, four-wheel drive has replaced four-legged friend.

For a country with no roads, in which distances are measured in hours over mountains and entrapments in bogs, there is an extraordinary sense of community. Most people seem to know most other people's names.

It is the remarkable air service and the radio that bind the settlements together. So for stagecoach read aircraft and for telegraph read 'the news'.

The bright red Islander does the rounds twice most days, from Stanley back to Stanley. It carries people, the mail, personal messages, small cargo. It can call at any one of the 37 usable airstrips, pretty well in any order. There are no schedules. Time, the developed urban sense of urgency, the restless huff and push, have no meaning here. You find out what flight you are on by listening to the radio the night before. You also find out who you will be travelling with, where you will be touching down and hence, at a guess, when you are likely to arrive at where you want to be.

My first trip in the Islander was not untypical of the Falklands flying experience and the role that the radio plays. I was booked from Stanley to San Carlos the next day and dutifully switched on the evening news.

The headlines came first. Trouble on the M25, more news on interest rates, someone big says this, someone just as big says that and tomorrow's wind-chill factor for newly shorn sheep will be 55 degrees.

News of the flights – where they are going, who will be on them – comes after in detail. '... the 8.30 flight will call at San Carlos, Port Howard, Hill Cove, Chatres, Goose Green, Stanley. Passengers Stanley – San Carlos: Mr Bound, Mr Clarke, Mr Larson, Mr Clifton and dog...'

I am at Stanley airport in good time. My case is weighed, my rucksack is weighed, my fishing rods are weighed, I am weighed.

I am walking towards the aircraft with Mr Bound (who runs Falkland Islands Tourism) and Mr Larson (a Danish journalist) when there's a kerfuffle in the tiny terminal behind us. Graham Bound answers an unspoken question in a matter-of-fact kind of way. 'Terry Clifton's dog. They're just putting it into a plastic bag.' Moments later Mr Clifton arrives, carrying a medium-sized dog. Its body is concealed inside a black bin-liner, fastened at its neck. Only the dog's head sticks out, turning from side to side in a half-anxious, half-bemused kind of way. We settle into our seats, fasten our seat belts and take off. The dog is sick on Mr Larson, but not much.

The countryside below is typical Falklands, though on this flight we miss out on the stunning seascapes that are a part of most trips.

The ground is like a vast, camouflaged Army blanket: all greys and browns, olives and ochres. Again there are no trees (there are no trees anywhere in the Falkland Islands, they cannot survive the constantly rummaging, frequently blasting wind). There are Land Rover tracks, peat bogs, rock meadows, cinnamon grasses, dwarf heaths and dried-up streams that wrinkle through it all like withered veins.

It is small-scale country and the names and places made familiar by the Falklands war are everywhere. Only minutes out of Stanley and the thin, seemingly innocuous ridge of Tumbledown is vibrating slowly past us to port. Bluff Cove and Fitzroy are just beyond it, Teal Inlet is not far to starboard. As usual we fly low to stay beneath the scudding cloud. Suddenly there is a break in it and a shaft of sunlight streams through. Our shadow undulates and skips over yomping-terrain.

There are two kinds of tourist in particular that the islanders want to attract: anglers and naturalists, mostly ornithologists.

The Falklands, like Tierra del Fuego, have some of the best sea-trout fishing that exists. There are three main centres and I get to two of them – San Carlos (for the San Carlos river) and Port Howard (for the Warrah River). My timing is not good. Sea trout, as we all know, are born in rivers, go to sea to mature and grow fat, and then return to the rivers to spawn. But they can only be tempted from the estuaries into the rivers if there is water in them. Migratory fish need some rain.

I arrive in a drought. As a consequence, the fish are still in the estuaries and most days on either river I catch little or nothing. One day, however – at Port Howard – I did hit it exactly right and had a dozen great fish on the fly. They included two at 5lbs, two at 7lbs and, at last light, one iridescent silver fish of 11lbs that was a lifetime's best, so far.

For the ornithologists and other naturalists the islands are a living laboratory. Human beings are so scarce here and they intrude so little that the birds and animals have learned no fear: their innocence was in every sense touching. The bird species are extraordinarily diverse. In one afternoon, on Pebble Island, I came close to black-necked swans, red-backed buzzards, night herons, sooty shearwaters, king shag, rock shag, black oyster catchers, upland geese, flightless steamer ducks, the black-browed albatross and many other birds besides.

The highlight of the trip was, unquestionably, Sea Lion Island, one of the most southerly inhabited places on earth. On a rare still day beneath a piercing blue sky, its coastline was sufficient to take the breath away; all brilliant white sand, low rocks, high cliffs and immense, golden-olive strands of kelp that moved sinuously, almost sensuously in the crystal water, as though to a mermaid's song.

It was all no more than backdrop for the wildlife. There were Magellanic penguins with their jackass brays, Rockhopper penguins with Denis Healey eyebrows, Gentoo penguins as smart and pressed as Grosvenor House waiters.

Sea lions bobbed in the water, heads out, studying me point-blank as though I were an exhibit in a zoo. Elephant seals – 18ft long and over two tons apiece – pigged it on the beach, lying amid the rotting weed and their own excreta: the bulls challenging all intruders, rearing up and collapsing on one another like sumo wrestlers without any arms, all cascading blubber and wide, pink jaws. Killer whales patrolled close in to the beach, vultures turned in wide circles, albatross skimmed. Slow waves arched and collapsed.

As I sat amid it all, looking and listening and utterly alone, with the earth as God had made it and His creatures as intended, I had no doubt about how privileged I was in those moments. I have no doubt, now, either, with the perspective of distance and time. It is exhilarating to know there are such places out there; still on the edge of an encroaching world; still hanging on.

The Grannom and the Mayfly

THE angler who studies his fish – above all, where he can, the angler who watches its behaviour in the water – is the angler who catches most. In the way they go about their lives, fish of all kinds give up secrets to the man who is prepared to leave his rod in the bushes, stay hidden and simply observe. Everything he sees will enable him to fish more effectively, when the time comes.

Few fish are as visible as trout when they are feeding at the surface and few aspects of trout behaviour are more worthy of study. We can see what flies they take and how they take them. Just as important, we can see which flies they leave alone.

* * *

FLY FISHERS have always been interested in why trout will sometimes take one kind of natural fly instead of another, when two are on the water together. Indeed, such considerations are first base for anyone wanting to improve: if an angler does not know which kind of fly the fish want at any given time, how can he increase his chances by tying on a matching artificial?

This capacity of fish to become preoccupied with one fly to the exclusion of all or most others – sometimes preoccupied with one species at a particular stage of its development – is one of the fascinations of trout behaviour.

A letter I once received from Mr Malcolm James, of Hammersmith, in London, took the question to its extremes. He wondered why trout appear willing almost to starve rather than eat some insects, yet will gorge on others. He gave as an instance of the first the tiny caddis fly, the grannom – and the mayfly as an instance of the second.

In my experience, the grannom is unique. On some rivers, hatches of this little brown fly can be so dense that they cloud the air. For hours, there will scarcely be a square inch of water that does not have an adult grannom or an empty grannom shuck, on it.

On my local river, chub seem to love grannom. As soon as the flies start to emerge in April, every chub in the river begins to sip them down. The grannom provides the year's first chance of food in abundance and chub take full advantage of it.

But the trout? Even though they have, like the chub, lived through a long, bleak winter and, unlike the chub, are lank from recent spawning, the trout ignore the grannom hatch until it is almost over. It will only be very late in the flies' three or four week emergence that the fish start to eat them. Mr James said it was as if the trout are reluctant to feed on the grannom until finally, at some point, steadily mounting hunger wins out. Could the trout not simply be behaving as we do, he asked: could they refuse the fly because they simply cannot stand the taste of it?

Now, one has to be careful not to anthropomorphise wild creatures – that is, not to attribute to them human qualities and sensitivities and behaviour. But there are some things that can be said.

Trout, like most creatures in the wild, are opportunistic feeders. If there is food available, they will take it and if there is lots of food available, they will go on taking it until they are sated. And with good reason, in the case of fish – early in the year especially. Trout have been sapped by the need to produce eggs and milt for midwinter spawning. In winter, bug-life is dormant or undeveloped. Around the Ides of March, when the season opens in most places the trout, like Cassius, has about it a lean and hungry look.

Common sense would suggest that, under such circumstances, half-starved fish would eat everything in sight. And yet on the rivers I fish most and apparently on those fished by Mr James of Hammersmith, trout shun the grannom for weeks, though there are no obvious differences between it and similar caddis flies that, later in the season, the trout take with abandon.

There can be very few reasons why. One possibility has to be that different flies do have different flavours and that the grannom – to trout if not to chub – tastes yukky. Exactly what it might taste of, I am not in a position to say. I have, however, long known what the mayfly, the second of Mr James' examples, might taste like.

In 1977 I had a day on Lough Maske with Robbie O'Grady, of Ballinrobe, an Irish international fly fisherman, a renowned ghillie and one of the great characters of Irish angling. At one point, conversation turned to this big and beautiful fly: to the immense numbers in which the mayfly hatched, to the way it drew every fish to the surface, to the way trout would eat it until utterly gorged.

Of course, I said, part of the reason had to be the huge feeding opportunity that the big fly presents. The sheer size of the fly, when coupled with its profusion, gave the trout the biggest and easiest meal of the year, at a time when it was still regaining condition.

'Ah, yes', said O'Grady. 'But there's another reason. They have to like it, you know. It tastes so good.'

I faltered in mid-cast, appalled and fascinated by the import of the statement. Then I turned slowly and looked at him. 'You haven't. You didn't. You wouldn't. Does it?' He nodded. 'I would and I did and it does. I ate a couple a few weeks back. They taste just like soft butter.'

A year or so on I was fishing with a friend in the middle of the mayfly season here. I told him what O'Grady had said. To my horror my pal promptly reached into a nearby bush, retrieved a mayfly and put it into his mouth. There was a pause, and then: 'Do you know, he's right. Exactly like soft butter.'

I was prepared to take my friend's word for it, just as I had been prepared to take O'Grady's. Frankly, I am prepared to take any reader's word about how any fly might taste, the grannom not excluded. All that is important is whether or not the fish are willing to eat it because in acceptance or refusal the fish is telling us all that we really need to know: imitate this one and this one and this one, but not that.

Good enough for the squeamish, Mr James.

The Hair Rig

CHANCE observations, the results of experiments gone wrong, outright strokes of luck in this circumstance and that, have led to all manner of discoveries. They have entered the history books, brought fame and occasional fortune for those involved and, sometimes, great benefits to humankind have resulted.

Most discoveries and developments, though, are hard-won. They come about in less glamorous ways: through carefully designed, meticulously executed research and experiment, often tirelessly pursued over years.

In such a context – in almost any wider context – angling is a trivial pursuit. Yet here, too, in this tiny, leisured, inconsequential side-stream of life, flair and insight have a place.

* * *

ADVANCES in angling come in all manner of ways – through improved knowledge of fish behaviour, better rod-making materials, more effective reel designs, hi-tech ways of alerting an angler to a bite and other routes besides. But they are all as nothing unless the individual can convert them to fish on the bank.

Terminal rigs are key to this in coarse angling and, over the centuries, a myriad ingenious set-ups involving all manner of technologies have evolved. All the more remarkable, then, that a rig based on a flash of insight and a single human hair should have been declared 'the greatest terminal rig of all time'.

Many questions went unanswered in the survey on rigs published by one of coarse fishing's popular weeklies – not least among them how a terminal rig is actually defined and what precisely constitutes 'great'. Few, however, will deny the simple brilliance of the idea that those readers and writers chose – and that has become a mainstay for millions in the years since it was conceived.

Like key developments in most spheres, the 'hair rig' did not come about through luck: it was specifically designed to solve a clear, identified problem. In the mid-1970s, the already-distinguished angler Kevin Maddocks and his friend Len Middleton became obsessed with one of the acknowledged frustrations of fishing for carp. It is that when groundbait is thrown into the water to induce the fish to feed, carp will suck up every offering in sight except the one with the hook in it. Carp do not do this once in a while or regularly, they do it all the time. It is one of the things that has given carp the reputation of being the wiliest fish in fresh water. What exactly, the two men set out to discover, was alerting the fish to danger – and how might the problems it presented, be overcome?

In 1978, Maddocks set up a large tank in his home and put carp in it. He fed the fish on sweetcorn – a typical angler's hookbait – and when he dropped a handful in, the fish promptly consumed it. Then he began lowering hooks baited with sweetcorn onto the groundbait in the tank. Each time he got one of two results. The first was that the fish ate everything in the tank but ignored the hookbait completely. The other was that the hookbait was left until last – and then, if taken, was promptly spat out again.

These and other experiments Maddocks and Middleton conducted eliminated every potentially fish-scaring feature of the tackle except the line. Even the extra weight of the hook inside the sweetcorn was considered as a possible problem – and eliminated when the sweetcorn was given neutral buoyancy by fastening tiny slips of polystyrene to it, without improving results. So the question became – was the line too visible, or thick, or stiff, or what? And if it was any of these, what could possibly be done about it given that a hefty line was necessary to land fish as large and powerful as carp? More experiments, more failures, more frustration resulted.

Then, some months into the experiments, Middleton tied a conventional carp hook to a conventional carp line. Then he plucked a hair from his head. He tied one end of the hair to the hook bend and, two inches away at the other end, he tied a loop. He put a piece of sweetcorn into the loop, pulled the loop tight and trimmed off the loose end. Then he lowered the rig into the water. This time the bait settled a couple of inches away from the hook and, crucially, the line. It was sucked in immediately, with all the confidence of the groundbait all around it. Same next time, same every time. And each time a bait on the end of a hair was sucked into a carp's mouth, the hook attached to a strong line whistled in behind it. Bingo.

In the first full-scale test of the rig, Maddocks used two rods, one conventionally rigged with a baited hook attached to a conventional carp line, the other equipped with a hair rig. He took 11 carp on the hair rig but nothing at all on the other. Middleton and friends had similar results.

In due course the hair was replaced by ultra-fine nylon, news of the technique travelled and other users, as usual, sought refinements. A general goal was to minimise the ease with which carp could suck a hair-rigged bait in and safely eject it: just as a sucked-in bait towed the hook bend-first behind it, so a blown-out bait did the same – and too often the point made no contact with the fish. The result was that a patiently awaited, brilliantly engineered take turned into a missed opportunity.

Over time, experimenters showed that the greatest chance of an ejected hook taking hold was when the hair was fastened not to the hook bend but to the shank directly opposite the point. That way the hook went out sideways, greatly increasing the chances of contact. Tying fine line to the middle of a hook shank – the first solution – proved fiddly as well as effective and many subsequent attempts were made to achieve the sideways effect more simply. One of the neatest and now commonly used solutions involves slipping a short length of silicone tubing up the main line, then tying both the line and the hair rig to the hook eye. When both are secure, the tubing is slid back down to the line end and over the eye and the upper part of the hook shank. It leaves the lower part of the hair, and its attached bait, projecting half-way down the shank, where needed.

Variations on the hair rigs are now used by coarse anglers in every kind of water where shy fish are found. Over the years they have accounted for millions of fish – including several record fish – that would otherwise never have been fooled. There has never been a lower-tech or more effective solution to a major coarse-fishing challenge. The hair-rig is a product of genius.

The Itchy Wellie Factor

MOST of us love an invitation to fish a new water. It is not just the new friends that can result from such a day, it is the anticipation and challenge aroused. What kind of water is this and what does it hold? Will we hit the weather right and how will I do?

That is usually the way of it: a one-off chance to see a new river or lake, an offer casually made and as casually accepted. Unless, that is, longer-term needs are pressing – which, from time to time, they are.

* * *

SO IN spring the fancy lightly turns to thoughts of love, does it? Not in angling, it doesn't. At least, not when the water is clearing and the trout are rising and a new season is set to open. Then, it is not the opposite sex that anglers are getting to grips with, it is the challenge of fishing new waters.

The decision to leave a water or club that has been a part of life for years and move on is not lightly taken but, according to one estimate, up to 20 per cent of fly fishers do it every year.

The reasons, naturally, must be legion. Among those commonly given are a desire to join friends who have already moved, disillusionment with the way the existing water is managed, the cost of the fishing and so on. I suspect, though, that a subtler personal reason underlies many decisions to move. It is that the existing water has, over time, simply lost the ability to interest and challenge.

Some waters, rivers especially, can offer a lifetime's interest because of their size or special nature or the quality of the fish they hold. But such places are relatively few, have long waiting lists and are often prohibitively expensive. The kinds of trout streams that most anglers get to fish are small to medium-sized waters carrying average fish. Often enough on such rivers, every nook and cranny can be reached with a well-placed cast, if not from the bank then while wading. Sooner or later they surrender their secrets, with fascination ebbing swiftly behind. Then, if the other features that make up the fishing experience are not sufficient to hold – the scenery, the wildlife, the friendships formed – Itchy Wellie Factor takes over. We begin to look around.

And so it is that if the 20 per cent estimate is anywhere near accurate, tens of thousands of fly fishers are on new waters each spring, beginning yet another of their cyclical odysseys.

The staging posts on the way follow a pattern. At first a new water is all unknowns. Its shallows and deeps, its bends and eddies, its undercut banks and the holes in its bed, all have to be discovered and have their potential explored. The quirks in the currents that will cause a fly to skid and scream 'fake!' to a fish though it appears to be drifting perfectly to us, need to be accommodated. The tactics that will winkle out the biggest, the shyest, the least accessible fish need to be tested and honed. For a season or two, it can all be fascinating stuff.

On to the next stage. Now we know that there will be a trout in front of that weed bed but likely not one in front of that rock. We know that though the water opposite the barn may be fishless, trout will line up in pecking order opposite the willow, biggest fish first, because there the current funnels hatching flies into a tight, thin line, straight into their gaping jaws. We discovered long ago that there will usually be a good fish where the stump sticks out and the wagtail often perches.

Stage three, now, and attitudes are changing. Now, when we are fishing seriously as opposed to wandering the water, we skip the fallow bits and go straight to the places that are likely to provide action. We approach these places in the right way, cast accurately to the right place and a fish often responds in the appropriate manner. The pleasures of the familiar take over, the satisfactions of being completely on top of this game in this place. But we know that the ability to be surprised has gone. The water that once tested and absorbed us is pretty much an open book.

And then to the final stage, which creeps up from behind. The familiar becomes the too familiar, the too familiar becomes the predicable, the predictable becomes the boring. And so, unless those other features of the river or club are strong enough to bind, the decision to move is made.

In trout fishing, the process is accelerated by the way many river stretches are managed. Most waters have to be stocked because the fishing pressure is so great, yet astonishingly few are stocked with the angler's psyche in mind.

A feature of the best waters is that the angler never quite knows what is going to turn up next. On too many waters, when fish are stocked, they are all introduced at much the same size. Every fish weighs four ounces or eight ounces or 1lb or 3lbs. The effect would be the same if they all weighed 30lbs. There is no element of surprise. At a stroke, interest is needlessly diluted.

In his famous story about Mr Theodore Castwell, G.E.M. Skues got it exactly right. When Skues wanted to send Mr Castwell to hell, he did not send him to a place where there was no fishing, but to a stretch of river that was stuffed with fish. Castwell was condemned to go on casting through all eternity, with a trout of 2lbs exactly taking his fly every time.

And so whatever the reasons they gave to the owners of their former haunts, or to the other members of their clubs if they were in one, vast numbers of anglers launch themselves onto new waters each year because interest in their old has simply ebbed away. They are starting another of their periodical journeys, seeking absorption and challenge anew.

In spring, anglers have no time idly to turn their thoughts to love. In spring, they have fishing in mind.

Francis Maximilian Walbran

ONE of the best things about writing a newspaper column, especially a column written for a national newspaper, is the response that comes from readers. Even the error that brings correction – and the smallest slip can bring corrections by the fusillade – shows that someone out there is taking an interest.

Other responses come from readers, too – sometimes adding this or that perspective to a piece already written, sometimes asking questions, sometimes coming up with new information. The best letters of all are those that stimulate a fresh article, perhaps on the original subject. This is an example of the latter.

* * *

AN article I wrote about the heaviest bag of big grayling I have ever taken – it included eight fish between 2lbs and 2lbs 12oz, plus two three-pounders – caused quite a stir. The ink can scarcely have been dry before readers were reaching for their telephones and letterheads.

All raised interesting points about the grayling and about significant grayling catches. Two contacts in particular stood out. One was a letter from Mr Tim Conroy, a Halifax solicitor; the other a call from Dr Tony Hayter, author of *F.M. Halford and the Dry Fly Revolution*, an absorbing life-and-times of the father of dry fly fishing. Both men linked big grayling with a Yorkshire angler whose fame flickered briefly over a century ago – and whose long-forgotten book has resurfaced.

Mr Conroy was dutifully reading *The Times* on holiday in Barcelona when he encountered my grayling saga. On his return he sent me copies of several pages from *Grayling and How to Catch Them*, published in 1895 by Francis Maximilian Walbran, of Leeds. In them, Walbran recorded how, in 1891, he had taken 12 grayling weighing between 1lb 3oz and 2lbs 6oz one day and from the same swim two days later, a monster of 3lbs 9oz.

Dr Hayter, a professional historian and author of an introduction to a reprint of Walbran's book, came up with more information. He gave me references for two catches of grayling said together to have included three fish over 4lbs and added for good measure that on November 6, 2001 he had himself taken a remarkable bag from a small Wessex stream – six grayling over 2lbs including three over 3lbs. Like Mr Conroy, he also drew attention to Walbran and to his lesser, though still significant, grayling catch.

In truth, Walbran's life and historical context are more interesting than his fishing, not least because he formed a living bridge between the north-country and southern schools of fly fishing at the time of their most intensive development. Walbran, the man, has been too long forgotten, as the reprint of his grayling book makes clear.

Max Walbran was born in 1852, fished as soon as he could hold a rod and began to write as soon as he could grip a pen. By the time he was in his twenties he was writing regularly for the *Fishing Gazette* – which went on to become the most famous periodical in angling history – and other journals. When he was 31 he produced a well-received revision of Theakston's *British Angling Flies*. In 1888 he opened a large and initially successful fishing tackle shop in

Leeds. In 1889 the first book from his own pen, *The British Angler*, came out.

Walbran's writings brought him into contact with the most famous southern anglers of his day, including Frederic Halford, William Senior, Major Anthony Carlisle and the enigmatic George Selwyn Marryat, collaborator in the researches for Halford's greatest books, *Floating Flies and how to Dress Them* (1886) and the monumentally important *Dry Fly Fishing in Theory and Practice* (1889).

Walbran entertained several of these big names, including Halford, on his local rivers and in 1891 Halford reciprocated, inviting the Yorkshireman to try for the huge grayling of the Test. It was when fishing with Halford on November 5 that year that Walbran took his 12-fish bag and on November 7 that he caught his 3lbs 9oz monster.

By now, Walbran was flying high. Within a year he was setting up one of England's most soundly established clubs, the Tanfield Angling Club, on the River Ure. The club still thrives, has its own hatchery and keeper – and miles of glorious fly water, chosen by Walbran himself, upstream and down from Tanfield village, near Ripon. The first keeper that Walbran appointed, Tom Sturdy, designed the famous Sturdy's Fancy fly.

(It is an aside but in April, 1992, I was the guest speaker at the Tanfield club's centenary dinner. That remarkable event was the first social gathering for members that the club had staged in its entire 100 years: the club did nothing to mark 25 years; nothing to mark 50 years, though apparently a flighty few suggested some gathering, only to be dismissed by the club's stern elders; and nothing to mark 75 years, either. No doubt some had misgivings about partying after a century but, as I pointed out in my speech, one dinner in 100 years – say 10 in 1,000 – does not rank as hedonism, even in Yorkshire).

Walbran's career as a writer and businessman peaked some time between the founding of the club in 1892 and the appearance of *Grayling and How to Catch Them* three years later. Thereafter, for reasons Dr Hayter discusses in his introduction to the reprint but cannot quite tease out, Walbran's fortunes went into a decline from which they did not wholly recover. In 1909 he met a sudden and untimely death, which Dr Hayter graphically recounts.

On February 13 that year, Walbran warned in his column in the *Leeds Mercury* that the bed of the river around Tanfield was covered in limestone slabs that were 'as slippery as glass'. They needed, Walbran said, 'very careful wading'. Two days later, intent on some grayling fishing, Walbran went to Tanfield, waded onto those same limestone slabs just downstream from the bridge, lost his footing, was carried away and drowned. A beautifully carved memorial to him, raised by public subscription, still stands over his grave in Tanfield cemetery, a few yards away.

In death as in life, Max Walbran has lain in the long shadows of those who refined the art of dry fly fishing on the southern chalk streams – and naturally in the shadow of Halford, above all. It is an irony that even now he is remembered not for *Grayling and How to Catch Them*, nor for his own written account of his time on the Test with Halford, nor even for the fine fish he caught there. Walbran has been remembered, where he has been remembered at all, because Halford also chose to write about their days together in one of his own books – and it is Halford's books, as always, that are read.

The Otter

I ONCE saw a trout drown a pike: the pike had taken the trout so awkwardly and far back in its jaws that it could not dislodge the fish and so could not close its mouth to breathe. I have had an osprey dive onto a river when I was chest-deep in it and pluck out a fish scarcely casting-distance away. Hidden by overhanging branches, I have seen a trout back downstream onto my wader and take up a holding position just inches in front of it.

Over a lifetime, most anglers see some remarkable things. It would be difficult to spend so much time by the water and not. Why, I once saw an otter, close-up.

* * *

I WAS about 12, I suppose – 13 at most. I was on the Tees at Croft, about a quarter of a mile upstream of the old stone bridge that stood beside the old stone church with which Lewis Carroll had once vaguely been connected; a little beyond the lovely, light-laundered piece of water that once rumpled its way downstream towards them both before some Ministry of Truth destroyed it with 'improvements.'

The mouth of the Skerne was on the opposite bank, down-stream. Klow Beck came in on my own bank upstream. The bank behind me was high and shawled with trees. Many trees leaned out over the water and lots of hanging branches trailed in it. The near water, tangled with branches and roots, was the haunt of chub. Further out there were dace and trout. In the middle, too far to cast, there were in those faraway days when imagination ruled, who-knows-not-what. Monsters, for sure.

I fished in two ways, then: float or ledger. On those sleeking, peat-stained, north-country waters that was all that most lads did. The idea of free-lining or fly fishing or the like would not have occurred. Anyway, fly fishing was for toffs.

That is why, that afternoon, I was there with my glinting new Wallis Wizard, the dreamtime rod that I'd done a paper round to buy. It had a black, silky-smooth Speedia centrepin on the bright, clean corks. (Both rod and reel are beside me right now and I often use the Speedia, still). I was already tackled up. A tiny, spade-end hook was clicked onto the catch-ring. A bob float and shot rattled against the rod on the taut line as I walked.

I had been on that bank a few days before. Then, walking directly upstream past the jumble of trees and leaning branches on my way to the Beck, I had come to the place where the trout lay. It was an enormous fish – 12 ounces, 14 ounces, a pound, who knows? Huge, anyway.

He was lying at the downstream end of a small clear space in the line of trees, in front of a fallen branch. The branch lay out into the water, easing gently. Its foliage held back and deflected the flow. The trout was on the pad of slowed water in front of the branch. He saw me in the instant that I saw him, there was a swirl and he was gone. How could he have not seen me and gone? It had been a chance sighting. I was high on the skyline, stark as a steeple.

That is why, this time, 30 yards downstream from the gap in the trees, I slid down the cliff-faced bank. At water level I was completely off the skyline, but my approach was slow. In places I had to clamber over fallen blocks of earth, in places I had to make looping, one-handed lunges at the loose roots that stitched the bank together or dangled out from it, half the time concentrating on not missing when I grabbed, half the time trying to avoid the places that might crumble underfoot and invite me in, half the time – my mathematics was as poor then as it is now – trying to keep my rod-end out of the branches and the debris trapped in them.

I approached the place where the trout had been and stopped and looked. There was the branch leaning out, easing on the current. In front of it, following the line of it out across the flow, a crease of deflected water crinkled the light. In front of the crease, a foot or two in front, a slow ring ebbed.

The world closed in. I crouched lower and edged forward, freezing every time a twig snapped or a few small, dry pieces of earth tumbled underfoot and trickled into the water. It was, looking back, probably the first time I had hunted a single, known fish: the first time I had felt the current of a high-voltage stalk. The fish and I were alone.

I came up to the branch and edged past it. The trout went on feeding. I could hear his soft sips, see the precise full-stops ebbing out. From time to time I glimpsed his back or a fin or a suggestion of flank. Yes, he was big. Enormous. Definitely a pound. Definitely.

I don't know how long it took to reach the top end of the gap where the branches of the next tree trailed, but it was a long time. The total distance between the trees, under the high bank, must have been six or seven yards. The fish, from that position, was now diagonally downstream, about 12 feet out.

When I had gone as far as I could I turned cautiously and faced the trout, keeping my rod low.

Sip-sip. All well.

I did not need to look away from the fish. My left hand knew the route to the catch-ring so well. I cradled the rod in the crook of my right arm, found the ring, unclipped the hook and transferred it from my left hand to my right. Then my left hand began the other practised route, down into the bag suspended at my waist.

I had a simple plan. I would sprinkle a few maggots into the water. With any luck, if I did not disturb him, the trout would take them. When he had forgotten the flies and was looking for maggots, my float would follow. Beneath it, maybe two feet under the surface, my hook and its cargo would find him.

Still I did not take my eyes off the fish.

Sip. Sip-sip.

Sip-sip-sip.

My hand went into the bag, among the maggots. I do not remember the detail because so much of my focus was on the fish, but I know how it will have been. I will have felt the warm teeming and heaving; will have delved into the bottom where I knew the biggest and liveliest ones would be; will have taken a few out into the palm of my hand. Then, because I will have needed to, I will have looked down and clicked one on by the skin at the broad end – maybe have noticed the little black sac surging back and forth. I will have clicked on another, ditto.

I do remember what happened next because I can see it so clearly. I looked back up at the trout. Still there. Still slow rings ebbing. But something else, now: a tease of light in the corner of my eye, far out beyond the branch and the fish.

I glanced aside, glimpsed a grey-brown head moving towards the bay. I had never seen an otter before but, of course, instantly knew what it was. The animal seemed to be looking straight into the bay, but not to see me. Then the head tilted down a little, melted and was gone. There was only the wake being carried downstream and a bow-wave heading upstream, into the bank. Light winked on the wake, rolled and curved on the wave.

The trout went on rising. Another sip. Another. I saw a trail of bubbles streaming and wobbling, drifting, approaching. I saw the trout go sip-sip-sip. And then there was a surge, a swirl and big water moved.

When the otter surfaced it had a trout – a trout so big that it had to be my trout – in its jaws. The fish flexed and quivered. The gleaming, grey-brown head turned and the eyes locked on. For a moment the otter seemed to study me full-face, as though to check that I was still not there: then turned upstream and swam in a leisurely diagonal to the far bank, where I lost him. As quickly as it began, the magic moment ended.

I had not moved, maybe had not breathed. The hook and bait were still in my left hand, the rod was still in my right. The float and shot hung in a shallow arc. I can see it all now, feel it all now, a lifetime later: the vividness of the images in crystalline detail; the cast I had planned, stillborn.

The Professor's Big Trout

WE LOVE our tall stories. Get a few of us together – get a few of us together and start the amber fluids flowing – and our exaggerations become ever more hilarious. The unlikely becomes the everyday, the impossible becomes the commonplace, the totally preposterous happens to some of us all the time.

The truth, of course, is that the strange and unusual does crop up. Over the years, many of us spend so long by the water that the bizarre one-off, the accumulation of unlikelihoods, is bound to happen. It can happen anywhere and take any form. The most notable incidents, in keeping with tradition, involve a whopper.

* * *

A FRIEND of mine once rang to say that he had caught a brown trout weighing 13lbs 8oz from a river. Now 13lbs 8oz brown trout do not come ten a penny on any river, so he had my attention straight away.

When I was told that the fish had come from the small and mostly shallow upper reaches of a river I had fished myself, I sat upright. When he told me that the beast had lifted to sip in a dry fly, I expressed surprise. When he said the monster had lifted to a size 16 my reaction verged on astonishment. When he said the fish had lifted to a size 16 dry fly and that he had landed it on a 3lbs point, I began to chuckle. When he said the leviathan had taken a size 16 dry fly and that the 3lbs breaking-strain leader had actually had a wind knot in it, I'm afraid I invited him to pull the other one. We were in bar-room territory, now. Any two or three of these factors – monster fish, small river, rise to the dry fly, 3lbs leader, wind knot, size 16 – creeping into a true fishy story, yes. Any four – well, okay. But the lot all together? I mean, come on.

Yet it was all true. The fish – no doubt a stocked fish but that, in all the circumstances, was almost immaterial – was caught by Professor Hermon Dowling, then Professor of Gastroenterology at Guy's Hospital, in London. Hermon planned to put his fish into a glass case and had called to ask the name of a good taxidermist. It was only in the course of the conversation that the extraordinary details of the capture came to light.

Hermon's fish had been successfully hooked, played and landed in a partially snagged river, albeit by an experienced angler who made something of a speciality of light-line fishing. Just to get it out of that place had been something of a triumph, given that most anglers would not attempt to play a 13lbs 8oz brown trout on a 3lbs leader if they knew the beast had heart trouble and was lying anaesthetised in the bath.

I told Hermon that a fish caught in such circumstances deserved more than simple preservation in a glass case, perhaps with its weight and date of capture on the front. It needed the whole saga in some way preserving: who caught it, where and how; the details of the fly, the leader, the knot; the story of the races up and down the bank to keep pace with its runs; the way its doubled-up weight nearly broke the net, the way the fly fell from the fish's mouth the moment the trout was on the bank. All that stuff. Yes, I said, this fish needed the works.

Certainly, I said, such a trout should not be abandoned to the fate of most glass case fish. Too often, fish in glass cases are reduced to anonymity. Junk shops, auction rooms, the walls of fishing hotels and pubs are awash with such melancholia. There is simply the fish in the case with, perhaps, a line of peeling gilt that tells us next to nothing. Yet, like Hermon's trout, every cased fish is likely to have been, for one reason or another, the highlight of some angler's life or it would not be there.

Mostly, the reason will have been the fish's exceptional size. But not always. There are a lot of modest fish in glass cases that someone has gone to the trouble of having preserved. We rarely know the reason. In most cases, we can never find out. Fish in glass cases do not always stay with their captors and often outlast them. Separated from the living story of why it was kept, what made it so special, a fish loses identity and meaning: a sublime wild creature is reduced to mere furniture. Perhaps, on occasion, even a moment of angling history is lost.

Yet what angler has not looked up at some fish in a case and wanted to know more? What angler has not wondered whether this anonymous monster – if it is a monster – was a known fish stalked and deceived or simply a whopper that came out of the blue? Who has not wondered what made it so special to someone that he spent hundreds, maybe thousands of pounds on having it set up?

I only once felt compelled, like Hermon, to put a trout into a glass case. I caught it years ago. It, too, came from a small stream. I kept it not so much for its size but because of the way it was caught and because, in catching it, I experienced a hair-raising moment of an extraordinary kind.

That moment – the details of it are not relevant here – was as intimately linked to the fish as the fly which seduced it. I wanted to preserve them all. And so my brown trout is indeed in a case. On the outside is the fish's weight, date and place of capture and my name. Inside the case, pinned to the back, is a panel carrying the neatly printed story of the capture: what the fish did, what I did, what it did next; and a description of a moment that, in the remembering, can still bring up the hairs on the back of my neck.

A brown trout of 13lbs 8oz caught on a size 16 dry fly on a 3lbs leader with a wind knot in it deserved no less. If the fish had been mine, I told the professor, I would have all the traditional stuff on the outside of the case, in gilt. Inside, I would have the remarkable story of its capture, set out in some way.

I said I would also have in there the size 16 dry fly which the great fish, against all odds, lifted to and sipped in and, still attached to the fly, that wisp-of-nothing leader complete with its knot. A hundred years on, the size of that fish alone would be guaranteed to attract attention. The story and that leader would bring its capture back to life. They would silence the doubters and the leg-pullers at a stroke. They would make the utterly preposterous, real.

The Benefits of an Aquarium

WHO cannot recall it? We have been given leave for the day or taken it. Work is off the hook. So are house, garden, other domestic duties. The bank manager. That duty trip to an aunt. We are, let us say, on the banks of some lake or reservoir and a fish rises.

Swish, swipe. We hurl out whatever we have on the end, possibly get somewhere near the fish, and retrieve. No response. We cast out again, with less certainty this time because we do not know in which direction the fish was headed. A similar result. We cast again and again. Still nothing.

More fish, more casts. The watch is chipping away at the day. The morning goes. So does lunch – and tea. By now frustration, which began niggling like a weevil somewhere between our heart and our psyche, has taken control. It has grown teeth. It gnaws and consumes. It becomes desperation.

An hour is left, maybe 30 minutes. The fish are rising steadily and we are now wild-eyed. The fly-box comes out again. Red flies, green flies, yellow flies, blue flies. Bright colours pulse and tinsels wink. A fish swirls and splashes, close in. It is huge. Our hands begin to shake. We've tried this and this and that and that. What about that other one, tucked in the corner? Looks a bit like a pullet, but so what? And anyway, we've already tried parrots and parakeets. Pullet also begins with a 'p' so maybe it'll be third time lucky.

On it goes, out it goes, back it comes. Nothing that cast or the cast after. Not a sniff and it's time to go.

For most anglers, days like this are merely rites of passage. Most anglers find there is another way and move on. But still a lot do not. It doesn't have to be like that. Here's why.

I WAS with a group of anglers that any straw poll would place among the finest fly fishers in Britain. The conversation ranged over every issue and new development affecting the sport and, as might be expected, every shade of view was expressed. There was though, complete unanimity on a question that exercises countless thousands of anglers, especially as a new season starts.

It was this: what one step could any angler take if he wanted to improve his results dramatically? The resulting views were expressed in different ways, but all had the same basic message. It was that any angler serious about moving on had, at a modest level at least, to become a naturalist. Every one of those present had himself been there and done that: had realised at some point that he needed to worry less about his immediate convenience, the quality of his tackle, the distance he could cast and all else and respond exclusively to the fish in the water: to its needs and behaviour and to the environment around it.

This sounds a pretty onerous commitment to make, but it is not. To put it in the context of fly fishing on lakes will make it clear.

The flies that stillwater anglers use can be grouped into three broad categories. Lures – typically those large and often gaudy designs beloved of advertisers in glossy magazines – are cast out and pulled back, usually at high speed. Attractors are smaller and generally subtler versions of the same thing and are fished more slowly. The third category, the imitative flies, are designed when wet and moved to look like the aquatic insects and bugs that trout habitually feed on – and they are generally fished at the kinds of speeds at which real insects swim.

Whatever the merits of lures and attractors – and on their day, in the right hands, they can be legion – there is a profound difference between these two groups and the imitative flies: it is that no-one knows for certain why fish take them. Most lures and attractors look like nothing any fish can have seen before and success often depends on ringing the changes until a winning combination of size, colour, fishing depth and speed of movement is found. For vast numbers of anglers, fishing lures and attractors is a process of trial and error.

The imitative patterns, however, are specifically designed to trigger an ongoing and known motivation not only of the trout in the water but of every living creature: the need to eat.

The angler who knows which insects and bugs are available to the fish in a given lake, and who has acquired the knowledge to use artificial flies designed to represent them, is putting himself in with a chance every time he ties a fly on and casts it out. He knows what imitators to use, how big they need to be, what colour they are – and that they need to be retrieved in a way that adds life-like movement to lifelike appearance, with one or two tactical exceptions.

For this naturalist angler, the lucky dip of fly choice and the roulette of technique have become things of the past. Every fishing action has been given a sense of purpose. It has been based on thought and reason: on an assessment of the conditions he finds at a given time of day at a given time of year – and on the likely reactions of insects, bugs and the fish he craves, to them. And, of course, if no trout happen to be feeding, lures and attractors are still available as a backstop.

There are lots of books and DVDs that will help in all of this, but there is a short-cut that will turn any inquisitive angler into a naturalist – and a much more successful fisher – in a fraction of the time it would otherwise take. It is to create his own miniature lake and to study what happens in it day by day, week by week, at home. It was something I once did myself and wrote about at length in my first book, *The Pursuit of Stillwater Trout*. It led to an increase in my catch rate of 600 per cent, between one season and the next.

The easy way is to fill a small, clear container – or a small, shop-bought aquarium – with water from a local lake or pond; to add a shallow bed of silt and small stones from the same source and then to lower into it a sprig or two of the kind of oxygenating weed available from any pet shop. The last step is to tip into this lake-in-microcosm a few examples of the insect life acquired from the same source as the water with a few sweeps of a child's minnow net.

By watching over a period of weeks at home how these fascinating and often beautiful scraps of life – olive nymphs, damselfly nymphs, corixae, shrimps and all else – live, mate, hatch and die, the new naturalist will learn more than months of reading and years of bankside sploshing about will show him.

What is more he will, for all the tiny scale of the artificial world he has created, come to some understanding of the world in which the trout itself lives. He will see the effects of the reflection and refraction of light, from close up. He will see what creatures live on the bottom and what in weed and how fast they swim. He will see what tends to hatch in the morning and what in the evening. He will be able to test how his imitations compare with the real thing when placed alongside them, below water. He will be able to see how his dry flies appear not when viewed on the surface looking down, but from beneath the surface, looking up – as the trout sees them.

There is almost no end to it. Taken together, insights like these will inform every aspect of his fishing – and give it new depths and satisfactions. Moreover, his catch rate will soar.

Too Many Deaths

RESEARCH regularly shows how dangerous angling can be. Indeed, some studies have shown that as many lives are lost to angling as are lost to extreme sports like rock-climbing and skydiving. This does not mean that proportionately as many anglers get killed as potholers and mountaineers, of course, but it is a reflection of what happens when vast numbers of people spend large amounts of their time beside water. Water kills. Rough or calm, it is dangerous. Every one of us needs to be aware just how dangerous, to go to it properly equipped – and to treat it with respect. Alas, not all of us do or, at least, not all of us do all the time. I have been guilty myself, in the past.

* * *

I ONCE rang the Royal Society for the Prevention of Accidents, to find out how many anglers had drowned in the previous five years. The call was prompted by the news that two anglers had drowned while boat fishing and I thought I should look into it.

I was shocked by what RoSPA told me. Their figures showed that over a five-year period they thought was probably typical, 150 fishermen – not all, but many of them anglers – drowned while boat fishing at sea; that 86 anglers had drowned in rivers, that 51 had drowned in lakes and that more had drowned in canals and ponds. The figures almost defied belief and yet, talking to those who compiled them, the totals stood up. Drowning deaths mostly occur one here, one there and are reported only by the local press, which the rest of us do not see. It is only when the figures are aggregated that the true toll becomes clear.

Many fatalities occur when anglers are moving about in small boats, typically those of a size to be equipped with outboard motors. Attempting to cast while standing up in such craft can, even in calm water, generate small rocking movements that lead to disaster. It is wading, though, that produces most problems.

Most wading problems occur when anglers are inexperienced, or are over-confident, or are tempted by a big fish or an appealing stretch of water, to go too far. Strong currents, objects arising from the river bed, slippery rock ledges and steep drop-offs on gravel that can slide underfoot like mountain scree are all ever-present dangers.

Chest waders, for all their usefulness on big rivers, pose a special hazard. Only the foolhardy wade deeply in chest waders without polarised glasses (which can make the river bed easy to see), or without a wading staff weighted with lead at the end (which makes it easy to maintain contact with the bottom). Most important of all, though, is an inflatable life jacket armed with a carbon dioxide cartridge that delivers 150 Newtons of buoyancy – enough to keep a big, fully dressed man afloat.

I know whereof I speak. I had no such equipment when, as a boy, I had a narrow brush with drowning, myself – and nor did I have it when, decades later, I had a second mishap. That second incident came on the day the two anglers were reported drowned and proved chilling in every sense.

The incident as a boy happened when I was 13 or 14. A pal and I had gone fishing on the River Tees at High Conniscliffe, a bicycle-ride from our homes in Darlington. We parked our bikes against the old stone wall high above the river and headed down to the water. For all that the heavens had opened the night before, the river was at its normal height. It looked in great form.

At the bottom of the steep meadow, we struck off through the woods to our right, heading upstream. The bank along the woods was steep and cliff-like, sculpted by the river from a yellowish-white rock. Usually, once some way into the woods, we would climb down the steep bank and fish from the ledges and footholds at its base. This time, though, while my pal prepared to do that, I pressed on. I had decided to chance my arm from the far side, the rights to which were owned by a local club. I knew that the field of view from there would be good and had calculated that, if a bailiff came, I would have time to hoof it, waders or not. And so I worked my way upstream to some shallows on a bend, crossed the river and headed downstream until, at some suitable point mid-river, I began to fish.

I don't know how long I had been there, trotting my float towards the trout and grayling the reach held aplenty, but it was a while. Then, as if at the end of some slow, mental dawning, I realised something had been happening little by little, for a while. It was something to do with the water.

Then I felt the pressure on my waders and realised what it was. The river was rising – and at frightening speed. I shouted a warning to my pal, turned in closer to the bank behind me, stumbled and sploshed my way upstream to the place I had crossed earlier and headed back whence I had come.

I was almost across when, with the now-coloured water pushing and rummaging and trying to jostle me off balance, I glanced upstream. And there it was, something I had heard stories about but had never seen before and was never to see again: the Tees bore.

The Tees has a large catchment high in the Pennines. Rain runs off the rocks there, gathers in the gullies and creases, congregates in the little streams and races headlong down the slopes. Under freak circumstances, vast amounts of water can hit the main channel with a pent-up urgency and weight. The result can be that the river rises at astonishing speed with, at the leading edge of the flood, something akin to a low wave.

That is what I saw surging towards me. I got to the nearest point of the cliff bank that I thought I could climb up, passed my rod up to my pal who lifted it clear – and then leapt for an overhanging branch. My fingers had no sooner closed around it than the water hit me. For long moments I trailed from the branch like a piece of caught debris; then I managed to swing my legs clear, gain a foothold on the rock and to pull myself upwards. I was safe: but safe only by seconds.

The second event occurred on a bitingly cold day on a different river. The temperature had been below freezing for a week, the puddles on the meadows were crusted with ice, the pitted and rutted tracks were locked solid. The last light was going and, after a long day out for meagre returns, I was tired. On the long walk back down the valley, a short-cut beckoned. It was through a part-flooded bankside wood.

There was no path, but I had crossed the wood before and knew there was a way through. Half way across, just feet from the river edge and without the water ever having been higher than mid-calf, I stepped into nothingness. Before I knew what had happened I was close to chest-deep and floundering, then grabbing at vegetation and then hauling myself out again.

That was it. The whole episode, from going in to being back out, took seconds. But I was soaked to the skin and the icy water had knocked the breath clean out of me. By the time I had walked the last quarter-mile back to the car in temperatures well below freezing, I had lost all feeling in my feet, my legs were like ice and I was beginning to shiver.

Twenty minutes later, heading home with an old pair of trousers on and the heater going full blast, I was not much worse except for the shock of it. It was not the shock of the icy water any more, but shock at the speed the thing happened; shock that, after so many years I could still misread the seemingly safe, shallow water directly in front of me. Then I turned on the car radio and heard of the two anglers lost. The incident in the wood took on a darker hue, the images from the Tees flooded back.

Angling is a hazardous business. It causes scores of deaths every year, as many deaths as skydiving, scuba-diving, rock-climbing, potholing and some other activities put together. Deep in the countryside and distracted for any reason, we forget it at our peril.

Which Fish Fights Hardest?

In SUMMER, *we are at the water as often as we can get there or, at least, most of us are. In summer, the attractions of mist-wreathed dawns, warm days, balmy evenings and feeding fish are simply too great to be resisted.*

In winter, when the nights have closed in and most fish have shut up shop, the pull of the waterside is not so strong. In winter, quite a lot of us fish mostly by proxy, especially if we are members of a club or an association. On club nights tackle-swapping sessions, fly-tying demonstrations, guest speakers, debates and discussions on this or that attract the biggest attendances of the year. Some subjects for the last two – indeed, for debate whenever anglers get together – come round time after time.

* * *

ANGLERS have their own silly season. It comes in winter when temperatures drop, fish become less interested in feeding and so sport, along with the bites, falls away. In winter, anglers do more talking than fishing and, on club nights especially, some hardy perennials come up for debate.

Many club debates are on subjects of real importance: the value and effectiveness of close seasons, the ethics of livebaiting, the impact of fish-eating birds on species under threat are all typical themes. Amid the serious stuff, most winter programmes offer a little light relief. A subject that often crops up, formally or informally, is that hoary old question – which species of fish fights the hardest?

It adds to the fun of such discussions that there is rarely an attempt to define what everyone actually means by 'fight hard'. Is it dash or duration? Is it high aerobatics or rod-bucking dives? Is it scorching runs or sheer brute strength? Is it – if only it could be – all of them displayed at once by a single species? Despite the lack of ground-rules, the same few species are regularly championed: bass and mackerel among the sea fish, trout, carp and barbel among the freshwater fish with, always, some wag backing the minnow, 'pound for pound'.

Now here's the point: whatever caveats each of us might like to inject, we all know that some species do give a better account of themselves than the rest. The interesting question is – why?

Many factors go into the mix and there will be no dispute about the most obvious. Different fish fill different niches and have evolved differently to fit them. All fish fight better when they are in the prime of their lives, are healthy and well-fed. All fish fight better if they are not full of eggs or milt and have not recently spawned. All species fight better when water temperatures are close to the middle of their preferred range. All fish fight better if the tackle used to play them is light enough to give them a chance.

Beyond these, environmental factors have to loom large. First, until it has time effectively to become wild, any fish reared on a fish farm will be a wimp of a fighter compared to its naturally spawned cousins. Fish that need to expend energy in their day-to-day lives – for example, by accommodating a current – tend to be more highly mettled than the slow-water moochers. Fish in big lakes tend to fight more strongly than fish in ponds. Sea fish overall tend to fight harder than freshwater fish overall. All of these except the first are generalisations, but in my experience, all have truth in them.

The depth of water in which a fish is hooked has a major influence on the kind of fight it puts up. Pretty well any fish hooked in shallow water – especially clear, shallow water – will fight with more dash than a fish in the deeps or, at least, a fish hooked at depth. Most fish hooked in deep water fight doggedly, with minimal lateral charging about. The fact that such a fish can dive as well as run and that, when it runs it has to tow a length of sunken line behind it, may contribute – as, possibly, might the weight of water against which the angler has to pull. A fish hooked in the shallows has little sunken line to tow, little water on its back and it has to fight in two dimensions instead of three. If this fish wants to put distance between itself and the angler it has no choice but to go thataway – which, in most cases, is exactly what it does, sometimes repeatedly.

An interesting aspect of these debates is the way that exotic species are increasingly being proposed as the hardest fighters. It has come about, of course, because more anglers are travelling regularly and many more are investing in that once-in-a-lifetime trip. Among the travellers, it is remarkable just how many of those who have fished for it, unhesitatingly chose the bonefish as the hardest fighter they know. The bonefish would get my vote, too.

The bonefish seeks its food – shrimps, small crustacea and the like – on crystalline shallows in the tropics and sub-tropics. It is mostly stalked by wading, usually with the help of an all-seeing local guide, or from a shallow-bottomed skiff which the guide, eyes skinned, poles quietly along. The bonefish is not easy to see.

It is so iridescently silver, so mirror-bright that it reflects all that is around it – effectively becoming invisible. When hunting it, neither guide nor angler is looking for a fish. Both are looking for signs that a fish might be there: a shadow, perhaps; a glimpse of reflected light where a fish has tilted down to take something from the bottom and, in the shallow water, its glistening tail has broken the surface, catching the sun; a patch of muddied water where a fish has rummaged something up from the sea bed before moving on. Once seen and hooked, the fish's speed, power and stamina simply suck the breath away.

Even modest fish will make runs of 50 yards, 100 yards and more and bigger fish will do it time after time after time, contesting every inch, never relenting. On Christmas Island, in the Pacific, I once watched amazed as the angler next to me had 250 yards of line and backing ripped out in a single, unstoppable run and then was broken in an instant when the fish hit the reel. For all the pressure put on it, that double-figure specimen seemed not to notice. It did not deviate from its dead-straight line. It was headed for the Antipodes and probably got there.

Part of the reason the bonefish fights as it does, has to be because it earns a tick in so many boxes. It is a sea fish. It is caught in extremely shallow water – typically knee-deep. It grows to a goodly size, with the average between 2lbs and 6lbs and with fish to twice that size being occasionally taken. In addition – it is the cherry on the icing on the cake – the bonefish is readily caught on fly tackle, some of it the lightest tackle of all.

None of this, though, even when taken in large dollops, accounts completely for the bonefish's fight. It is beyond understanding how this luminescently silvered, torpedo-shaped slip of life can run so hard, so far, so fast, so often.

The nearest we come to such fishing in Britain is by stalking bass with a fly-rod across tidal shallows. The bass is a wonderful fish and a savage fighter, offering marvellous sport when at bonefish sizes. But it is not a bonefish. Only a bonefish is a bonefish. The bonefish is a fish that passes all understanding. It is the father and the mother of the reel-smoking run. I cannot imagine how it fights as it does, what dynamic forces are at work inside it, where it gets that energy from.

Yet get that energy, it does. The bonefish in shallow water is a fish without parallel – the minnow, pound for pound, not excluded.

Promises, Promises

LIFE is so hectic, these days. The pressures come at us from all angles. There seems no relent. Do this, achieve that, fix the other, make a commitment about so-and-so now. It is bad enough for ordinary folk, I know. Just imagine what it is like for a fishing writer.

Fishing writers, of course, are not ordinary folk. We are, naturally, mystical creatures bordering the superhuman. In the maelstrom in which fishing writers live it is all too easy to leave some things undone: to forget this commitment or to let that resolution slide.

That is why, when someone sent me a new book to look at, I was thrilled to be able to make not one use of it, but two. It has enabled me to map out the year ahead and given me the tools to stay focused.

Next year – next New Year – will be different. It will be organised. It will go clickety-click.

* * *

I RECEIVED, a little while back, what was very nearly the perfect fishing book. It was a beautiful thing, part-bound in leather on richly marbled boards. It came complete with thick cream pages, gilt edging, a tasteful green ribbon marker, the lot.

Indeed, no matter how carefully I scrutinised this delight, no matter how diligently I pored over its pages there was, so far as I could judge, but a single deficiency. This deficiency, this lack, this absence was – how can I put this? – of words. Every page was a blank page, from beginning to end.

Naturally even I, a notoriously slow reader, got through it in no time. It was only as my wife was remarking that a fishing book without words was much to be preferred to a fishing book with words – I know, I know – that I noticed a letter still in the packaging.

This letter made everything clear. Here was no ordinary book. Here was a book that was meant to have no words. Here, indeed, was an innovative product from a company that normally specialises in reprinting old books. What I had was a spanking new – and entirely blank – Fishing Journal: a kind of log in which an angler can set down details of his performance over the year, in superlatives of his own choosing.

Now if there is one thing we fishing writers are, it is busy; and if there is one commodity we are short of, it is time. A fishing writer's year is pretty much spoken for before it begins and so no matter how appealing the idea of keeping a fishing journal might be, the practicalities of keeping one going make it a complete nonstarter.

The greater part of a fishing writer's time, as might be supposed, is taken up with landing whoppers. Some days we are kept so busy landing whoppers that it is difficult to find time for a kip. Some sessions, when we are camping out at night on the canal bank, rubbing our hands together and blowing on them as ice crinkles across the water and our lips are turning blue – and sometimes canal banks are crowded with angling writers doing this kind of thing – it is difficult to squeeze in a second kip. So a full third of a writer's year is spent by the water, bagging up.

A second chunk of a writer's year is spent being treated for the pulled muscles, strained backs, popped elbow and shoulder joints that our battles with great fish inflict. The fact that this treatment sometimes means long hours spent in the hands of leggy young masseuses at The Fishing Writers' Club brings no complaints from us. We simply lie back and endure it. Even so, that is more of the writer's year gone.

The rest of an angling correspondent's time is spent in writing it all up so that our readers might gawp and learn and it was here, fishing journal in hand, that a penny dropped. If I filled in my year's fishing journal in quiet moments in advance – an easy matter, given the meticulous way we fishing writers plan these things and the infallible way our plans work out – I could save time later on. I could have my journal and yet lose no time next year in landing whoppers, writing them up for readers and all the rest of it.

So that is one good use I have found for my fishing journal: I have set out some of next year's highlights in advance, as they will happen, under the appropriate month's headings throughout the book. I have, in addition, found a second use for it. At the front of the journal, I have set out something else well in advance: my resolutions for the New Year to come. I have written them prominently, in ink, where everyone can see them, for reasons that I will explain in a moment.

But first, next year's highlights. I am not going to beat about the bush with these. Overall, next year, I will take more fish of more species than have ever been taken by a single angler, in a single year, before (numbers supplied on application).

These fish will, naturally, include my usual tally of monster coarse fish – roach, dace, barbel and pike among them – all taken, alas, with not a witness in sight and my camera infuriatingly left in the car. But it is from my trout fishing that the most dramatic results will come. Against all odds, I will again break the records for both the rainbow and the brown trout on rivers. I feel under no pressure to reveal here what the weights of these fish will be but, suffice it to say, they will prove surprising.

More surprises will come from the big reservoirs, not least because my bags from these waters will pretty well duplicate, fish for fish and date for date, catches I wrote up in an earlier book, after a similarly stunning year.

On Grafham, Chew and Rutland Water, where the bag limit is supposed to be eight fish and the average catch is one, I shall catch eight fish on every visit, all of them over 10lbs. Some visits I shall catch 28. On June 26 I am scheduled to get 103 trout and on August 5 a further 122. 'Uncanny', *Angling Times* will call the coincidence. 'Incredible' is how *Trout and Salmon* will describe my reports (and, if I may say it, rightly so).

The record-minders will be able to slumber for weeks, after that. In fact, I will trouble the Record Fish Committee just twice more in the year, on both occasions for sea fish. The first time will be for the exceedingly rare Spiney Glop I plan to take on September 12. The second occasion will be for the Three-Fingered, Piano-Playing Zither Fish that I plan to catch on October 9. This latter creature, a curious animal named because its pectoral fins, when splayed out, move in a manner reminiscent of a pianist's hands when playing Rachmaninoff's Piano Concerto No. 3 (Second Movement), will be the first example of its kind known to British waters, or for that matter known to science.

Of course, I expect the usual carping and niggling when all of this comes out, the same tired old calls for 'evidence' and the like. But as a fishing writer I have been here before and, as before, I shall give it all short shrift. Frankly, I could have put in plenty more.

If catching whoppers is my strength, organisation is my weakness. I have made countless New Year resolutions in my time to try to improve things, but they have never worked out. I make them in December. Come February my resolve is flexible, by March it is floppy and by April it has turned to liquid and run away. So far, no angling resolution I have made has survived the season through.

Enter my beautiful, leather-bound fishing journal, complete with its marbled boards, thick cream pages and gilt edging. This now not only has my next year's catches set out for all to see but, in ink, right at the front, my resolutions for next year as well. Placed there, I will not be able to miss them or ignore them. If I begin to slip, they will reproach me every time I open the book. I am confident that, under such pressure, I will for the first time keep them.

And what are these demanding resolutions? Mostly they concern how I get organised before a trip, how I get organised after a trip and getting things right by the water.

For example, next year when I go fishing, I will know where I am going before I get into the car. When I get where I need to be, I will have permission to be there. So will my companion, if I told him the same place. I will not have left my rod at home. I will not even have left a section of my rod at home.

Next year, I will not inadvertently misread 'Private' signs, or find myself absentmindedly worming under several strands of barbed wire unless the coast is manifestly clear. I will not wade above my wader tops. I will not allow a large fish just out of casting distance to lure me into a deep hole. If anybody is to fall in when I am fishing, it will be my companion. Likewise, I will not break a rod in a car door unless it is someone else's. Certainly I will not break my own rod in a car door again.

If I am trout fishing, I will only cast to trout. I will definitely not cast to rings made by dabchicks, or ever again spend the morning stalking a dabchick, a trick I have habitually performed. I shall instruct every shrub, bush, fence, notice and piece of rusted farm machinery I see – and many I shall not see – to stay perfectly still while I am casting. No shrub, bush, fence, notice or piece of rusting farm machinery will step smartly to one side and snag my backcast while I am concentrating in front. I will even stop all the above stepping aside to catch backcasts made by my daughter because she seems as plagued by the problem as I am.

I will hook no passing cars or motorcyclists on my backcasts, for all the adrenalin hits they can give. No birds will take my bait or fly in mid-cast, for all the fascination of finding the rod bending upwards and the line jag-jaggling somewhere in the sun. No bird will take a fish from the water while I'm playing it, as happened several times off Christmas Island. No shark will take the fish I am playing. No shark will take me.

I will not exaggerate the size of any fish that gets away, beyond what I deem necessary given the competition at the time. I will not exaggerate the size of any fish I land if there are witnesses about. I will never attempt to play down the sizes of any fish caught by my companion unless he is smaller than me or obviously inexperienced or comes from Eastern Europe and cannot speak the language.

I will leave the river when I promise my wife I will leave. I will arrive home when I say I will, regardless of the timbered old Free

House where everyone else is going to swap stories. When I do arrive home late, I will have a plausible excuse.

All this I have committed to my splendid new fishing journal, along with my planned catches for the year plus my physio dates. With it all written down in advance I can make sure that every goal is hit, every resolution is kept, every appointment is booked in and takes place.

Yes, a fishing writer's life is a hectic life all right, but thanks to my journal help is at hand. Next year – next New Year – really will be different. It will be organised. As I said, it will go clickety-click.

Champion of Champions

COMPETITIVE *fishing is not for most of us, survey after survey shows that. Yet for those involved in it, match fishing is as intensely pursued as competition in all sports and requires similar levels of knowledge and skill.*

The biggest matches are run on coarse fisheries, the qualifiers for some attracting fields of thousands. Sea anglers fish competitions as well – mostly out there, on the literal fringes, when the rest of us have gone and the beaches are deserted. I reported on one.

* * *

JOHN BROWNING, winner of 80 sea angling awards in the last 10 years, victor of several major open championships and a tournament-caster of some repute, looks along the 12ft Seacaster behind him, addresses it with a gaze of intense concentration, holds his breath for an instant and whirls.

The rod, one moment almost straight, dropping slightly beneath its own weight, the next arched back in a screaming bow, flashes around and 130 yards out to sea a small plume of spray erupts. Down the beach, as far as the eye can see, rods arch and flash in the November sunlight and the water is perforated by a line of white splots. It is 10.00am and the most prestigious sea-fishing contest in years – to find the Champion of Champions – is under way.

Like everyone fishing today, John Browning got here by winning or coming second in a special pre-match contest for the honour of representing his club, one of the 523 sea fishing clubs in England and Wales. He is one of 350 qualifiers on this five-mile strip of cornflake-crunching shingle between Brighton and Hove.

When he's satisfied his bait is in the right place, Browning tightens his line and slips the rod into its rest, the top high up against the sky to telegraph a bite. It is cold and he paces in tight formation around the rod-butt, partly to keep warm, partly because he's tense.

For a long time nothing happens. He reels in and casts again, a little nearer. It's 10.30... 10.50... At five-past-eleven the top of his rod jerks around and in an instant he's leaning hard over, rod swept high over his shoulder and backing up the beach.

'Bass!'

The single word conjures power and speed. It cuts down the morning air and the man on either side reels in to give Browning a better chance if he needs it. But it's not a big fish and after one driving run towards the groyne on his left it turns and slowly, doggedly, comes into the edge before rolling onto its side. It's 2lbs, perhaps 3lbs, the first fish of the day and the first bass anyone's seen on Blue Zone. It's a good start.

Another long wait and then at 12 o'clock the word comes down the line. The chap at the end, half-a-mile away, has had a beauty. Another bass, around 5lbs. 'If it's who I think it is,' says Browning, 'he's from Cornwall or Devon. They say he's got masses of peeler. They can get it down there.' Peeler crab is the classic bait for bass which Browning, who comes from Brighton, couldn't get.

A few minutes later and a photographer from the oil company

that's sponsoring the event arrives to take his picture. There's a publicity man, too. They're working down the line, photographing contestants as they go, so that the nation's local press will have the story if their man wins.

'That's a nice fish. Name, address? How long have you been fishing, John?' and then click-click and they're away so quickly we hardly know they've been.

At one o'clock the men on either side get fish simultaneously. Flounders both, small and brown and flat. Fish, but make-weights not match-winners. Fifteen minutes later, Browning gets two himself in quick succession. 'What'll I do with them? Not eat them, that's for sure. Never eat sea fish. Only fish I eat is in those sandwiches.'

I ask him what it is. 'Salmon.'

Nothing doing again for a while and he decides on a bite to eat. 'Favourite? There's no favourite in a field like this. You've got the cream here today. The local man must be in with a chance, though. He's in with a chance everywhere, the man who knows where the fish are.'

But he's a local and with the fish he's got he's in with a better chance than most, surely. 'True. It won't be a big weight today, not with the wind in the east. Five, six, maybe seven pounds will do it. We'll know at the weigh-in, that's for sure.'

All the time we've been talking, his eyes haven't once left his rod-top. Suddenly, the end dips down. It's another flounder. And then, straight away, a fourth. At 1.45 it's neck-and-neck. It must be, if the spectators who've come down the beach are anything to go by. Then the grapevine passes the word. 'The bloke with the bass has lost another beauty – 7lbs, they reckon.'

'Bad luck, that.' Browning means it too. No-one likes losing a big bass, competition or not.

Another half-hour and his own rod nods again; another flounder, a good one this time, flutters in through the water, towed behind the weight above the hook. Five flounders and a bass.

Five-past-two. Another flounder. 'Bloke with the bass has got one as well,' says a professional spectator who happens to be passing.

'I doubt that,' says Browning. 'He's fishing peeler for bass. He's after the big fish.' He's getting more hopeful as the minutes tick by but keeping level-headed with it, trying not to sound anxious.

Twenty minutes later and the last flounder slides into the big bucket beside him, down into the water that will prevent it from drying out. Then, at 3.30, it's over and everyone reels in. A bass and seven flounders: Browning's in with a chance and delays arriving at the weigh-in until he's one of the last, keeping himself on tenterhooks, nervously spinning it out.

The crowd pushes around the table where the scales are set up and for all the hundreds of competitors, everyone knows it's between the local man, John Browning, of Brighton, and the man with the bass. The weigher-in works through the queue, shouting out the weights like a referee in the ring, as someone else notes them down on official white dockets.

'Two pounds, one-and-one-half-ounces,' he shouts punctiliously... 'Ten-and-one-half-ounces'... 'One pound thirteen ounces exactly.'

Suddenly, the big bass is on the scales and there's a murmur from the crowd. The man at the scales inches the little balance along the bar and bends down to get a closer view. 'Five pounds, seven-and-one-half-ounces.' There are more murmurs from the crowd.

A few minutes later and it's Browning's turn. He looks away with counterfeit detachment, but everyone else cranes forward to see. Again the balance is tapped along and again the weigher-in stoops. 'Five pounds...' and there's a theatrical precision about it this time, '...five pounds... five... and-one-half-ounces.'

That's it. It's all over.

'Bad luck...' 'Bad luck, John...' 'Hard lines, mate...' And instantly, for two ounces short, John Browning's day is just one more reminiscence in a long season's fixture list. The Championship of Champions has just got away.

Yippee!

THERE is, I suspect, a common misapprehension about angling writers. It is that they, which is to say we, spend our time monotonously reeling in whoppers. There is the water, here is an angling writer, he is holding a rod, let there be fish – that kind of thing. Hmmm. Not on the planet I inhabit. I live in the same world as everyone else, as most angling writers do. We – at any rate, I – fail to find fish, our casts go awry, takes or rises are not forthcoming, big fish and little fish alike come unstuck.

But, of course, like everyone else, we do have our moments. Here is one of mine. It occurred on November 12, 2004.

* * *

FIRST, for that moment of triumph, I need to thank my agent, my producer, my director, my mum and dad, that schoolmaster who encouraged me all those years ago and finally, of course, my wife and family who have stood by me through thick and thin.

Well, kind of. The truth is that for any angler to make the sort of catch I have made, who has not only achieved a life-long ambition but beaten it by a moon-shot, good fortune and luck need to be dancing close attendance. And so let me acknowledge that without the two friends who found the fish in question, without the owners of that rarely fished, off-the-map piece of water who gave us access, without the benign weather, the clear water and the good light that enabled me to look down through it and see just what was in it, none of it would have happened.

But it has. I have caught a weighed, witnessed and measured monster grayling, a genuine, no hankey-pankey whopper. Actually, I have caught two.

I have hankered after a whopping grayling ever since I caught my first from the River Tees as a boy. I was still in short trousers. The day was so cold I had to push the ice from the margins before I could start.

That was only a small fish, of course, but then, grayling run small. Hardly any have been caught overt 4lbs and most years only a handful are caught over 3lbs. Most places, grayling average maybe 4oz to 6oz. A 1lb grayling is a good one, a one-and-a-half-pounder is a very good one and many a two-pounder ends up in a glass case. It took me 30 years to catch my own first two-pounder. For the 20 years since then I have been irrationally keen to get a three-pounder. Two of my friends, both of whom have reached this sublime figure themselves, have known it and been anxious to help.

And so, after a phone call to say they had found fish of a size mentionable only in whispers, I found myself on a short stretch of water not a million miles from Southampton. I was on my hands and knees in dense woodland, looking down at a shoal of grayling that defied belief. They were all monsters. They were hard on the bottom – and they were feeding.

Ronnie, who had come with me, refused even to put up a rod. He just wanted me to go for my biggie and I was eager to oblige.

I had gone expecting to float fish and had taken a trotting rod and some sweet-corn as bait in readiness, but it was obvious from the outset that a trotting rod was impractical in that confined space. It would have to be the nymph. I put up an 8ft 6ins 4-weight with a 9ft leader and tied a heavy nymph onto the point.

The lack of room meant that conventional fly-casting was out of the question. Instead, I held the nymph between the forefinger and thumb of my left hand and pulled back against the flex of the rod held in my right. The rod took on a taut curve, I targeted a fish on the edge of the shoal and let go. The rod jerked straight, the line and nymph were catapulted through a gap in the overhanging branches and the nymph went in a couple of yards upstream of the fish I was aiming for. It sank as the current carried it downstream and arrived on the bottom, right in front of the fish's mouth. I saw the mouth blink white and I tightened.

On the bank, I guessed that fish at around 1lb 12oz but Ronnie thought it more. He produced the full business – a weighing sling and a set of digital scales with a large dial that had every ounce on it clearly marked.

I had underestimated. The fish weighed 2lbs exactly. Minutes later a weighed grayling of 2lbs 3oz was being returned. A couple of smaller fish quickly followed.

Around noon a large, light-coloured fish that neither of us had seen before, drifted into view. At the second or third catapult cast through the branches, it also took. I tightened and the rod went over. In the net the fish seemed huge. On the scales, the needle scarcely seemed to believe its size either and dithered this way and that. Then it stopped and there it was: my weighed and witnessed, no hanky-panky monster grayling, 3lbs exactly.

Several more fish followed until finally they stopped taking. I replaced the nymph with a size 12 hook, baited it with a single piece of sweet-corn and pinched a single BB shot a little way up the leader to carry it to the bottom. Then I cast again. A fish of 3lbs 2oz took instantly, then a couple more.

I ended the day with 15 grayling caught and returned, almost all of them taken while still kneeling down, eight of them between 2lbs and 2lbs 12oz, plus the three-pounder and the 3lbs 2oz. As Ronnie said, it had to be one of the most extraordinary catches of grayling ever taken.

I am not falsely modest. While I know that a whole range of factors – above all, the generosity of my friends – put me in that place at that time, I also know that I must have got everything right, as well. In angling, such coincidences almost never happen and now they have, and for the right fish.

Call me excitable if you want – but yippee!

Faked Orgasms

OKAY, so there you are on the bed, side by side and the build-up's been great. Suddenly, her movements become more urgent and she starts to rub her body rhythmically against your own. You steal a glance and her mouth's wide open and her eyes are rolling. She begins to tremble and shudder. Yes. Now. Yes-yes-yes.

Or, quite possibly, no. At least, it seems, if you're a trout.

* * *

SWEDISH researchers (they would be Swedish, wouldn't they – maybe it's something to do with those long, dark nights) have shown that in 59 per cent of matings, the female trout fakes her orgasm. Then, before the cock fish can say 'that was wonderful, darling' and light up a piece of ranunculus, she's at it with someone else, in all probability someone hunkier than he is.

The news will all come as a surprise to trout anglers who, with their own tackle untouchable in the winter close-season, have in the past been content that Mr and Mrs Salmo trutta at least were using theirs.

The spawning of trout in winter, like the hatching of the mayfly in spring, is one of the hidden dramas of the British countryside and few other than anglers and naturalists ever get to see it. Even those who have never seen it in the flesh, so to speak, know how the process works. Male and female fish congregate on the shallows. The hen fish digs a hole in the gravels and a male fish slides alongside her. When their flanks touch, it looks as if an electric current is running through them. The fish go into spasm, they tremble violently, their jaws are wrenched wide and she sheds her eggs as he releases milt over them. In moments, it has always seemed, a new generation of trout – and for anglers a future season's trout fishing – has been set under way.

Alas, Erik Petersson and Tobjorn Jarvi, of Sweden's National Board of Fisheries, long ago discovered that all is not as it seems. In a scientific paper published in 2001 they reported that hen trout are – I'm afraid there is no delicate way of putting this – cockteasers in the most literal sense. In the 117 spawnings they observed, females faked orgasm 69 times. The hen fish adopted the characteristic jaws-wide, body-trembling posture on the stream bed, the cock fish did likewise and after a few moments, he shed his milt – but she held onto her eggs. Then, just when everything seemed to have gone swimmingly and with the poor male drained and spent, the female would back away and start up with a stranger.

One of the reasons the female cools off, Petersson and Jarvi say, could be that – sound familiar? – the male fails to hit exactly the right spot. 'If she feels he is not in the right position, she just stops the process', Petersson says. 'But the male, he is so excited that he misinterprets the female's cues and goes the whole way. He's a little bit tricked.'

Other researchers suggest the reason the female fakes orgasm could be that the male that gets to her first is simply too weedy. Then, they think, she goes through the motions to get it over quickly for him so that she can move on, looking for better genes elsewhere.

Some hen trout have been seen to fake it not just with one male but several, one after another. It is, observers say, as though all the time she is trying to find Mr Right, who tends – surprise, surprise – to be Mr Big: a cock fish with bigger fins, bigger kypes, presumably bigger everything if you know what I mean. Petersson reported that when the hen does find a partner that can make the gravels move for her, she goes all the way, leaving a string of spent suitors behind her, 'looking confused.'

None of this will be apparent to the casual observer on the river bank – or even through the big lenses that naturalists sometimes train on the fish. Not one angler in 1,000 will have known anything about it. But it's all true and, now that it's out in the open, the grapevine will be buzzing.

Even so, surprise and not shock will be the reaction among anglers. In winter, anglers are forever fiddling with their flies. In summer they will discuss the evening rise openly. It is not faint-hearts we are dealing with, here. A few faked orgasms are going to make no-one blush.

Angling and the Future

MILLENNIA do not come and go so quickly that, when one ends, the occasion can easily be ignored. When the cosmic wheel clicked and the 1900s tripped over into the 2000s, it seemed an appropriate moment to consider angling and the world in the round.

Like many others, I had long been aware of movements both inside the sport and out. These movements – in some cases, it seemed to me, seismic shifts – had nothing to do with catching fish but with more profound, more subtle and more disturbing matters. I thought then and think now that, collectively, they put angling's very existence in danger. It is on this cautionary note that I want to end this book.

* * *

MEN have pursued fish with rods for as long as they have been able to carve hooks from bone and paint images on rocks. Fly fishing has been around since Claudius Aelianus. Both coarse fishing and game have been written about in English since the *Treatyse of Fysshynge wyth an Angle* appeared in 1496.

In the 300 years that followed, the sport moved forward in fits and starts. In the last 200 years progress has been made in a rush. The end of the 20th century and the beginning of the 21st, the end of the second millennium and the beginning of the third, seems a better time than most to take stock: to look at where we have recently been and where it seems we are headed.

It is clear that the 19th century ended on a roll, for trout fishers especially. Alfred Ronalds had taught us the importance of reflection and refraction, W.C. Stewart had shown the advantages of casting upstream, G.P.R. Pulman had pointed out the effectiveness of the dry fly, Frederic Halford had shown how to fish the dry fly upstream. The last decades of the century saw the development of eyed hooks, split cane rods and lines that could be cast into a wind. They brought the rainbow trout to Britain.

The twentieth century proved no less creative. G.E.M. Skues showed us the ways of a trout with a fly, A.H.E. Wood greased the salmon fisher's line, Hugh Falkus took us fishing for sea trout at night and Tom Ivens brought method to stillwater trouting. Head-and-shoulders above them all stood Richard Walker, who made a practical contribution to fly fishing and who, almost single-handedly, brought coarse fishing out of the dark ages into the light; who changed the way generations of coarse anglers will think about their sport. The 20th century saw the fixed-spool reel overrun the centrepin, carbon fibre replace split cane, synthetics displace gut and lines developed that will present a fly at every level in the water from surface to bed. It gave us *cul de canard*. It gave us the Dog Nobbler.

And so, poised between past and future, how do things look? Did the 20th century, like the 19th, go out on a roll? Are we destined to forge onwards to some bright green upland?

In my view, no. As one millennium fades and a new one dawns, angling is in turmoil and its future, uncertain. I believe our sport is threatened on several fronts, each of them compounding the pressures of the rest.

Three are worth setting out in some detail. The first threat is changes to the physical environment on which all angling depends. The second – more subtle but just as sinister – is changes in attitudes inside angling itself. The third threat is one that, reading what much of the angling press says and listening to many anglers talk, one might imagine did not exist at all and yet it is the most important of all: it is shifts in the way non-anglers see the world.

In discussing these threats, I am not talking about game fishing. There is a dangerous myopia in the way game anglers talk about their sport: it is as though game fishing were the whole of angling or the greater part of it. Where the major threats and the public are concerned there will be no picking and mixing. We are – game fishers, coarse fishers, sea fishers – all simply anglers together.

The environmental problems facing us are broadly known. Global warming is increasing air and sea temperatures which in turn are changing wind flows and rainfall distributions. In the United Kingdom, one effect is that winters are getting shorter, summers are getting hotter and those areas most in need of water – the east and south – are getting less summer rain. Frequent and prolonged droughts are more likely.

We are compounding the rainfall problem by the rate at which we build and where we build.

As the new millennium dawned, there were plans to build 4.4 million new houses inside 20 years, around 2.2 million of them in greenbelt and open countryside. Around 840,000 were scheduled for the driest areas of all, the south and east. Every person in every house will need to be supplied with water.

Say it fast and 2.2 million houses on green field sites is just another huge, meaningless figure. But break it down, work on just 1.5 persons per new home and it becomes the equivalent of 82 new towns of 40,000 people apiece. Yes.

We are making the supply problem worse by what we do to the water we have. Lower flows already mean less physical space for fish and the food chain on which they depend. They already mean more silt deposited and more eggs suffocated in the gravels. Add the drive for greater farm production and we see more fertilisers and insecticides on the land and in the water – which further reduces insect life and promotes choking blooms of algae. The drive for more productive industries is leading to more acid rain and to the release, among other things, of chemicals into the environment that mimic female hormones. An effect of the latter is that male fish are becoming feminised (and did we hear that sperm counts in men are for some reason getting lower?).

The impact of this and more on our inland fisheries is relentless. Matters are no better in the estuaries and the sea.

Who has not heard of the threat to salmon stocks – or that multi-sea-winter salmon numbers are in steep decline? Fish farms are allowing sick fish to escape into the wild and to transmit their diseases to such wild fish as remain. Escaped farmed salmon are breeding with wild fish in most rivers that have salmon farms near them – and so the genetic integrity of wild stocks is diluted. The qualities required for life in cages are being bred in, the migratory and other instincts are being bred out.

Away from the coasts, changes in ocean temperatures are likely to be having their own impact on salmon numbers. Over-exploitation by netsmen certainly is. The inroads that nets are making into the food chain on which wild salmon depend, could be doing likewise. Predation by seals and birds is causing alarm. The result is that the very fish on which our sport is based are under assault from the land, from the sea and from the air.

The second threat comes from a different direction – from the ranks of anglers themselves. It is a real danger, insidious and growing. To describe it will mean using some quaint terms – maybe unpopular and unfamiliar terms.

Little by little, I believe, we are seeing a haemorrhage of principle from angling, an erosion of the moralities on which our sport has always been based. These are the moralities which say that angling – angling as a whole, not just gamefishing – really is a sport and not a business; that the quarry should be respected and not abused; that the ancient, unwritten codes of restraint and fair play should be upheld and not ignored or bent for personal gain.

Commercialism is at the heart of the problem.

In an over-subscribed and under-regulated market, fisheries must compete for anglers, the tackle trade must compete for customers, angling's media must court advertisers as carefully as it courts readers – and so must not only hype and froth but talk up causes that further advertisers' interests.

In this clamour, everyone has to shout louder to be heard. To secure a niche, offers and antics must become ever-more extreme. Our needs and vanities are tapped into with the precision of doctors using surgical probes. More fish. Bigger fish. Fish that are easier to catch.

Fish that often end up abused.

We have already seen the cynical manipulation of trout records, for commercial gain – dazed porkers ricocheting from stew pond to waiting angler to lodged record claim, sometimes in less than an hour.

We have seen huge carp, fish that are worth thousands of pounds apiece because of the business they can attract, stocked in ponds to act as targets for chest-beaters – fish doomed to be harried and caught repeatedly from the moment they are stocked to the day they die.

We have seen salmon of 40-odd pounds apiece being trucked from fish farms in Scotland to small ponds in England so they can be caught by 'anglers' who must have had all sense of sportsmanship removed with scalpels.

The close-season for coarse fish – a device that, however imperfectly it coincides with the breeding seasons it is designed to protect, does show respect for the quarry by giving it some respite – has already been abolished on lakes and canals. The existence of the close season on rivers is the subject of relentless challenge by the tackle trade because no fishing means no sales.

Some lakes are deliberately overstocked so that competition between fish for food is increased, natural caution is through desperation reduced and the fish become easier to catch. Easier fishing attracts more business which means more cash to the owner.

It is a list that is near-endless and which tarnishes us all.

The bottom line of it all is that, in the interests of profit and chest-beating, the creatures we publicly claim to love and protect are being reduced to the status of commodities and objects – and are being systematically abused. Not by everyone, everywhere, but by some of us, somewhere. And in the only arena that really matters – the real world around us, a world to which we often seem blind – a few is quite enough.

Cue the third threat: changes in public opinion.

Though to listen to the commercial lobby you would never know it, the world is changing around us. While we keep our heads down and look inwards, the familiar reference points we have so long lived with are moving. The certain is becoming less certain, the once-acceptable, less so.

The reasons why things are changing are not hard to find. Opinions are changing because fewer and fewer of our fellow-citizens have contact with the land and the wild lives lived upon it. They are changing because Beatrix Potter, Walt Disney and a host of others have turned animals into little people with human sensitivities and emotions. They are changing through the power of television, which has brought the secretive and unfamiliar into every home directly, in zoomed-in and cuddly close-up. They are changing, as well, because a segment of society – intelligent, articulate, impassioned, ruthless and with a view it has every right to express – wants things to change and has the wherewithal to exploit every weakness we offer it.

At present, most of the goings-on I have been describing have been happening out of the sight and consciousness of Joe Public. Mr Public, insofar as he has been concentrating anywhere, has been concentrating on foxhunting. For the man on top of the Clapham bus, angling has been just the rather dotty pastime pursued by this neighbour or that chap on the bank. (This bemused and generally benign attitude on the part of non-fishing folk towards angling is, it is worth noting, one of our current greatest strengths. We may be slightly dotty – but we are harmless).

But once foxhunting has been forgotten and the national media has been softened up some more and our opponents have begun to video some of the things being done in angling's name, the Bloggs will turn their refocused gaze on us. Thanks to the camcorder and the close-up and some slick, selective editing, the Bloggs will see angling presented not as the benign and dotty pursuit they had always imagined but as a mean and petty business in which living creatures are cynically abused for profit and ego. They will see angling presented as a pursuit that has lost all touch with sporting values and that has forfeited the right to tolerance and support.

This is not the way things will be – but it is the way they can be presented, will be presented and are likely to be perceived. At the start of the 20th century, we would have had to rummage in the short grass to find opponents of angling. At the end of it, an opinion poll showed, 29 per cent of the public already would have been happy to see angling banned.

And so to the future.

Several issues are on the agenda now that, when taken together, are as dangerous as matches near a fuse. I will mention three which show the range of the front we must defend. The first is the reintroduction of the otter, the second is livebaiting for pike and the third is the catch-and-release debate that has been going on in salmon fishing for years. All three are already the focus of interested, outside eyes.

The steady increase in otter populations presents little danger to river stocks because of the creature's nomadic habit and its huge territories. On even the most prized river, the vast majority of anglers are likely to regard the sight of an otter as more than adequate recompense for the loss of the occasional fish from a given length. But the threat to inadequately fenced commercial fisheries – espe-

cially commercial fisheries stocked with large and valuable carp –
is a different matter for those who own them. The most obvious
danger is when an otter has a holt near such a water.

Just one frustrated fishery owner, seeing his living disappear-
ing before his eyes and taking drastic measures, would not put the
problems with otters on the agenda but the rest of us in the dock.

Livebaiting is a longer-standing hostage to fortune. Among
many coarse anglers and some game anglers there is a view that
livebaiting must continue as of right. It is a perfectly legitimate
view to hold. The arguments, variously, are that livebaiting has always been practised and that any ground surrendered on it will be
the thin end of the wedge; that there is no substantive difference
between putting a hook through the back of a living fish to keep
it on the line and putting a hook through its lip to catch it in the
first place; that to ban livebaiting with fish would mean a ban on
the use of maggots and worms because they are livebaits, too – and
then the game would be up. And so the posture is, give nothing:
never a yard, never an inch, no surrender.

There is an alternative view which I (and, of course, many others) happen to hold. It is worth setting out to show the scale of the
gap between honest opinions. This view says that we live in a community which, for all our cynicism, has a love of animals and a
sense of fair play written through it like the lettering in Blackpool
rock – and that it is a mistake to give our opponents such leverage
upon it.

The livebaiters' view suggests that logic and science are what
will influence the public. I do not believe that. I believe that what
will sway public opinion will be perception and emotion. The real
issue, I think, will be how different do the various practices seem?

I suspect Mr and Mrs Bloggs will see a big difference. They know that lip-hooking a fish is what angling is about and right now, according to the quoted poll, 71 per cent appear to find that acceptable. Would 71 per cent of the millions who have enjoyed all those television programmes showing anglers catching fish in the understood way, have been as content to see the same fish having treble hooks pushed through their backs in close-up? Would they really see no difference between angling with a living fish impaled through the back and baiting, say, with a maggot? There is a mind-leap between identifying with an individual fish – individual fish are often kept as pets – and identifying with creepy-crawlies. The idea of simply touching a maggot would have Mrs Bloggs recoiling in revulsion – before, that is, she boiled up a pan of live mussels for dinner.

Though some would argue that the clinical similarities are not so far apart, the exploitable perception and emotion are very different. My own view is that a voluntary phasing-out of livebaits would be more in our long-term interest than the retention of such a hostage to fortune. But either way, the issue is coming towards us fast.

The catch-and-release debate in salmon angling is just as fraught and, again, opposing views are legitimately and passionately held.

Quite a few salmon fishers believe all fish caught should be killed because that way we are fishing for the pot. It is a position that makes us less vulnerable to our opponents, they feel: we are not using fish as what Hugh Falkus termed 'playthings' – catching them only to put them back.

An alternative view is that angling's greatest quantifiable

strength is our numbers. In those numbers, coarse anglers out-number game anglers by umpteen to one – and coarse anglers today kill nothing. To justify our sport on the grounds that every-thing should be killed will seem sensible to some but myopic to many. At a stroke it would split angling in two – but not down the middle. It would leave game fishers isolated and vulnerable. Another challenge.

These issues, I repeat, are mere examples of what the future seems to hold. There are many more. They are coinciding not only with one another but with a reduction in our numbers. Every sur-vey taken in recent years shows that angling's numbers are falling. At one end of the sport, old hands are dying off. At the other our traditional recruits – the young – are not coming in at the rate they once did. The young have so many pressures, so many alternative pleasures, so many opportunities to sit in a room with a screen that they scarcely have reason to come blinking into the sunlight.

The young are also, it is worth noting, the most idealistic sec-tion of society. They are even more imbued than their parents with a love of animals and a sense of fair play. They are in all likeli-hood more susceptible to propaganda than their elders and, as the third millennium gets under way, may increasingly not only not support us but join with the opposition.

And so the conclusion?

At this pivotal point in our history, pretty well everything our sport depends on is either threatened or up for grabs. Deep wounds are being selfishly self-inflicted. Practices that once went unquestioned are either on the public agenda or heading towards it. Some of what is done in the name of angling is open to manip-ulation and distortion. On major issues, anglers themselves are honestly divided on principles.

It is all happening at a time when public opinion is itself on the move, when technologies are available to carry emotion-charged images into every home, when the numbers of young recruits on which we could historically rely, are beginning to drain away.

It is also, it needs to be said, all happening at a time when angling's long lack of leadership and need of a single, coherent voice have caught up with us. The Salmon and Trout Association, the National Federation of Anglers and the National Federation of Sea Anglers posture under the titles of 'governing bodies' but govern nothing and no-one outside their own minority memberships. From time to time 'co-ordinating bodies' do come – but they also go.

In quieter times such posturing could be ignored, but it cannot be ignored, now. Why not? Because these groups have a habit of consulting within their own narrow ranks and then declare positions on a range of contentious issues – and when angling's 'governing bodies' declare positions, the outside world naturally assumes that they are speaking on behalf of the sport as a whole. The result, as we have sometimes seen, can be a public relations disaster – each one of which colours a little more of the outside world's perception of what angling stands for and is.

Underfunding is a further intractable problem. It is likely to remain so without a leadership that can persuade us to dig into our pockets for good reason, without a body that can negotiate coherently on our behalf, without some group that Government agencies and other purse-holders can point to and say with confidence over the long term 'that organisation represents angling in the round'. The one outside group that might help – serious commercial sponsors – is kept at arm's length by our own behaviour, by the antics of a largely uncritical and sometimes irresponsible angling press and, of course, by the changes in public opinion that make the other two so damaging. For businesses that do not have a direct interest in fishing, the perception must often be that there is increasingly more to be lost by association with us, than gained.

Of course, not everything is doom and gloom. In our rivers, the black filth of industrial pollution is largely a thing of the past (though diffuse pollution from farmland has largely replaced it). Access to fishing for most has never been easier. Angling conservation bodies and coherent political voices are at last appearing. Dialogue is under way with non-angling groups which otherwise might prove adversaries, in the hope of finding common ground. And so on.

But it is also the case that, like most anglers before us, we concentrate so hard on what is happening under our rod-tops that we scarcely look over our shoulders to see what is behind. In the developments I have described, I can see the potential for a collision coming faster than it need: a collision between a sport moving in one direction and a public opinion moving in the other.

What is important is that we are aware of what is happening and pause to take stock: that we look at ourselves, at the world about us – and seek ways of ending the drift.

We can begin as individuals by promoting everything that is positive about angling – a sport that gives so much to the millions who practise it and to the environment in which everyone else lives. We can stop shooting ourselves so obviously in hands and feet together and waving red flags in the faces of the public. We can highlight and resist abuses, the worst of them commercial and vote with our feet and our wallets.

Angling has been a major influence in my life. It is a sport that I love. I want my children's children to be able to fish and their children to fish, as well – or, at least, to have the freedom to choose whether they fish or not.

Such choices may not be available unless we acknowledge that the compass points which have guided us so long, are moving: unless we recognise that, degree by degree, north is becoming west and south is becoming east. If we continue blithely along the course set now, we may end up at some place not intended.

Index